The Fighting Nun: My Story

by

Margherita Marchione

Cornwall Books

New York • London

Cornwall Books
2010 Eastpark Boulevard
Cranbury, NJ 08512

Cornwall Books
Unit 304, The Chandlery
50 Westminster Bridge Road
London SE1 7QY, England

Cornwall Books
P.O. Box 338, Port Credit
Mississauga, Ontario, Canada L5G 4L8

The paper used in this publication meets the requirements of the American National
Standard for Permanence of Paper for Printed Library Materials Z39.48-1984.

*Library of Congress Cataloging-in-Publication Data
is available from the Library of Congress*

SECOND PRINTING, 2003

ISBN 0-8453-4876-0
PRINTED IN THE UNITED STATES OF AMERICA

In memory of
my beloved parents,

Crescenzo and Felicia Marchione

Acknowledgments:

The author is indebted to Barbara and Peter Bye for their computer assistance, to Shirley Horner for reading my manuscript and to Sisters Filomena DiCarlo, Josephine Palmeri, and Helen Sholander for secretarial help. She expresses gratitude for a grant from the Ralph M. Cestone Foundation.

Contents

Foreword

The name Margherita Marchione illumines the ranks of many constellations: educator, scholar, writer, professor emerita, college president, administrator and treasurer of the Religious Teachers Filippini. She has fulfilled a remarkable role in the twentieth century. Her significant contributions to the history and culture of both America and Italy ensure the lasting resonance of her fame, no surprise to those who have long observed her resolute faith and courageous spirit.

Author of thirty five books and over one hundred articles, she is the recipient of a Michael from the New Jersey Literary Hall of Fame (1993). With her recent research on the Holocaust relating to Pope Pius XII's efforts in saving Jews, she launched a crusade in his defense that has advanced her status as one of the world's leading scholars.

Sister Margherita Marchione's mission fulfilled a dream that found its origins in God. Her confidence in Divine Providence never drifts, permitting no leeway to any challenge. No passive personality, she has participated in the life of the Religious Teachers Filippini, serving as treasurer for twenty-five years; in the affairs of the state of New Jersey for fifteen years as a member of the New Jersey Historical Commission under three governors; in elementary, secondary and higher education for fifty years; in many national educational, cultural and religious organizations; in international affairs, for she is known to respect each individual and assist all who approach her with their problems. Such is her legacy.

Among Italian-American women who have succeeded in their careers, Sister Margherita continues to perform an inspiring role. For her, service is no burden; it is a privilege. Charming as well as courageous and compassionate, she takes overwhelming pride in her heritage. She is known as a "liberated" member of society and a gifted member of the Religious Teachers Filippini.

Working through her conviction that one can inspire people only by example and love, she has sought to help others live intensely and enrich their lives. As a person and as a polestar of faith, Sister Margherita will always be esteemed both nationally and internationally.

Ralph M. Cestone

Prologue

This book is not strictly an autobiography. Responding to those who wish to know me, it describes how my wonderful family and friends have enriched my life. It is the story of their goodness and love.

In February 2000, I was negotiating with three publishing houses during the production of my latest books. How could I possibly contemplate an additional task?

Some forty years ago, Dr. Peter Sammartino suggested I keep a "Diary." I did not. Recently, however, I was invited by Dr. Francesco Crocenzi and his wife Angela, to speak in Boca Raton, Florida, on my new book, *Pope Pius XII: Architect for Peace.*

Francesco and Angela are very dear friends. In my book, *Yours Is a Precious Witness: Memoirs of Jews and Catholics in Wartime Italy,* I had already written about their aunt, Sister Assunta Crocenzi. She was instrumental in saving the lives of 114 Italian Jews during the Holocaust. As treasurer of the Religious Teachers Filippini she provided food for both the Sisters and the Jews who were hiding in our convents.

It was a difficult task. I knew that one day she had fearlessly gone to the German Commander in Rome and had demanded a permit to go to northern Italy for a truckload of rice! Permission was granted. But I did not know that, when Francesco was about seven, the Fascist government sent his father to Africa as an engineer. Soon after, Francesco and his younger brother lost their mother. Their father became a British prisoner-of-war. The two boys, alone in these perilous times, were helped by their aunt, Sister Assunta. To protect them, she sent the two youngsters to live in a convent outside the city of Rome where they survived the horrors of World War II. Not until he was seventeen, did Francesco and his younger brother finally reunite with their father. Francesco and Angela, forever grateful, have established an endowment in memory of Sister Assunta.

When Dr. and Mrs. Crocenzi told me the rest of the story about their aunt, I realized how much of my life and the life of others needed to be put on record. In the same month, four members of my family—Jean Messner, Marie Lotito, Ceil Gallis, John Pirro—urged me to write a family history and the story of my life.

These two experiences motivated me as never before. I began to write my story. Writing it became an obsession. The story was completed in two months.

This book is a friendship-fest that makes me delight in the love of family, students, friends. If I have done little else in life, I have accomplished this: firming bonds that withstand distance and silence, bonds of mutual understanding and deep affection.

I hope that I have fulfilled my commitment to all who asked for this book. I gratefully acknowledge the blessing and inspiration of God.

Chapter One: Early Life

> "There is an appointed time for everything …
> a time to weep and a time to laugh."
> *(Ecclesiasticus 3:1-11)*

Labor Day, September 2, 1935. The news hit the family like a bomb when I announced my religious vocation at our family dinner table! Everyone stopped eating to stare at the thirteen-year-old who had just blurted out: "Today, I am leaving to become a nun. I want to say goodbye to all of you." My parents, siblings and guests were shocked! My story begins with this scene because the affection I have felt for my family and for the home I left in 1935 is always with me.

For many years, New Jersey was truly the Garden State. Seventy years ago, when you said that you lived in a farming community called Little Ferry in northern New Jersey, no one blinked. The three-story home where I was born on February 19, 1922, was on 59 Liberty Street, a symbolic name. The house was part of a dairy farm and I can still picture the six acres of vegetables and fruit trees, the roomy barn that housed the cows and the dairy building that bustled with activity.

As a child I was strong-willed and independent. In an Italian syndicated newspaper article thirty-five years later, Professor Giuseppe Prezzolini would describe me as "a mixture of Catholicism and American independence." ("Un misto di cattolicesimo e indipendenza americana.")

Like most Americans who were changing the demographics of America in the early twentieth century, we were a first-generation family in transition. My parents came from the province of Salerno in Campania, Italy, where they were married in 1900. My father, the son of Luigi and Rosa Marchione, was born September 6, 1879, in Pontecagnano. My mother, the daughter of Michele and Alfonsina

Schettino, was born July 22, 1882, in nearby Montecorvino, Pugliana. No young married man could hope to raise a family and live comfortably in these small towns where the farming area was controlled by large proprietors. So, when cousins from Philadelphia invited Crescenzo to the USA, my father decided to leave his home.

My parents came over during the Great Migration of the late nineteenth and early twentieth centuries that brought 4.5 million Italians to these shores. They had the courage to cross the Atlantic Ocean and live in a strange new world. Like their contemporaries, they sacrificed personal dreams to help their son and daughters realize theirs. They had no professional careers, yet they insisted that their eight children learn fluent English and receive a good education.

My mother, Felicia Marchione, was well-organized, hard-working and economical, but she found time to instill in us her love for God. One of my earliest memories is my weekly task of bringing the flowers she had selected from her garden and placing them on the altar of Saint Margaret's Church, a block away from our house. Why do I remember that those bouquets were always arranged artistically? Perhaps because I still admire and try to emulate well-thought-out arrangements. Not necessarily flowers, but lectures, symposia, books, etc.

Saint Margaret's Church has other fond memories. For several years during the month of May, I was selected to be dressed as an angel to lead the First Communicants to the altar. A photo shows me in a beautiful white dress with white wings attached to my shoulders, representing their angel from heaven.

Crescenzo Marchione, my father, had a personality that matched the English derivative of his first name: energetic, entrepreneurial—but always jovial. The thirties were hard times for working people, but my father's industry never faltered. His construction business collapsed, but he ran the dairy and later vegetable market from Little Ferry, even building that town's first gasoline station. Many family snapshots preserve the happy feeling he always generated, whether dancing or singing or—to my mother's chagrin—smoking his Italian cigar.

Leaving his wife and first child, Rose, to his parents in Pontecagnano, Crescenzo joined several male relatives for the trip to

America in 1900, hoping to prepare a suitable home for his family. He was one of seventeen million immigrants who approached the Statue of Liberty with fear in their hearts. Most of them did not know the language, but they did know the dignity of labor.

Herded into the Great Hall of Ellis Island, they harbored hope within their hearts, hope that the inscription on the Statue of Liberty would sustain them:

Give me your tired, your poor
Your huddled masses yearning to breathe free...
(Emma Lazarus)

Three years later, my father had enough money to send for Felicia and young Rose. After they were reunited at Ellis Island, they first went to live with relatives. Their next step was a farm in the Catskills, in Bloomville, New York, a similar environment to their former home in Italy. My parents now owned about one hundred acres of land. My mother's sister Alfonsina and her husband, Michael Moccio, were responsible for the workers on the farm. Since it was necessary to feed the many workers in the large farmhouse where the family lived, they were called to meals by hitting a hanging iron plate with a hammer.

The following year a second child blessed the Marchiones. A family photo shows Rose standing, Jean in her mother's arms, next to Crescenzo with his brother Peter, and Crescenzo's parents who had just arrived from Italy (they would remain here several years).

Within the next two years Marie was born. Grandparents Luigi and Rosa Marchione were so enamoured with this baby that, two years later in 1912, they insisted on taking her to Italy to visit the family there. Later, when relatives informed my mother that Marie's arm was in a cast, she insisted that Luigi and Rosa return immediately with her child.

My sisters Jean and Marie recall that Mamma had reluctantly agreed to let our grandparents Marchione, returning to Italy after a brief stay here, take Marie with them. However, Mamma's terms were that Jean (age 4) must accompany her little sister (age 2) to watch over her. In Italy the little girls went to nursery school accompanied by their grandpa on horseback, Marie on his lap and Jean holding his waist. Less than two years later, on learning from relatives that Marie had broken her arm when kicked by a donkey (the child loved to play with his tail!), mamma threatened to hire an attorney, if Jean and Marie were not sent home immediately with cousins who were coming to America. When the ship docked in New York in 1914, the little girls, leaning over the ship, recognized papa who had blue eyes and red curly hair: "Look" they cried, "There's Papa. The man with the curly red hair!" They continued, "Papa, Papa!" until they were in his arms. Indeed, Marie, too, had curly red hair as did Rose, Mildred and Louise.

After Jean and Marie returned from Italy, they contracted whooping cough. They too went to the large house in the Catskills and soon they were able to attend a one-room schoolhouse. When this property in Bloomville was lost for non-payment of taxes, the family moved to Bound Brook, NJ, where papa had bought forty acres of farmland. When my mother complained, he smiled, pinched her cheek and asked: "Are you healthy? Is there enough food on the table? What more do you want?" The farm always brought in enough money to feed the family. Our bills were always paid. I remember that when I was a child, my older sisters Jean and Marie worked and contributed toward expenses.

Families then were "bumper crops." The Marchiones' first child, Rose, was married a few months after I was born and fourteen-year-old Jean was among her many bridesmaids. Each one of my seven siblings graced my life, and even as I sit here composing these words, I am joined by three of my remaining sisters, Jean, Marie and Ceil who remind me of those days in Little Ferry.

Rose was sent to business school during the Depression to help Papa with his commercial endeavors. She negotiated the buying of an apartment building in New York City in partnership with another man, who later broke the agreement, leaving papa the loser. She married Thomas Pirro in 1922, and moved to Brooklyn, where Tom had a bakery and grocery store. Here, she not only wrote letters in Italian for all her neighbors but, during the Depression, she provided food for the poor around Saint Mark's Avenue and was often asked to be godmother for the children. She herself had two children, Palmina and John.

My parents never received government help. They were proud and would have refused the benefits available to today's immigrants. As property owners, they suffered terrible losses, but were never deterred by misfortunes. They would begin all over again. Before I was born, when the family lived in Union, NJ, they had a dairy, a thriving business until, one night, during a terrible thunder-storm, lightning struck the barn. Fifty-nine cows perished in the fire; only the bull survived! Unfortunately, there was no insurance. Papa merely remarked: "Why cry? We have plenty of food on the table!"

Papa had courage and began a new business but, with the Depression, disaster struck again. In the twenties, he and his partner had built the foundations for several houses on Merhof Road in Little Ferry. His partner abandoned him, took the money papa had invested, and the houses were never completed. Today, a flourishing restaurant is located on that property.

On the Little Ferry farm where I was born, the old house still stands, but the large porch has been "mutilated" and it is surrounded by condos. In my youth few families lived there. Our house was shingled when I was a little girl. Nearby stood a round iron fire alarm that alerted people about a fire in Little Ferry after someone struck it.

The kitchen had running water besides a water pump that provided the most delicious H_2O. As children we carried water jugs to laborers on the farm in the hot summers. Pumping water was a chore, so papa always asked: "Are you sure this is water from the pump?" There was no need to add ice. It was always ice cold!

As soon as papa had some money he would invest in a new project. He loved music. We had a piano with music rolls, and my sister Louise took piano lessons. Papa loved to dance. Mamma preferred to crochet and sew. She was strong, serious, but loving toward all and devoted to her family. Her cooking was superb. Cleanliness and order reigned everywhere. The artistic arrangements of her garden and her flowers were the envy of the neighbors. I recall an oval-shaped, sepia photo of myself sitting in her flower bed at age two, a lovely example of Mother Nature in action—a happy child delighted with the beauty that surrounded her.

As youngsters we picked berries, then helped mamma sterilize the jars and preserve fruits and vegetables for the winter months. We picked berries for her to make jellies. Her preserves became gifts when we visited relatives and friends throughout the year. She also made mozzarella and we helped her when she made sausages.

Felicia Marchione had innate intelligence. Without any book-learning, she anticipated the success story of the canning industry. Her father had studied in a seminary. Mamma was the oldest of three children. Her sister Alfonsina and her brother Michael Schettino also came to America after her arrival in 1904. Their mother died when they were very young and their father remarried.

The Schettinos had relatives in this country who were educated. One of them became president of a bank in Philadelphia and used to visit mamma in Little Ferry. When mamma first moved there, she learned that her neighbor, Mr. Petretti, had been married on her wedding day. In fact their carriages criss-crossed on the way to church. He came from her village and his bride came from papa's village. They had never met until now—some twenty-five years later! One of their children, Lillian Petretti, married the son of mamma's cousin, the banker from Philadelphia.

Mamma was a wonderful cook. No one could ever match her chocolate-filled "pasticelle," her homemade "ravioli," her Easter bread or rice-pie. Nothing was ever lacking in Little Ferry during the Depression. Nothing was ever wasted—so we always had plenty of food. We also had a player piano, a telephone, and a radio and we commuted to private Catholic schools. Mamma prepared a chart with the phone numbers she used frequently. But she was ahead of her times. Years before the telephone company used numbers in place of letters, she had prepared her own.

Toward the end of her life, the older daughters shopped for mamma's gifts to be placed under the large family Christmas tree. She refused to waste anything and would store away papa's gifts: sweaters, ties, shirts, etc., until they were needed. When the supply increased and she had no storage room, she would re-wrap these items for Christmas and other occasions. Instead of buying new ones she presented these to him. Papa confessed later that he had caught on, but pretended to be excited as he opened the gifts. Once he slyly remarked: "Darling! But didn't I have one just like this? It looks familiar!"

Everyone remembers his remarks. When in pain after working on the farm, he would say: "Guess I need a new pair of knees!" Little did he realize that someday knees could be replaced.

While many young girls worked in factories, my parents, who were determined to provide their children with opportunities they did not have in Italy, refused to allow their daughters to work there and insisted on education. While some Italian parents did not want their daughters to become nurses, mine permitted Louise and Mildred to become R.N.'s; Jean and Marie became secretaries and commuted to New York City.

To return to my sister Rose's two children, who would eventually marry their childhood sweethearts from Brooklyn, Palmina married Nicholas Monda and John married Clare Di Maso.

John graduated high school when he was seventeen years old. By that time the United States had joined the Allies during World War II. After one year of college at St. John's University in Brooklyn, John enlisted in the U.S. Navy on his birthday, May 1, 1944. First sent to Oceanside, CA, and later assigned to PA123 USS Kittisan, an attack transport, he was aboard ship on Christmas Day, 1944, soon to arrive in the Pacific—Hawaii, Philippines, Martial Islands, China, Okinawa, and Japan.

John recalls that on Easter Sunday, April 1, 1945, at 8 a.m., his group invaded Okinawa. Assigned to a landing craft boat marked "GAS," their job was to fuel amphibious tanks. Japanese suicide planes were circling over the area and he and the other sailors prayed that the Japanese could not read the word "GAS." If so, they would be blown to pieces, as did happen later to a ship in their vicinity, causing many casualties. Shortly after, John was assigned to the Destroyer USS Rapertus and, on June 9, 1946, he received an honorable discharge. Leaving the Navy, John continued his education, went on to a happy marriage and raised six children. While working as an accounting clerk for Blue Cross of New York, he earned a BS and MBA from New York University. He soon attained the position of vice-president of Blue Cross of New York and retired after a forty-year career. He is proud of his twenty grandchildren and one great grandchild!

Within two months after I entered the convent in 1935, my sister Jean married Harold Messner, who became vice president of investments of Midland Marine Bank in New York. They had two children: Joan became a teacher and Harold, Jr., followed his father's footsteps into finance. Jean lives in Bronxville, NY, and is ninety-two years old. (She looks twenty years younger!)

Although our parents never returned to Italy, they remained Italian citizens until the last few years of their lives when they received their citizenship papers. They were so proud of their achievements. They had always hoped to return to Italy—dreams that never materialized. Although they were often treated unfairly, as were many twentieth-century immigrants, they were proud and never accepted handouts. Rather, they tried to help others while supporting their own large family.

Louise graduated from Saint Mary's Hospital in Passaic, NJ. She married James Monroe who was in the U.S. Reserves and who had a wonderful sense of humor. They had two girls: Marlene and Lorraine. When Jim returned from the Korean War he decided to go into business and build a diner. In the midst of the project, while also building a new home in River Edge, he had a heart attack and passed away. Louise completed the projects and raised the two girls alone. Marlene became a nurse and Director of Case Work Management in Ashtabula, Ohio. She married Tom Sartini, an attorney and County Prosecutor. Lorraine, a secondary school teacher, taught English and History and became Dean of Students in Toledo, Ohio.

Louise later married Joseph Vecchione. They moved to Saint Petersburg, Florida, and spent many happy years together. She outlived her second husband. About fifty years ago, Louise was one of the first patients at Deborah Hospital in South Jersey where she had heart surgery, and, until her death, she lived with a pace-maker.

Mildred was a delightful character. Ambitious and lovable, she graduated from Saint Cecilia's High School in Englewood and went on to study nursing at Mount Vernon Hospital in New York. She fell in love with Art Norton and wanted to marry him. But my parents felt she was too young and should continue her nursing career for a while. Art dated a girl at work who invited him to the opera regularly. But opera wasn't his only weakness. When the girl became pregnant, he married her and broke Mildred's heart.

Mildred lived in Mount Vernon. She convinced my parents to purchase a lovely, large two-family house in Fleetwood, New York. However, Papa would not move there because the property did not provide space for a large vegetable garden. Instead, my parents rented it to Mildred and Jean where they lived happily for more than twenty-five years. They eventually became the owners and only recently sold the large two-family house.

Throughout her life Mildred was a devoted nurse, lovingly caring for family and friends. People have remarked even years after she died, "We cannot forget what Mildred did for our family." She had married George Constantine during World War II and had one son, George, Jr. Apparently to avoid a car packed with people, he swerved and crashed into a rail, dying instantly. Mildred later became directress of a nursing home. However, while caring for others, she neglected her own health, waiting too long before she finally had a physical examination. When x-rays showed cancer of the bone, she realized her days were numbered and wished to remain in the New York Hospital. God called her shortly after. She died at age sixty.

Our family reunions in Fleetwood were memorable. In 1986, as we gathered for Thanksgiving dinner, Jean's daughter, Joan Messner, announced her wedding to Dr. Manfred Epstein. Dinner was served in both dining rooms, "upstairs" and "downstairs." I was assigned "upstairs." Being the youngest in the family, I volunteered to serve. I placed a pretty apron over my habit, and greeted the Epstein family as they arrived, paying special attention to Manny's mother. My first chore was to serve cocktails. Conversation was delightful and dinner was a success. When her son accompanied her "downstairs" to meet the others, Mrs. Epstein continued praising the good food and Joan's family. Suddenly she paused and exclaimed: "And, Manny, what a lovely *upstairs* maid they have!"

Louis was the only boy among the eight children. He loved to play the harmonica and would sing to me, "Margie, I'm always thinking of you, Margie!" He was a prince with seven sisters. In his youth he was athletically inclined and enjoyed baseball, football and boxing. He was sad whenever he recalled how one day he was practising with his bat and unintentionally hit our niece, Palmie, age five. She was bleeding and had to be rushed to the hospital, requiring several stitches near her eye. After that unfortunate accident, Mom and Pop were opposed to all types of ballplaying, yet Louis continued his career and became a successful local ballplayer. He even won amateur bouts as a boxer, but his first fight was lost by a technical knockout. Mom had gone to Church to pray he would lose.

At that point my sister Jean convinced my parents to send Louis to Staunton Military Academy in Virginia where he attended high school for two years. We were so proud to see him in his uniform whenever he returned home to visit. I recall baking cakes and mailing them to Virginia.

On our farm on Liberty Street in Little Ferry a picturesque brook added to the bucolic setting of my early years. There was a bridge that separated the area near the house and barns from the farmland. At the far end of the acreage, my father built a gasoline station. It was operated by hired help, but occasionally Papa would ask Louis to help for a few hours.

Louis knew my parents particularly objected to his Saturday afternoon football games. Although he had certain chores, he managed to get away for practice, having decided that a career as a ballplayer was more important to him than substituting for employees on weekends. During the summer, if he wanted to sneak away to play ball, he showed young nephew John, age seven, what work chores had to be done. The young boy never told his grandfather, but he remembers clearly that he substituted for Louis on several occasions.

When Louis was recruited during World War II, he joined the Signal Corps. Although he was trapped with several others for five days by the Germans, he returned home uninjured physically and inherited Papa's business. He was able to re-join his wife Elsie with their three children—twins Louis Jr. and Dolores, and younger sister Diane—and was present for each of his offsprings' weddings. Louis, Jr. still works for Mercedes-Benz in NJ; Dolores' husband is with Toyota in California; Diane became a nurse and married Dr. John Mulflur and they now reside in Maryland.

My brother, Louis, Sr., belonged to the Knights of Columbus and was a member of the Board of Trustees of Saddle Brook Nursing Home. There for three years he cared for Papa who, after my mother died, had a stroke and was paralyzed. Louis died at age fifty-two from a heart attack.

Cecilia (Ceil) was the second youngest offspring. She taught in Saint Francis Xavier elementary school in Newark for twenty-five years and was also activities director of the Nutley Summer Camp. She met Nicholas Gallis, a young man of Greek origin and later married him. Theirs was the last wedding held from the house at 59 Liberty Street in Little Ferry, NJ. By that time I was already in the convent and, according to regulations then, was not permitted to attend.

Ceil and Nick had three children: Elaine, Elizabeth and George who later became a physical therapist. Elaine, an elementary school teacher, married Dr. Robert D'Alessandri, vice president for Health Sciences and Dean of the School of Medicine at West Virginia University. They had two children, Ann and Dawn. Elizabeth, a social worker, married Leonard Ferrara, a high school science teacher. They had three children, Christopher, Steven, and Michelle.

Steven's application to Cornell University included the following essay:

"Whoosh! A whirl of black fabric rushes by. 'My Gosh, there's the flying nun!' one exclaims.

"Indeed, there is a nun, but she is not flying. It is my aunt, Sister Margherita Marchione. Much like the Energizer Bunny, my aunt never stops. Her perpetual motion has contributed to her success as she crams meaningful activity into every minute of her day.

"It is only with deep love and pride that I can speak of Aunt Margherita. She displays a unique blend of qualities that I both value and admire. First and foremost is her dedication to her family, her religious order and to God. Then there is the boundless energy which radiates from this remarkable woman. She has used this energy to author, edit, and/or publish over thirty books. She has also served as president of Corfinio College in Italy, and as a professor of Italian Language and Literature at Fairleigh Dickinson University. She is a natural teacher and no one leaves her presence without some gain in knowledge.

"A selfless individual, Aunt Margherita gives away just about every gift she gets and receives great pleasure from this giving. She is completely devoid of materialism. As treasurer for her Community she no doubt has managed millions of dollars, yet finds no need or desire for personal wealth. Her present goal is to raise funds for the care of the retired nuns so they can spend their retirement years with independence and dignity.

"My aunt is a woman of focus, determination and compassion. In 1935, at the age of thirteen, she left for the convent despite her family's surprise and objections and has since never left. She has persevered in all of her projects, especially in her research on the Italian revolutionary and correspondent to Thomas Jefferson, Philip Mazzei. Her books about him have added a new historical perspective regarding the role he played in the formation of our democracy. It has been out of love for her heritage that she has toiled relentlessly to bring the name of Philip Mazzei to the attention of historians and scholars. Through her efforts, she has gained both national and international recognition, although that was not her original intent.

"As most people who have had the good fortune to know Sister Margherita, I, too, have grown from being in her company. Her boundless love and energy, her generosity and her willingness to put material things last, have served as an inspiration of what life is all about. I much admire her eagerness to learn and her desire to share all she knows. She has taught me that with hard work and tireless effort, it is possible to do it all." [Steven became a financial analyst and is now with Prudential Insurance Company.]

George Gallis, a physical therapist, married Jennifer. They live in Spokane, WA. I am the baptismal godmother for their three children, Alicia, Michael, and Julie Ann. When George was in the first grade, he came home with a large box of chocolate bars and told his mother he had to sell the candy to his neighbors. But before ringing doorbells, he decided to taste it. He then convinced his neighbors to sample the chocolate before purchasing it. He sold every bar and triumphantly announced to his mother: "I gave everybody samples and here's all the money I got!" Of course, she paid for the samples.

And now to me. The youngest, I was called Margaret, or Margie as my playmates called me. Each summer I also played with my sister Rose's children Palmie and John, who came to live with us in the country. John still recalls how I told him and his sister stories to put them to sleep and was even obliged to sleep with them. I was an avid reader and the children learned from me about *The Bobsy Twins, Little Women, Little Men*, etc. There was no central heating in the house on Liberty Street during the Depression. There was a very large kitchen stove and, during the winter months and terrible snowstorms, mamma would heat bricks in the oven, wrap them in towels and place them in our beds so that our feet were always warm.

In Little Ferry the older children had chores in the house or on the farm. John Pirro is my oldest nephew. He recalls his summers in the country, how mamma would remind him and his sister to say their prayers, "le cose di Dio." He also has jubilant memories of picking blueberries, huckleberries, elderberries and blackberries in our woods at the end of the farm property; vivid recollections of the horses, the cows, the chickens; playing in the wagons, jumping from the hayloft (from second floor of a large barn), making jelly and wine.

One day John was playing with his grandfather's nails and tools. He took the hammer, selected a tree where his grandmother usually sat in the shade while shelling beans, and hammered away until all the nails disappeared from the box. When his grandfather returned and asked him for the nails, the child smiled and said: "There they are on Grandma's tree!" Grandma smiled, and waited for Grandpa to react. Fortunately, John did not understand Italian.

Not only was that *her* tree, but her flower garden too was sacred. She loved arranging her garden and graciously distributed flowers to all who came to visit, but became indignant should anyone dare pick them without her permission.

John recalls having to count the tomatoes as they were placed in boxes for the market. He also delivered milk to neighbors. Mrs. Heckel was around the corner. Her son Peter was Louis' boyhood friend. One day they went swimming in the lake. When Louis noticed that Peter was in a whirlpool, he ran for help, which arrived too late, and sadly Peter drowned.

John Pirro loved life on the farm. He recalls receiving one penny for weeding a line of tomato plants one mile long. Today he grows his own tomatoes in Freeport, NY, and takes pride in sharing these large, specially grown, tasty tomatoes with friends. In fact, there is annual "professional rivalry" between him and his son Thomas who also inherited a green thumb. Each summer the tomato competition rages on!

One summer when John was seven years old, he insisted on going to the market in Newark with grandpa. He remained awake one night and hid in the truck. He succeeded in convincing papa to let him go to the market in Newark. From that excursion, John remembers that every owner had to pay one dollar to sell his products and that he sold papa's bunches of parsley at ten cents each.

Eventually his sister Palmie married Nicholas Monda, a childhood neighbor in Brooklyn, who also has contributed to memories of my father. Nick recalls the following incident that occurred when they were visiting in Little Ferry. Nick was asked to accompany papa, who was about seventy, to Newark where money was due him from some customers. Afterwards, the two passed a theater, and papa decided to treat Nick. But once they were seated comfortably, Nick realized where they were. "Grandpa," he said, "this is a burlesque theater!" That made no difference. Papa had paid for the tickets, and they had to stay. It was too late!

Papa was loved by everyone who knew him. He was most generous in supplying milk to poor families. Years later he laughed telling us how he supplied the Desiderio children with milk because their father was a junk collector in Newark and could not afford to pay him. However, the Desiderio family did not remain destitute. They became very wealthy when their business began to thrive in Whippany, NJ.

When my parents moved from Little Ferry, Marie, not yet married, went with them to a beautiful two-family house at 400 Jerolamon Street in Belleville, NJ. Soon after, Marie married Frank Lotito and moved to Woodridge, NJ. Of all my siblings' weddings, Marie's was the only one I attended because I had to substitute for the Holy Family Church organist who was not available on that day. But, according to our regulations, I was not permitted to attend the reception. However, more recently, I did attend several weddings of nieces and nephews.

Here, too, in Belleville, Ceil and Nick Gallis had an apartment with their three children: Elaine, Elizabeth and George. It pleased Papa that the house boasted a large vegetable garden. When he needed fertilizer for his own garden, Papa asked his son-in-law Nick and his nephew Donald Schettino, who was visiting one day, to get a truckload of manure. They complied but returned home with only one-half of what was needed. Reprimanding them because he needed more manure, he announced with a smile, shaking his head and looking at the manure: "You boys are no good for...(SH---T)!" That's about the strongest language he used in English. Of course, no one knew what he was saying when he spoke Italian!

For their fiftieth wedding anniversary, my parents received a beautifully hand-painted blessing in Pope Pius XII's own handwriting, requested by his niece, Elena Rossignani Pacelli. Years earlier during her sojourn in the United States, she had spent some time with our family. From Rome, she sent the blessing with the Pope's "zucchetto" (a white skull cap that he occasionally removes and presents to people). The anniversary dinner party was a great success. Papa proudly said: "Just remember one thing: If it wasn't for me, none of you would be here today!"

Years later, our parents decided to return to Bergen County where they bought a house in Rutherford, NJ. They lived at 189 Summit Cross in a smaller house than before. Every day a woman would walk her dog, stop in front of the house, and leave the dog's "duty" on the lawn. One day papa followed the woman to find out where she lived. He returned home, picked up the mess in a shovel, and carried it to her house. He rang the doorbell and said: "I think this belongs to you." The woman learned her lesson.

Again he planted vegetables alongside of the house, but this time the vegetables could be seen because the property was on a corner. Mamma wanted only flowers; papa wanted his tomato patch and other vegetables. When his plants grew too close to the front of the property, mamma would remove them!

His love of gardening never diminished. One day in the fall I visited my parents and found papa taking nails from strips of wood. When I asked why, he retorted: "Well, I'm saving this wood for the hothouse in the spring!" He was eighty-three years old.

My parents looked after each other. At times they were pleased when they outwitted each other. Mamma always complained about the Di Nobili cigars papa liked to smoke. In Little Ferry where there were mosquitoes and people complained, he would announce triumphantly that the insects gave him no problem. He kept them away with his cigars.

Papa enjoyed speaking about previous business negotiations. Whether he was buying property or selling it, he never signed contracts. He was satisfied by a handshake, believing in the golden rule: "Do to others as you would have them do to you!" Most often he was left "holding the bag," for several people took advantage of his lack of business acumen. Although, as he admitted, he lost many opportunities, he never lost his good nature and good humor.

Once with the $2,000 in cash he had realized from the sale of property, he decided to invest all in 1,000 baby chicks with the idea of starting a "chicken farm." This concept pleased him immensely, but the project did not succeed: an epidemic soon wiped out his assets. Although papa always regretted this investment—a complete loss—it did not dampen his initiative to take care of his family of eight children. He provided family support and maintained his independent spirit.

Even as octagenarians my parents were still very active. One evening they were sitting in the front row at the wake of an elderly friend. Thinking that my father was in the coffin, a stranger approached my mother and expressed his deep feelings of sympathy at her terrible loss. My dad overheard the stranger, poked him several times with his cane, and remarked: "What do you mean? I want you to know I'm here, and this" he said, as he continued to poke him, "will assure you that I'm here!"

At another wake, standing before the coffin, papa was heard to whisper a prayer for the deceased man that was followed by the words: "Better you than me!" And after my mother's funeral Mass, when Mr. Paul F. Freytag tried to console him by saying, "You will soon be happy to join her in heaven," papa responded, "But didn't you bury your wife some forty years ago?"

Shall I say that God blessed my wonderful parents only with joy? No, although they loved and admired their children, they were not spared the disappointments and sorrows that life imposes. Many were the financial failures, family experiences, sorrows and challenges. Yet, they would live to a good old age.

In June 1964, I visited my parents before departing for Rome as a Fulbright scholar. Mamma was in terrible pain and said: "You probably will not find me here when you return." I told her I would pray that she would recover from her illness. While her condition declined during the summer months, she refused to go to the hospital until my return in September. Only then did she agree. The nurses were amazed to find her saying her prayers and crocheting in bed before the operation. The doctors operated and realized there was no hope. They could do nothing. She was in excruciating pain. The cancer had spread throughout her body.

Mamma had appointed me the executrix of her will and wanted me to review it with her in the hospital before she died. I assured her that she had remembered all her children and grandchildren. Her suffering increased intensely and she prepared for eternity with God. Her prayers were answered and, within a few days, on September 28, 1964, she passed away peacefully.

Papa was devastated. Our parents had been very active and totally independent. They had even celebrated their sixtieth wedding anniversary! Now he was alone. Within a few months, papa had a stroke and lingered for three years in the Saddle Brook Nursing Home. He was paralyzed and confined to his bed. One day while visiting, he began ringing the call bell. I asked if I could help, but he ignored me and continued ringing. Then, with a twinkle in his eyes, he said: "I'm just testing."

Shortly after, during another visit, my dad was complaining and insisted on returning home. I tried to console him, encouraging him to be patient with the personnel, suggesting that he bear his sufferings for the love of God, as part of his future purgatory. Fundamentally a very good and honest man throughout his life, papa did not calmly accept his present suffering. However, he did have a sense of humor and, without hesitation, responded: "Never you mind, my dear. I'll take my chances!" Papa died October 29, 1967.

I think mamma and papa would be smiling if they knew that, on November 11, 1996, their youngest daughter became an honorary citizen of Pontecagnano, Italy, the town they left behind at the turn of the century.

Chapter Two: Life as a Teenager

> "The Lord is my light and my salvation
> whom shall I fear?
> The Lord is my life's refuge
> Of whom should I be afraid?" *(Psalm 27)*

We are back at the dining room table, on Labor Day in 1935, where I made my momentous announcement that I was leaving to become a nun. As I retrace the trail of influences that gave me direction, I am aware that like so many others in their formative years, I was inspired by a teacher. Her name was Sister Annunziata, a Benedictine nun, who taught the eighth grade at Saint Mary's School in neighboring Hackensack. Each morning, carrying my books and a lunchbox meal lovingly prepared by my mother, I commuted by bus from Little Ferry.

I realized that my choice of vocation was very sacred and I spoke of it to no one. It was a silent but insistent whisper that changed the course of my life. I knew I was to be enrolled at Saint Cecilia's High School in Englewood. I also knew that I had to respond to God's call and that this move would mark the turning point in my life. I confided in Sister Annunziata that I, too, wanted to become a nun. She invited me to visit her motherhouse in Elizabeth, NJ. Recognizing my eager interest to be genuine, she made arrangements for me to attend the Benedictine high school, beginning that September.

Earlier in June, I was confirmed at Saint Margaret's Church in Little Ferry. Here the confirmation class was taught by the Religious Teachers Filippini. Although I did not receive confirmation instructions from them because I already attended a Catholic school, fate would dictate the major role that the Religious Teachers of Saint Lucy Filippini were to play in my life.

The Pontifical Institute of the Religious Teachers Filippini was founded in 1692, by Lucy Filippini and Cardinal Mark Anthony Barbarigo. In her life and work, Saint Lucy anticipated the spirit and activity of the Roman Catholic Church today. She was in the best sense of the term a modern woman and a modern saint. With boundless love of God, she sought to reform the degraded customs of her times. She directed souls to virtuous living. Her activities were divided between the work of the schools for young girls and the social apostolate: spiritual exercises for women, visits to needy families and care of the sick. No surprise that her apostolate spread rapidly throughout Italy.

In 1910 Pope Pius X sent five Religious Teachers to care for the Italian immigrants in Trenton, NJ. A few weeks after their arrival, they opened Saint Joachim School for the children of these immigrants. Under the leadership of Mother Ninetta Jonata, the school developed, but the Sisters had to overcome many difficulties.

Several years later when Dr. Edward C. Griffin, the pastor, attempted to replace the Religious Teachers Filippini with non-Italian Sisters, the parishioners reacted. There were two colonies of parishioners: those from the region of Umbria and those from Campania. Determined to support the Sisters, the parishioners formed a committee. History records one member's remark: "Something must be done about this. If not, it's going to be too bad for Dr. Griffin, because a dish of spaghetti and the electric chair mean the same thing to me right now!"

Another incident occurred when a group of women, with clubs and sticks hidden under their aprons, rushed into the auditorium and barred all the exits. Commanded by the pastor to leave, they refused and said: "You get out of this parish! Woe to you if you send our Sisters away!" Only after the pastor promised to keep the Sisters did the women relent.

Mother Ninetta continued to work and suffer for the Church as she did during the first eight years in Trenton. She was dedicated to evangelization, education, sanctification of the faithful, seeking out and consoling the lost, the poor, the rejected. She loved to underline the signs of special esteem and benevolence extended by the Popes to the Religious Teachers Filippini. Reaffirming the Institute's founding history and its development, throughout her life she was at the service of the Church. She frequently reminded the Sisters that our Foundress had been called to Rome in 1707 by Pope Clemente XI, and that we were a Pontifical Institute and must always remain devoted to the Pope.

In 1918, Mother Ninetta met Bishop Thomas Joseph Walsh who became the superior of the Religious Teachers Filippini in the United States. In 1930, the motherhouse was transferred from Villa Victoria, in Trenton, to Villa Lucia (later renamed Villa Walsh) located in the suburbs of Morristown. Under the direction of Bishop Walsh and Mother Ninetta, the Institute flourished. Today the Sisters serve in elementary and secondary schools, child day care centers, retreat ministry, parish ministry, religious education and in other areas of need where they are missioned.

In June 1935, Bishop Thomas Joseph Walsh was officiating at the confirmation ceremony that took place in Saint Margaret's Church where I had been baptized. I remember this day of my confirmation as though it were yesterday. It was the first time in my life that I had seen a Bishop—so impressive, so majestic in all his robes, with his crosier and miter. While he spoke, his piercing eyes met mine, and I followed every word, especially when with his finger pointed—it seemed at me—he said, "And if there is any young girl of Italian extraction who wishes to become a nun, she **must** join the Religious Teachers Filippini. She **must** go to Villa Lucia in Morristown," For me, this was the Voice of God. I had no choice, but to follow this command.

My plans to become a Benedictine nun were altered. I was only thirteen, but I was not a silly child. I was a serious youngster, who loved to read, and perhaps because I was usually in the company of so many older siblings, I understood the significance of a career decision. But even more than that—this day, I felt that God Almighty was telling me what to do.

What happened next perhaps best illustrates my determination because I even wonder today at my courage. I approached Sister Mary

Falcone who had prepared the youngsters for the ceremony, and told her, "Bishop said I have to go to Villa Lucia, the motherhouse of the Religious Teachers Filippini." The following week, thanks to her having made arrangements, I was an observer at the investiture ceremony, that took place on the steps of the Southern Colonial Mansion, built in 1878. Sitting in the front row, I was completely in awe at the pomp and circumstance that infused the occasion and that only a personality like Bishop Walsh could orchestrate with such zeal.

The Directress of Novices was the above-mentioned Mother Ninetta, whom I now met after the ceremony. She invited me to visit her that summer in Morristown. Again, my recollection of a morning in July stirs me to wonder when I recall the courage that inspired me— a youngster who had never left home before. From Newark, where I was visiting a cousin, I climbed on a bus bound for Morristown in quest of Villa Lucia. As I began a two-mile walk on Western Avenue, the noon church bells were ringing. I approached the tower and walked up the hill to the mansion door, where I rang the bell and presented myself.

I was wearing my graduation dress with its hand-rolled hem. I noticed that the hem had begun to unravel, so by the time the door opened, I was crying, worrying whether it was all right to be seen in public in less than tip-top state. But I was greeted with love, and soon Sister Margherita Pecorini, assistant directress, came with a needle and thread and repaired the hem. This was the same kind of tenderness I knew at home with my family in Little Ferry—and perhaps, being the youngest of eight, I was a little spoiled and expected to be treated the same way here.

During my interview with Mother Ninetta, she planned that, on September 2 (scarcely six weeks later), I should return to Villa Lucia to start high school there—not at Saint Cecilia's High School in Englewood where my family expected me to attend and graduate as had my brother and sisters. I told no one until the Saturday that fell two days before Labor Day, when I went to confession, and then revealed to Father Maxwell, the pastor of Saint Margaret's mission church that I was going to become a nun and that on Monday, I had to be at Villa Lucia. His response? "Oh, I'll take you there."

Now at the dinner table, having made my announcement, I excused myself and went upstairs to change my clothes. My words were taken lightly. But it seemed that neither had Father Maxwell taken me seriously. At 1:15 p.m., his car was nowhere in sight. I called his office only to be told that he would not be in for the rest of the day. At this point, I must have been more than a little impatient to carry out my plan because I called Mother Ninetta to say, "You told me to come today and Father Maxwell said he would take me and he's not home, and I don't know what to do."

Mother Ninetta seemed not unfamiliar with such a situation. Neither she nor I had told my parents, but she told me confidently to telephone the Filippini Sisters who were in Hackensack and tell them to find someone to drive me to the motherhouse in Morristown. Within a half-hour after my telephone call, following her instructions, a large black limousine, the kind one sees in funeral processions, drew up in front of my house, and a chauffeur awaited me.

There was no need to take a suitcase because Mother Ninetta had said, "You don't need anything; we'll take care of everything." All my childhood treasures were left behind—even the beautiful pearl necklace given to me by my confirmation godmother.

By now, my family had begun to realize that my plan was not a childish whim. My sister Marie said, "Ma, you must go with her. I'll come with you because certainly she can't go alone with a stranger," and the two accompanied me to Villa Lucia in Morristown. Here, Mother Ninetta greeted us hospitably and sent for coffee and cookies.

I must say that, although my mother was cooperative, she had begun to cry. At one point, Mother Ninetta asked, "How many children do you have?" "Eight" was my mother's response. "How many girls," came the next question. When my mother replied "Seven," Mother Ninetta shocked her by saying bluntly, "Seven—and you are not willing to give one of these seven girls to the Lord? Aren't you ashamed of yourself." Mother immediately stopped crying.

Quiet negotiations followed. My mother permitted me a few weeks' stay at the Villa. Now, as a postulant, I went off to be dressed in a black dress and a veil, so pleased that I had won my battle.

Chapter Three: Convent Life

**"But by the grace of God I am what I am,
and His grace toward me was not in vain..."**
(I Corinthians 15:10)

Was it all smiles afterward? How could it be for a 13-year-old girl who was terribly homesick? I had never been away from home, but here in the mansion, on the third floor, I shared a large dormitory room with forty other young girls. Each one had a bed surrounded by a white curtain, a night table and a chair.

How better to begin to describe my change of residence than to view the visible magnificence of my new home? The mansion was the only building with living quarters on the property that was originally called Tower Hill. It was the residence of Louis Charles Gillespie, a multimillionaire businessman from Richmond, Virginia. In 1878, he built a summer home for his nine children. Several years later he remodeled the house into a Gilded Age mansion which became his family's permanent residence. He imported a variety of trees from Hamburg, Germany, two of which are not indigenous to northern Jersey: the Laurel Oak and the Bur Oak. They still stand on the south-west lawn area near the mansion and add majesty and splendor to Tower Hill.

The beautiful divided staircase of carved oak, the differently designed borders for the parquet floors, and the woodwork of highly finished quartered oak and mahogany with its extensive hand carving are among the mansion's extraordinary features. Each room had its own fireplace. One can only marvel at the twelve hand-carved differently-designed mantelpieces embellished with tile in various colorful designs that had been imported from Holland.

Constructed out of Philadelphia pressed brick, with white marble trim and green-tiled roof, this house has a porte-cochere and extensive wide porches with steps leading to the lawn. The mansion is Southern Colonial with Corinthian columns that support a second porch commanding a breathtaking view described by some visitors as "Little Switzerland." The complex is located on a 750-foot elevation, the highest point within a 30-mile radius of New York City.

In 1894, our water tower, a huge stone edifice, 26 square feet at the base with walls 42 inches thick was built. It is 70 feet high with a chimney 12 feet higher, and on the second floor there is an open fireplace of red Potsdam sandstone. It was erected over a 417-foot deep well; a steam engine on the ground floor pumped water into a tank on the fourth floor of the mansion. (Incidentally, living in the mansion was not always full of the amenities of life. Many comforts were lacking. I recall that, quite often, when we washed in the morning, the tank did not supply the third-floor residents with sufficient water as we washed our faces or brushed our teeth.)

The water tower is six stories, and from its lookout on clear nights, there is a panoramic view of New York City, and even the Brooklyn Bridge is visible. Undoubtedly, this property served as a lookout for George Washington's forces during the Revolutionary War. The mansion remained unoccupied for ten years when the Gillespie Family left Tower Hill, and until Bishop Thomas Joseph Walsh purchased the estate in 1929. On February 16, 1930, the Religious Teachers Filippini transferred their motherhouse from Trenton to Morristown. It was called *Villa Lucia* and a decade later renamed *Villa Walsh*.

In 1935, the Saint Lucy Filippini Chapel was built with a bridge connecting it to the mansion. Its interior recalls Renaissance art. Through the beauty and realism of paintings by world-famous Professor Gonippo Raggi and through the originality and gracefulness of its stained glass windows, this outstanding monument inspires a sense of mystery that uplifts the soul as it instructs and inspires visitors.

Multi-windowed bridges connected the other brick buildings that followed: Brown Hall (1936), Freytag Hall (1942), and the seven-story Ninetta Hall (1962) with its large auditorium. A walk-way now under construction, and adjacent to the chapel, will connect a home-care facility to house the aging members that once—a long time ago—were welcomed as young aspirants to the Sisterhood.

The chapel was not the only gift from Monsignor James T. Browne, pastor of Immaculate Conception parish in Hackensack. His $60,000 gift for a chapel was an inheritance he received as a boy scout when he saved the life of his friend who had been bitten by a serpent. Aware of the need for more adequate housing, he also proposed to finance a dormitory building to house the young girls in the Novitiate. This meant that he would donate an additional $40,000. With his unexpected death, it was his sister, Mrs. Matilda O'Neill who kept his promise. About a year after the chapel was blessed on December 30, 1935, we dismantled our beds and carried them with chairs and night tables from the third floor of the mansion to a new dormitory building.

It was while living in this building that I learned many practical things from Sister Margherita Pecorini, assistant to Mother Ninetta. She was an older woman who had arrived from Florence, Italy, and spoke Italian beautifully. She encouraged us to obey Bishop Walsh who said we were to speak Italian every day from 1 p.m. to 5 p.m. It was from her that I learned to express myself colloquially in the Italian language. She loved me and depended on me. I was always at her side and, helping her, I was also learning many practical things. For instance, I remember that, while she sewed our dresses, I cut the material with the help of a pattern. My name became "Margheritina." In the Tuscan dialect, "ina" was added to a word when the meaning was endearing.

Once, I became extremely ill with bronchitis and a very high fever. Concerned about my condition, she called the doctor and alerted Mother Ninetta and Mother Saccucci. Soon they were at my bedside and I remember that I was told to drink whiskey. In the excitement Sister Margherita Pecorini forgot to replace the cork on the bottle and I heard Mother Ninetta gently reprimand her because, she said, the whiskey would lose its potency. Actually, as a result of this illness, my left ear became infected and I lost the ability to hear properly. Years later when I realized I was handicapped, I recalled this incident. How I managed over the years without the use of my left ear is miraculous. My solution to the problem: In advance, I simply alert people on my left side to favor my right ear.

In 1910 and during the formative period of the American Province of Saint Lucy, it was Mother Ninetta Jonata who recognized the importance of learning thoroughly the English language and the need to document one's mastery with a diploma of higher education. She realized, too, that only in this way would the Sisters be able to compete successfully with other religious groups already dedicated to teaching. Thus, she envisioned and sent her followers to highly prestigious colleges and universities, both Catholic and secular. By her example, Italian immigrants soon learned that the most effective way to promote themselves and their children to a dignified status in the American social environment was through education. In fact, because of her efforts, the New Jersey Department of Education eventually placed the teaching of Italian on the same level as courses of other modern foreign languages.

With true missionary spirit the Religious Teachers Filippini helped preserve the customs and traditions of the Italian community. They encouraged participation in parish celebrations and feasts, and joined the immigrants in processions honoring their patron saints. They also directed church choirs and plays, fostered social organizations, visited homes and local hospitals, and conducted catechetical classes for those unable to attend their schools.

When the second and third generations of Italian immigrants became professors, doctors, lawyers, businessmen, and political leaders, many searched for more suitable dwelling places. As the population shifted its location and the character of national parishes changed, so too did the ministry of the Religious Teachers. But one thing did not change: respect for Bishop Walsh's command to teach the Italian language and heritage. However, his plans were no longer restricted to their elementary and high schools.

How would I later follow in this path? Inspired by Bishop Walsh and as a member of the Pontifical Institute of the Religious Teachers Filippini founded in Italy in 1692, I too continued the promotion of Italian culture at Villa Walsh and, on a vaster scale, at the university level. At first, after obtaining the Ph.D. at Columbia University, in an effort to spark renewed interest and develop a new awareness and concern for Italian, I taught Italian Literature courses at Seton Hall University, South Orange, NJ, from 1962 to 1965.

Subsequently, in September 1965, I was responsible for the introduction of Italian courses on the Madison campus of Fairleigh Dickinson University, New Jersey's largest private university, founded by Dr. Peter Sammartino. I even conducted FDU summer programs in Italy. Here I taught for twenty years and, for a brief period, I was chairman of the Language Department. My efforts culminated in a Bicentennial research project on Philip Mazzei funded by NEH and NHPRC and other foundations. I also sponsored the 1980 international airmail stamp in honor of Mazzei, a patriot whose friendship with the first five presidents of the United States is well-documented.

But to return to the beginning of my convent living in 1935. It was difficult being an aspirant in those days. For me, there was a big adjustment that had to be made to a life that differed from the one that had nurtured me earlier at home. Although the young girls were fortunate to be under the wing of Mother Ninetta, who was always understanding and encouraging, we were nevertheless only children. I missed my family. In a little hallway that leads from the mansion to the chapel is where someone might have observed me looking out the window. This was my secret place where I would cry almost every day until my home-sickness wore off. At that time, going home for visits was not part of convent life as it is today. Parents were permitted to visit once a month. Each time my father came, he insisted that I return home. "No," came my answer, explaining that I was happy, that I would become a nun.

When I look at photographs from those days, I recall especially the adjustments I had to make—and confess that there is one I never made.   At home, being the youngest on whom the family doted, I usually ate what I enjoyed most. Here the menu included foods that were unfamiliar to my taste. For example, sunnyside-up eggs. On my first Friday in the convent, I refused to eat the egg that was prepared *that* way. Meal-time came and went, and I was still sitting at the table, refusing to eat the egg. Today, I still cannot eat a sunnyside-up egg. These days, the medical advice is that eggs not thoroughly cooked—à la sunnyside-up—are possibly dangerous because the less-cooked yolk retains bacteria. But the year was 1935, in the midst of the Depression, and commodities like eggs were not to be wasted.

One month later I had another unhappy experience. During the monthly meeting of faculty, administration and students gathered in the presence of the chaplain and superiors, each student was asked to stand while her grades were read aloud by the principal. Preceding this ordeal certain students were assigned presentations. My religion teacher asked me to speak extemporaneously about the "Israelites," as I had done in the classroom. Although I knew the story, little did I realize that it was quite different to address a public audience. Well, I curtsied, gave the title of my presentation, looked at the audience, and froze. I could not speak! Instead I began to cry. The sympathetic superiors tried to console me. Encouraged, I pulled out the notes I had hidden in my pocket and read them as fast as I could. I finished, continued crying and rushed to my seat while the audience applauded. I was 13 years old. I never messed up again after that experience.

A few years later, on January 27, 1939, as a novice during my canonical year of spiritual preparation for the Sisterhood, I had the opportunity to speak before a very distinguished audience of friends and benefactors. The occasion was Bishop Thomas Joseph Walsh's anniversary of ordination and a concert was given in his honor. This was indeed a special privilege that, traditionally, served as a preparation for the next special occasion—the Bishop's onomastic day celebration, in the presence of a larger group of ecclesiastics, educators, politicians, and friends. Again I wrote the discourse and was privileged to deliver this more important speech on March 7, the feastday of Saint Thomas Aquinas.

Yes, I had made a commitment at age thirteen that time and the vicissitudes of life would not destroy. As young aspirants to the Sisterhood, we followed a routine of daily prayers and spiritual direction while attending classes in a State-approved high school with qualified teachers. I can still hear Bishop Walsh repeat one of the requirements for the Religious Teachers Filippini: to be able to teach Italian from kindergarten to university!

I thank God that I was able to please him. When he died, we were the beneficiaries of his will, jointly with the Archdiocese of Newark. About fifteen years ago we were informed that an oil well in Oklahoma had just been revived. As treasurer of Villa Walsh, I received a letter stating that we had a share in this well—.01%! The company wanted to give us $200.00 for the rights to this portion of the well. "No, thank you" was our answer.

Fortunately we did not sell it. Since then, although Archbishop Walsh passed away fifty years ago, a small check from him arrives monthly. As I deposit that check I whisper: "Thank you, dear Archbishop, for continuing to care for your spiritual daughters at Villa Walsh."

Frequently my thoughts turn back to him and to our struggling community at the turn of the twentieth century. In 1918, within three days of his installation, Sister Ninetta and her companion arrived at the residence of the new Bishop of Trenton to request an appointment. While waiting for the secretary, they saw the young Bishop in ecclesiastical robes descending the staircase. He noticed the two sisters and went directly toward them, speaking in Italian and greeting them warmly: "Siete voi le Maestre Pie Filippini, le Suore italiane?" (Are you the Religious Teachers Filippini, the Italian Sisters?)

Bishop Walsh took pride in recalling that the first congratulatory telegram he had received on becoming the Bishop of Trenton was from the Religious Teachers Filippini. During their conversation, he reviewed a memorandum that Sister Ninetta had prepared on the history of the Institute. Toward the end of the discussion, Bishop Walsh asked about their living conditions. When he heard that they had to carry their chairs from one room to another, he immediately handed Sister Ninetta a bill and said: "Buy a few chairs as soon as possible." The bill was folded in such a way that she could see only a zero. She recalled having seen a zero on a ten-dollar bill, but this one was different. As the Bishop continued speaking, she fumbled with the bill, curious to know the meaning of that zero. The suspense, she later recalled, was unbearable! After receiving the Bishop's blessing and bidding him goodbye, she unfolded the bill as they left the residence and yes, she had guessed correctly. It was not a ten-dollar bill. Indeed, she had never before seen a one-hundred dollar bill. Instead of walking home that day, the Sisters celebrated by taking the trolley car for the first time.

Soon after, because of the difficulties encountered in Trenton, Mother Rosa Leoni, Superior General, sent a cable asking the sisters to return to Rome. Sister Ninetta appealed to Bishop Walsh who succeeded in keeping them in the United States by sending the following: "Governo proibisce partenza." (The government forbids departure.) The Superior General did not understand whether the reference "government" was civil or ecclesiastical! The sisters remained and prospered, helped by Bishop Walsh's encouragement and personal interest. They followed him in 1930 after he was transferred to the Diocese of Newark. When he died on June 6, 1952, newspapers called him "an apostle of Catholic education and of charity."

Dark clouds hovered over the peoples of Europe in the late thirties, but no tensions surfaced at Villa Lucia High School in Morristown. As novices we studied each summer, and so we finished the required high school courses in three years. Then, after one year of intense spiritual and pedagogical preparation, we were assigned to parishes during the school year. Studies continued in the summer months as we completed Normal School requirements to qualify us to become teachers in the diocesan elementary school system.

On June 12, 1938, in the presence of relatives and friends, I received the religious habit during a most impressive investiture ceremony. I was sixteen years old. Dressed as a bride with a long white veil, I approached the beautifully-decorated altar slowly and, following instructions, before Bishop Walsh, Mother Teresa Saccucci and Mother Ninetta, I removed my veil and long white gown and threw them beyond the altar rail. (Bishop Walsh was an avid baseball fan and was delighted as he observed the throwing of the bridal gown and veil, a symbol of our renunciation of worldly things.) At the altar I remained in a long white petticoat that reached to my ankles while donning the religious habit. When fully dressed, the Bishop blessed me and I returned to my pew carrying a lighted candle as the choir sang my favorite song: "Suscipe Domine" (Accept, Lord, my will, my heart, my memory...).

Three years later, Sunday, August 27, 1941, during the profession ceremony, I finalized my commitment by my Oblation, a permanent promise of fidelity to Christ. Again I appeared before Bishop Walsh. As I knelt before him, he placed a crown of white flowers over my bonnet as the choir sang, "Veni, Sponsa Christi" (Come, Spouse of Christ, accept this crown prepared for you from all eternity!). On that day, I received the gold ring that I have worn since then, fully understanding the significance of my commitment. I understood that Christ promised to be present forever, and that He would love, honor, and accept me as His Spouse. At times faithful to my commitment, at times not so faithful, I have always loved Him and tried to do His Will.

Each day that I pass in front of the altar here at Villa Walsh, I remember the symbolic action I performed on Sunday, June 12, 1938, and the meaningful words of the ceremonial songs. I re-live as well the joy of that first festive occasion on the feast of the Most Blessed Trinity, when at age sixteen I completely and irrevocably dedicated myself to the service of God.

Canonical year was a time of religious preparation in the novitiate. During the summers I attended the Villa Walsh Normal School. For the 1939-1940 scholastic year, I was sent to Montclair, NJ, to be the music director at Mount Carmel Church. This was my first assignment. I directed the choir, was organist for weddings and funerals, and gave piano lessons to children. While I played the organ, Sister Isabel Diena, the soloist, sang beautifully. She was a dear friend, two years my senior.

For many years directing the choir and playing the organ gave me much spiritual consolation. Somehow I sensed that music was helping the congregation to move closer to God. In 1954, my duties changed when I was assigned to Villa Walsh, and I no longer had time to play the organ. I missed the melodies I had played on the organ, especially during the Christmas season. So, I treated myself on Christmas Day and I played all the carols I loved. With no one in chapel for this private "Serenade to the Infant," I reminisced about the past and felt closer to God. Since then, every Christmas Day, I have continued this "private" recital.

But to return to my first assignment in Montclair—Sister Isabel and I had other duties. We canvassed the parish for a church census of every member. In doing so, neither of us was prepared to cope with the worldly problems that people had to face, but we prayed for those we interviewed, roaming the streets, trying to encourage and help whomever we met. The parishioners loved us and invited us into their homes. Several years later, three of the young choir members—Irma Papaleo, Angelina Del Vecchio, and Josephine Ridolfo—joined us in Morristown and are, to this day, dedicated members of the Religious Teachers Filippini.

Meanwhile Eugenio Cardinal Pacelli had been elected Pope, March 2, 1939. The name he took was that of his revered predecessor. As Pius XII, he directed the church for twenty years. Who could foretell that someday I would be writing books in defense of his role in history?

I recall celebrating the coronation of Pope Pius XII, on March 12, 1939. As members of the pontifical family, we were imbued with love, pride and devotion for the newly-elected Pontiff. To participate in the official festivities in Saint Patrick's Cathedral, that day everyone was bussed to Newark.

Mother Teresa Saccucci, Provincial Superior, left for Rome soon after I became a novice and remained there as Superior General during World War II. I know she embraced the 114 Jews (men, women and children) hidden in three of our convents in Rome, for more than a year during the Nazi occupation, with the same solicitude and gentleness I experienced as a young Sister. At the end of World War II, the Jewish women expressed their thanks to the Sisters with the gift of a five-foot statue of the Madonna.

Fifty years later, during the month of November, 1994, I became acquainted with the Sisters who recounted to me the events of the war years and how, despite the dangers encountered, they demonstrated heroic Christian solicitude for their Jewish guests. I gathered these stories, as well as the memoirs of others whom I interviewed, into a book entitled, *Yours Is a Precious Witness: Memoirs of Jews and Catholics in Wartime Italy.*

Three years elapsed and I continued my campaign to make known the work of Pope Pius XII during the Holocaust. Then, one day, I came across a rare book. I read a reference to the Superior General of the Pontifical Institute of the Religious Teachers Filippini, founded in 1692, in *La Chiesa e la Guerra* (The Church and the War). I was truly excited. Indeed a treasury of information about the work of the Vatican during World War II, this out-of-print book, published in 1944, described the help given by the Religious Teachers Filippini.

Though the book did not name the Superior General, I saw her—Mother Teresa Saccucci—in my mind's eye. I felt once again the strength of her prayerfulness; I remembered her humble and dignified appearance, white hair, angelic smile; again I heard her maternal and affectionate words, extending an extraordinary peace among us—just as it affected me when I was in the novitiate at Villa Walsh in Morristown, NJ, from 1935 to 1939.

What I also learned from *La Chiesa e la Guerra* was the fact that the Religious Teachers Filippini helped the Holy Father in the Information Bureau of the Vatican Secretariat of State. According to the author of this book, the Superior General responded during an interview: "For this work in the Information Bureau, I had designated five or six Sisters with typewriters. But every day there were other young women and children of the school who wanted to work for the Holy Father and answer the letters of prisoners of war and the needy. I did all I could to satisfy the Pope's wishes. The work had to be kept secret. As followers of Saint Lucy Filippini, the Sisters dedicated themselves to this task. It was a good sign when there was work in the office and the pontifical initiative succeeded. It was a charity that had no bounds in the midst of hatred and destruction."

The lessons I learned throughout my teaching career came from various sources. One day after school hours, I visited the Children's Hospital in Newark, NJ. As I entered the Ward, I noticed a group of youngsters and, among them, was my little girl with rheumatic fevers whom I had come to visit. Kissing and embracing her, suddenly I felt someone tugging at my skirt. A beautiful black, five-year-old child, looked at me lovingly and said: "Do you have a cold?" Puzzled, I responded "No, dear, I'm fine." She then smiled and said: "Well, in that case, you can kiss me, too." I picked her up, kissed and hugged her and realized that every child present needed to be loved. How could I have been so insensitive!

In 1950, I was appointed Vocation Promoter while teaching in Saint Frances Xavier School in Newark, NJ, where I was also moderator for the Children of Mary Society. Young ladies from this parish soon joined—Grace Zizza, Vilma Cozzini, and Mary DeBacco, who, in 1994, became Superior General of the Filippini Sisters with residence in Rome, Italy.

I recall first seeing Sister Mary in church every morning with her saintly parents. One day I approached her and asked if she would like to attend a weekend retreat at Villa Walsh. She immediately said she had been praying for such an opportunity. I invited her to meet me at the convent and arranged to include her that weekend. Although she had an excellent position as a legal secretary with a law firm, within a few months she entered the Religious Teachers Filippini.

At this time I was not a licensed driver, so I depended on friends to help me get around. The Cozzini family had two young altar boys in high school, Robert and Dorino, who frequently came to my assistance after school hours. One day, I went to the Darlington Seminary to visit Robert, who was preparing for ordination to the priesthood. I had embroidered a "manutergium" that was needed for the ceremony. It was a long white strip of linen cloth, two inches wide, that would be placed around the newly ordained priest's hands by the Bishop. Louis

Fimiani, who was also from Saint Francis Xavier Parish in Newark, looked at me sadly and said: "But I don't have a Sister to make mine!" Moved by his statement, I promised to make a "manutergium" for him, too. And I did. I considered this a great privilege to be asked to sew the one item that a priest usually placed in his mother's coffin, acknowledging the part she played in nurturing his vocation.

Today, Reverend Robert Cozzini is parochial vicar in Epiphany Parish, Cliffside Park, and Monsignor Louis Fimiani is pastor of Blessed Sacrament Parish in Roseland, NJ. The words of Saint Augustine have inspired me throughout my life: "Where there is love, there is no labor; and if labor there be, the labor itself is love."

Those were fruitful years in Newark. I also began a Boys' Choir. Five-year-old John Caprio loved music, but was not of age to join. On Sunday mornings his mother accompanied him to the choir loft. He was fascinated by the beautiful sounds produced by the organ and insisted on sitting on the organ bench. He watched me as I played and listened attentively to the singing. This was the beginning of his career. He began taking piano lessons and his love of music increased. It was his passion. As an adult he became music director for the diocese of Paterson and, then, for the archdiocese of New York. In fact, when Pope John Paul II came to the New York Giants' Stadium, John Caprio composed and directed the music for this special Eucharistic Liturgy. He always attributed his interest in music to "sitting on the organ bench with Sister Margherita!"

One day, the pastor of a local church needed help because he had no organist for a funeral service. I telephoned a young lady to ask that she please take me to the nearby church. When we arrived, opening the music book to the *Dies irae*, I said, "Fortunata, do you know the Requiem Mass in Latin?" Not a bit happy to realize that she had been promoted from "chauffeur" to "soloist," she replied that she knew some of it but not the entire sequence. I tried to calm her, "Don't worry. We'll pull this one off. I'll help you. We can shorten the *Dies irae*. We will sing the first two and the last two stanzas. No one will know the difference!" Somehow we got away with the "new" arrangement. But, despite her baptismal name, that day "Fortunata" did not consider herself very "fortunate!"

Encouraging youngsters to follow a vocation to the sisterhood was not an easy task. I prepared exhibits for diocesan rallies and gave talks wherever I was called. During a Father-Daughter Communion Breakfast, I noticed two five-year-old girls who were listening attentively. After the breakfast they came to me with their dads. I immediately said to one, "Do you think you will be a Sister when you get big?" "Oh, no," she answered, "I have other plans in mind." I patted her cheek and turned to the other little girl, "You want to be a Sister when you grow up, don't you?" "Yes, I want to be like you," she said. Before I could respond, the first little girl looked at me and shouted, "Don't listen to her. She'll probably change her mind when she gets big!" Well, I was shocked to say the least. Indeed, I soon learned that many young girls forget that they once dreamed of serving God.

This experience was only the beginning. I still continued, even asking young ladies to join. I would first ask if they were married. When the answer was negative, I usually added, "Do you think you would like to serve God as a nun?" Years later, I was in a limousine and the driver was a young woman. I asked the usual questions and the answer was unexpected: "Why, I would be the first Methodist nun in the Church!"

To return to my preparation as a teacher, each summer I went on to continue my studies in Italian Literature at Georgian Court College and graduated with a B.A. degree in 1943, at a time when many Americans were little interested in the language of their heritage. Classes were held off-campus so I did not experience living on the beautiful campus in Lakewood, NJ.

My first assignment as a teacher was to the sixth grade in Our Lady of Pompei School in Baltimore, Maryland. These were the years of World War II. On one occasion I needed special protection from the good Lord to avoid a terrible misunderstanding about a letter I received. It happened because on Sunday afternoons I devoted some time to writing letters of encouragement to young men in the service of our country during the war. I had been corresponding with John Schettino who was fighting in Japan and was very homesick.

According to regulations the superior was obliged to censor mail. When John answered my letter, the superior kept it and, then, one day she gave it to the provincial superior during her annual visitation. During my interview, Mother Ninetta questioned me about the letter and told me to read it. I soon learned that it was from John who, while expressing his gratitude for my encouragement and prayers, wrote: "If I could, I would ask you to marry me." I realized how these words had frightened the superior. I looked at Mother Ninetta and said: "But John does not mean this. He's my cousin. We were playmates when I was home. He's just lonesome for his family and friends. There's no reason for concern." She gave me the letter and we both laughed over the incident. Mother Ninetta, who was very understanding, explained to the superior and the three of us agreed that the matter should be dropped.

The following years I taught the seventh and eighth grades, while also serving as organist, directing both the junior and senior choirs, and giving piano lessons on Saturdays. Soon after, four young girls whom I taught in Baltimore joined the Religious Teachers Filippini— Alma Blume, and three sisters Margaret, Mary and Ann Geraghty. They, too, remained faithful to their commitment as Religious Teachers. The Filippini Sisters are truly blessed.

Among the fond memories of my four years in Baltimore, teaching the senior choir is one of them. Members were older professional people who loved to sing and came to rehearsals regularly. They probably knew I was not a great musician, but they loved and supported me. Having studied music for several years while in high school, I recognized that my knowledge of the keyboard was extremely limited. Although I always prepared myself, it was a struggle to play the piano and organ without skipping some notes. And skip them I did. How did I ever attempt to teach three-part choruses we had learned at Villa Walsh? Yet, I remember teaching not only César Franck's *Panis Angelicus*, but Marchetti's *Ave Maria*, as well as *In a Monastery Garden*!

One year I directed an Italian operetta, *Una ciliegia tira l'altra!* (One cherry attracts others). This required a bowl of cherries which was placed backstage the night of the performance. Unfortunately, the stage crew began eating the delicious-looking cherries. When they learned that the bowl of cherries was one of the props, it was too late. Very few remained. It was certainly obvious to the audience that there had been a disaster. But I learned my lesson: Keep cherries under lock and key in future productions!

Then, too, there was Pasquale, a poor student, who had been promoted to the eighth grade because of age. Everyone loved this good-natured young man who was an excellent soccer player. True, he was incapable of following the lessons in class, but he was the best soccer player in the school. The young ladies and I followed him to the soccer field in Patterson Park after school and cheered him heartily. Invariably Pasquale was responsible for the team's success. Years later I learned that he had become a successful businessman.

When I was first assigned to teach in Baltimore, I did not anticipate the following exciting experience with the U. S. Immigration Office. I was nineteen years old and had been in Baltimore several months. Sister Emma Melchiorre, a young nun from Italy who had been in the United States for five years, received notice to report for her citizenship papers. I was asked to accompany her as a witness. The attorney questioned me about whether I had lived in the convent with Sister Emma during the previous five years. I had not. My answer: "Well, I know Sister and have been in communication with her for five years. We met on various occasions at our Motherhouse reunions in Morristown, NJ; we also spent our summers together there; we are now living in the same convent in Baltimore. I think this should satisfy the requirement." The attorney then turned to me with a twinkle in his eye and said, "You may be the witness. However, should you ever decide to leave the convent, please come back to join my firm!" I did not join his firm, but in the past fifty years I have assumed enough tasks to make me eligible: processing immigration papers and passport requests for our nuns, assisting with wills, and every other kind of legal red-tape imaginable.

In September 1947, my assignment was suddenly changed to Holy Rosary School in Jersey City. Why? Because the young musician there was too "short" according to the Sister who was the principal. I was a mere two inches taller, and I knew less music. Still I was given charge of the music department. Besides teaching the seventh grade, I was responsible for the annual stage production for kindergarten to grade eight. There were over one thousand children and everyone was required to participate. The Sister who was too "short" became my assistant and, together, we prepared the program.

One number included the children from all the grades who did not have special parts meaning that several hundred would be included in "The Grand Opera Group." This portion of the program consisted of a few songs. "McNamara's Band" was one number that always made a hit. The first graders were in costume and carried toy instruments. They marched solemnly from the entrance to the auditorium down the main aisle and then proceeded to the stage, midst the cheers and clapping of parents and friends! Once the "Band" arrived on the stage, the "Grand Opera Group" performed beautifully.

Holy Rosary School in Jersey City has many memories. We had over one thousand children and fire drills were held regularly. Silence was required. One day, as my class was lined up in the hallway, a boy was talking. I walked toward him and said, "I'm angry!" He looked at me innocently and retorted very seriously, "Sister, I'm Frank." How could I refrain from laughing?

Accompanied by one of my students, I commuted from Jersey City to Columbia every Saturday for two years. The student who came worked with me in the Paterno library of Casa Italiana and learned to take notes for my research project.

When I enrolled at Columbia University to study Italian, I was instructed by the Mother Superior to sign my name as Margherita Marchione. My namesake, known as Saint Margaret of Cortona, was a thirteenth-century Italian who, after living a sinful life, repented and at age twenty-five became a Third Order Franciscan nun. To avoid complications at Columbia in 1945 when the Admissions Office noted that the name on my transcripts was Margaret, I was told to have it changed officially as Margherita. And so, I now bask in the sunshine of the Latin meaning of margarita, *precious pearl* and the beautiful Italian flower, margherita, *daisy.*

My life has been a continuous miracle: a happy childhood and a loving family. I dreamed and aimed for excellence. I made decisions and implemented them with enthusiasm. I accepted challenges and, with God's help, I achieved my goals.

But what was going on with the Marchione family? World War II was in full swing. As I moved on in the path I had chosen, the siblings I left behind no less zealously pursued their ambitions and, although at times we went in different directions, the strong thread of the Marchione family—our ties to one another—did not diminish over the years.

Chapter Four: Religious Teachers Filippini

**"...like the Apostles, you will be able to sow seeds
of evangelical truth, of culture, and of Christian education."
*(Pope Benedict XV to the Religious Teachers Filippini
before their departure to the United States, February 20, 1921)***

In 1992, the Religious Teachers Filippini celebrated the 300th anniversary of its foundation in Montefiascone, Italy. This was the land of the Etruscans where, about 800 B.C., Etruscan civilization flourished before the rise of Rome. From the Tiber northwestward along the coast and across the Apennines to the Po River, their superiority and wealth was in part based upon their knowledge of ironworking, and they were experts in bronze, gold and pottery. Etruscans were fond of music, games, and racing; they introduced the vine and olive tree and improved agriculture by controlling the rivers for irrigation. Their cities were a loose confederation, each ruled by oligarchical government. It was here that Lucy Filippini was born; she lived in the Etruscan center of Corneto, the ancient Tarquinia.

Even today as one travels along the Tyrrhenian Sea, lovely panoramas of delightful vineyards and healthy gardens meet the eye. Green fields, spreading to the east, are intersected by ancient aqueducts; little white houses on the site of Etruscan tombs and pebbly mounds trimmed with grass and bushes dot the landscape.

It was here that the Pontifical Institute of the Religious Teachers Filippini was founded in 1692, by Lucy Filippini and Cardinal Marcantonio Barbarigo. At age twenty-five, Marcantonio Barbarigo became a member of the Grand Council of the Venetian Republic; five years later he decided to prepare for the priesthood. The founders had much in common: both were of noble families; both were interested not only in education, but also in the social apostolate.

Lucy was sixteen when, at the cardinal's insistence, she went to stay with the Benedictine Sisters of the Monastery of Saint Clare in Montefiascone. She foreshadowed her future apostolate as she taught the religious there to read and write. Several years later, when Cardinal Barbarigo asked her to direct the schools in his diocese, she consented.

This was a period of cultural decadence—a period when false doctrines and practices, such as Jansenism and Quietism, flourished. Among the causes for the dismal social, religious, and moral conditions can be listed the paganizing influence of the Italian Renaissance; the lack of necessary formation for the clergy; the scandalous conduct of the ruling princely families; the ignorance and worldiness of priests and religious.

Poverty, in the late seventeenth-century, was foremost among the many cultural and socio-economic problems existing in Italy. This was a heritage from an Italy dominated and divided, having meager resources. It was a time of regression, of epidemics, of wars and calamities. A new era was rushing in, challenging the old, but a robust Christian-Catholic culture would emerge to face the illuministic innovations of both religious and social life. With ecumenical and prophetic discernment, Cardinal Barbarigo and Lucy Filippini looked ahead to fulfilling their generous, ardent and profound mission of faith and charity. The schools they founded were intended to promote the dignity of womanhood and help influence a healthy family life. The social apostolate was an extension of the classroom. History records the dynamic response—a rebirth of Christian living and value-centered education.

In 1707, Pope Clement XI called Lucy to establish her schools in Rome. Not only in the Papal States, but also throughout the Grand Duchy of Tuscany, Lucy established centers of spiritual renewal where the teachers in these schools kept faith alive for uneducated, humble, unfortunate people.

In founding and consolidating her work, Lucy Filippini had much to endure; yet no lament escaped her lips in times of trial. When accused of the heresy of Quietism, she stood with humility and fortitude before the inquisitors of the Holy Office. She had no need to fear them, for there was no shadow of error in her "doctrine." Her perception of the pressing needs of a world that had lost the authentic meaning of Christianity and her response to those needs are two important elements of her particular calling. She was obedient to her Bishop and to the Sovereign Pontiff. From their hands she accepted the divine mandate.

Lucy divided her activities between the work of the schools she established for young girls and the social apostolate: spiritual exercises for women, continued guidance of her former students, visits to needy families, and care of the sick. Today in our foreign missions, Sisters conduct literacy programs, teach Christian Doctrine to children and adults, visit families, distribute food and clothing, assist the aged and abandoned, visit lepers and perform basic tasks of charity helping people spiritually, materially and financially.

Spanning several centuries, the Pontifical Institute of the Religious Teachers Filippini remains relevant and deserving of deep appreciation for its timely lessons of love and hope.

In Italy, as part of the ongoing three-hundred-year celebration of the Religious Teachers Filippini, the Postal Ministry on May 2, 1992, issued a commemorative stamp as part of their Philatelic Stamp program. The United States Post Office also issued a special cancellation to mark the opening of the year-long festivities for the tercentenary.

Celebrations continued to abound in all parts of the world where the Sisters were missioned: Europe, Asia, Africa, North and South America. Pope John Paul II's blessing included congratulations "for the educational and evangelical work that has been accomplished and continues to be performed for the poor and the humble." Recognition in 1992 included a Proclamation issued by New Jersey Governor James Florio and a Message from President George Bush referring to the Sisters' "wonderful example of Christian faith and charity. ...Your work shines today as a reminder that it is through helping others that we find the best within ourselves."

I celebrated our founders with my books: *From the Land of the Etruscans* (Edizioni di Storia e Letteratura, 1989) and *Cardinal Mark Anthony Barbarigo* (Religious Teachers Filippini, 1992). Indeed, Lucy Filippini's work as an educator has assumed universal and eternal values. On the strength of what she accomplished during the sixty years of her earthly life, she could easily and successfully pass the test and attain the rewards reserved to the Blessed. Just as in Dante's *Paradiso*, Piccarda Donati declares, "In His will is our peace," so too Lucy, in meeting and working with Cardinal Barbarigo, could very well repeat those words. Together they successfully face the challenge of history and stand the test of time.

Also for the occasion of our 300th anniversary, I prepared a new book entitled *A Pictorial History of the Saint Lucy Filippini Chapel* (Edizioni del Palazzo, Prato, 1992), located at Villa Walsh in Morristown, NJ. It is the story of the Pontifical Institute of the Religious Teachers Filippini since 1692. What has transpired since then testifies to the zeal of many women who, in the light of the Gospel and the mission spirit of their founders, dedicated themselves during the past 300 years to the needs of the world. The Institute's development in the United States of America has been rich in deeds and accomplishments.

The book attempts to be a monument of Christian inspiration to convey the spirit and sanctity of Saint Lucy Filippini visualized through the originality and gracefulness of paintings by the renowned artist, Gonippo Raggi, and through the exquisite stained glass windows, mosaics and imported marble. Some thirty pages of black and white sketches, explaining each symbol in the chapel, followed by twenty pages of colored photographs depicting sections of the chapel also enhance the book.

Lucy Filippini's work of evangelization continues and her wishes have been fulfilled. She often repeated these words: "As for me, I long to be present in every corner of the earth to cry out everywhere and plead with all peoples of every sex, age, and condition; 'Love God, love God!' O my God, make me into many Lucys so that, multiplied, I may spread Your glory far and wide!"

For three centuries, the Religious Teachers Filippini have inspired generations of young people who have joined with distinction the ranks of doctors, political leaders, attorneys, businessmen, clergymen, and teachers. They have brought new hope to God's people through vibrant Christian living as they carry on their ministry of dedicated teaching and social involvement.

After teaching in Newark, and serving as local Diocesan Vocation Promoter, I later became increasingly involved in the administration of Villa Walsh, filling positions in various capacities. Mother Ninetta Jonata, who was now Superior General in Rome, appointed me Directress of the Aspirancy and Vocation Promotion Directress for the entire Province of Saint Lucy by an official letter of July 31, 1954. This was indeed a great honor.

I revered Mother Ninetta, not only as our foundress in the United States, but principally as a saintly person. With great humility, in her most difficult trials, she remained serene and tranquil when unjustly accused by some of the very people she loved. Yet, nothing disturbed her peace. There was no appeal, no word of defense, no act of resentment. She was intimately united to Christ and His Blessed Mother. To the end of her life, her lamp burned with the oil of pure charity.

At Villa Walsh, while a full-time high school teacher, I was also house-mother, guiding future candidates to the Religious Teachers Filippini. They would become role models of decency, honesty, compassion, courage and honor for our young people. Several young ladies in my tutelage—Ascenza Tizzano, Rita Tassinari, Jo-Ann Pompa, Roseann Fernandez and Marie Antonelli—became superiors and elementary school principals. Today, Sister Ascenza is the superior of Villa Walsh. Others also developed into responsible and creative members of the Filippini community.

Later, other administrative positions were assigned to me. Besides the office of Directress of the Aspirants, I became Secretary to the Provincial Superior, Treasurer of the Province of Saint Lucy, Coordinator for the Foreign Missions, President of Walsh College, Provincial Councillor, and Treasurer of Villa Walsh.

In order to accompany the young aspirants to town when necessary, I was obliged to learn to drive. Someone gave me a few lessons, and I passed the driver's test for a license. But I really had not learned very well. One day, there was no traffic whatsoever as I was driving to town and enjoying the open space and the beautiful spring blossoms. Totally unaware that I was speeding, I raced down Western Avenue. An officer motioned for me to pull over. Still distracted, when the officer approached the car, I smiled and began the conversation saying, "Officer, can I help you?" The officer was stunned and requested my license. As I handed it to him, I said, "Is something wrong, Officer?" Evidently disarmed, in a serious tone, he inquired whether I realized I had gone over the speed limit and gently suggested I be more careful in the future.

Parking a car and driving one continued to be a problem for me. At the Fairleigh Dickinson University campus, students generally came to my rescue and parked the car when I did not succeed. Getting out of a parking lot when I visited my dad in a nursing home in Saddle Brook always posed a problem. One day, I just couldn't manage. Traffic moved constantly and there were no traffic lights or officers in sight. So I lowered the window, prayed, and waited for a passer-by. I explained my predicament, and immediately the gentleman stopped all the traffic, motioning me to pull out. I graciously nodded to the left and to the right acknowledging everyone's courtesy and triumphantly drove out of the parking lot.

In 1960, I served as secretary to Mother Carolina Jonata, Provincial Superior, the guiding star for many years at Villa Walsh and also in Brazil. A woman of prayer and charity, she attracted the respect, admiration and love of all the Sisters. She had great musical talent, and under her direction the Villa Walsh Choir was famous in New Jersey. With her younger sister, Katherine Jonata, an artist who directed the young Sisters in the Novitiate, Mother Carolina was a dedicated collaborator, working closely with Mother Ninetta Jonata, her cousin.

From 1966 to the Millennium, among other duties, I have been filling the task of treasurer in the Bursar's Office, serving several

Provincials: Sisters Helen Ippoliti, Mary Paglia, Clare Testa, Mary DeBacco and Frances Lauretti. I was elected Councillor in 1988 for six years and also continued to be treasurer of Villa Walsh. Presently we are engaged in building a health-care facility for our retired Sisters at an estimated cost of 15 million dollars. This building will be a lasting tribute to the Religious Teachers Filippini, their families and their friends.

Pope John Paul II referred to the elderly of the world as "a treasure for the Church, a blessing for the world." We can apply these words to our aged Sisters who helped educate young people in their faith. Thousands of students have benefited from their instruction, counsel and loving care. These students have taken their place in society and have become role models as priests, deacons, religious, professionals and dedicated lay ministers.

Chapter Five: Columbia University

**"The Casa Italiana, under the able, resourceful,
and tireless efforts of Giuseppe Prezzolini (1930-40),
was a veritable beehive of scholarly and educational activity."**
(Columbia University Souvenir Booklet, 1927-62)

My enrollment at Columbia was the beginning of a long friendship and literary relationship with Giuseppe Prezzolini who, over a period of forty years, proved to be a major influence in my endeavors. From his encouragement came such fortifying inspiration that I welcome the opportunity to relate the story of our friendship, beginning in 1945 and continuing until the time of his death, in 1982, at age one hundred.

During high school at Villa Walsh, everyone studied the Italian language. In 1945, having achieved some fluency, and because of my interest in the language and culture of my roots, I was assigned to a parish in Garfield, NJ, to translate sermons into Italian for the pastor and fill the role of the parish musician. Moreover, I was directed to enroll in September for one course toward an M.A. in Italian Language and Literature at Columbia University.

I was twenty-three years old, very young for a nun to attend a non-Catholic university. Along with my very dear friend, Sister Mary Paglia, I registered for a course in Machiavelli, but we needed the professor's approval. Like our fellow-students, we arranged to meet Giuseppe Prezzolini, the well-known Italian professor in the department. When we arrived, he greeted us cordially and then said bluntly: "I teach Machiavelli. The kernel of Machiavelli's thought is that politics is a human activity incompatible with Christian morality, the basis upon which the Western world was founded. A course on Niccolò Machiavelli and Machiavellianism will not be in your best

interests. I think you nuns ought to go sign up for something else."
Our answer was definitive: "Our superiors told us to register for this
course!" And we did.

Prezzolini was considered a leading authority on Machiavelli, an
important figure of the Renaissance, especially distinguished for his
insight into politics. Though Machiavelli may be called the Galileo of
political activity, his ideas were essentially anti-Christian and drew
ferocious opposition from both Catholics and Protestants.

In his courses, Prezzolini closely examined Machiavelli's works
and doctrines, illustrated the application of his philosophy and pointed
out the misinterpretations and modifications through which so-called
Machiavellian ideas developed and gained notoriety. Each age has
interpreted Machiavelli according to its own matrix; every national
spirit finds lines to admire or despise. Prezzolini, a brilliant scholar,
highlights the ramifications of Machiavelli's thought emerging in
modern Western philosophy—in the national policies of France,
Germany, England, Russia, and America.

All the students affectionately called him "Prezzy." In his revised
edition of *L'italiano inutile* (Vallecchi, Firenze, 1964), Prezzolini
dedicated a chapter to the Filippini Sisters who attended his classes.
He begins with: "How a devil like me knows these Nuns is a story I
must tell!" He says that the whole atmosphere in his classes changed
with the presence of nuns. Previously, students would snicker and
make all sorts of irreverent statements regarding morality in the
courses on Machiavelli. There was none of that anymore.

As my mentor, Prezzolini recommended that I write my M.A.
thesis on Girolamo Savonarola, a Domenican Friar, a contemporary
and political opponent of Machiavelli. He was delighted when, rather
than dwelling only on the differences between Savonarola and
Machiavelli, I located passages indicating areas in which they agreed.
For instance, if a choice had to be made between a devout leader who
was lacking in intelligence and one who was intelligent and capable of
ruling but less devout, it behooved the citizens to select a person with
intelligence.

When, in January of 1949, I successfully defended my thesis on *The Politics of Girolamo Savonarola,* Prezzolini concurred with the professors that I should add to this work and use that material toward a doctoral dissertation. The thesis committee arranged that I begin immediately. However, after much consultation, my superiors at Villa Walsh decided that I should not continue my studies in deference to my duties as full-time teacher and parish musician.

Years passed and I lost contact with my professors at Columbia. In September 1954, as mentioned, I was assigned to Villa Walsh and, several years later, I was given permission to return to the university. I registered for one course. Although Prezzolini was no longer teaching, he did, however, maintain the same office in Casa Italiana as before and greeted me cordially whenever I sought his advice.

One day, I arrived in his office at Casa Italiana just as he was checking his mail. He had received a miniature pamphlet of poems, *Curriculum Vitae* by Clemente Rebora and asked me to read them as an example of Rebora's life and poetic genius. Prezzolini told me that, in the early 1900s he had published some of this poet's writings in the literary review, *La Voce*, and then suggested that I go to Italy to meet with Rebora and research his life and poetry.

Officially Professor Peter Riccio was my Ph.D. mentor, but it was Prezzolini who directed me behind the scenes. One day, while encouraging me to obtain a Ph.D., he stated categorically: "You are not a genius, but you have the potentiality for good work." Within months I was given the Columbia Garibaldi Scholarship with the condition that I interview Clemente Rebora and do my dissertation on him.

Thus began a new period of my life. Funds were now available, but the idea of permission to travel alone in Italy was unthinkable. Who could imagine such a liberty for a nun! To travel alone was not allowed. The Provincial Superior wrote to the General Superior for permission. The answer: "Absolutely no! Consult the local ordinary of the archdiocese of Newark." However, Archbishop Thomas Boland—who had succeeded Archbishop Thomas Joseph Walsh—responded:

"That's wonderful! Sister Margherita may be permitted to accept the scholarship and travel to Italy alone."

When informed, Mother Ninetta still was not convinced. She wrote to the Provincial, Mother Carolina: "I do not agree, I'll have to ask our Superior, Archbishop Diego Venini, the Secret Almoner of the Pope." Fortunately, he knew Clemente Rebora who was now a member of the Rosmini Fathers in Stresa on Lago Maggiore. His answer was, "Yes, she may be permitted to travel alone."

What followed were many wonderful experiences in Italy—except for one. It was the worse misunderstanding of my entire convent life. Before leaving the United States I had consulted Mother Carolina about my plans. Time was of the essence because the subject of my study was very ill. To avoid delay I arranged to fly TWA from New York, then go directly to Stresa from Malpensa Airport in Milan in order to interview Clemente Rebora.

My planned visit to the Mother General in Rome would take place during the last week in August; afterward, I would fly back to New York. However, once I learned that the professors I planned to visit in Rome would be away on vacation, I telephoned them to arrange alternate appointments before their departure. I also informed Mother Carolina about the changes, asking her permission to go to Rome earlier than August, specifically asking what I should do about the planned later visit to the Mother General before returning home. Mother Carolina responded by telegram, delivered via telephone, and received by the Rosmini Sisters with whom I was living in "Arca Pacis Convent." Unfortunately, Mother Carolina's words, when they reached me as a written message, made no sense perhaps because they had been received by an Italian nun who understood no English.

This written message listed Italian cities (I still have the note!): Palermo, Roma, Otranto, Novara, Italia, Firenze, Roma, Ancona, Novara, Torino, Empoli, Domodossola, Empoli, Italia, Torino, Hotel Empoli, Roma W Ancona Y Carolina). The only word I understood was Carolina. A few days later another telegram arrived: "Permission granted either way Carolina." From this message I understood that I was free to use my own judgment.

Today, forty-three years later, as I write these words I finally understand the meaning of "W Ancona Y" (WAY—Ancona is a city on the Adriatic and was used to indicate "A" of the word WAY). That is, the operator probably said, "W, A as in Ancona and Y. I took a night train to Rome and kept my appointments. I even met with Pope Pius XII's niece Elena Rossignani Pacelli who accompanied me to an audience with him. I was so happy with this visit that, upon my return from Rome, I immediately wrote to the Mother General and told her about my wonderful visit with the Pope. Because I had failed to pay my respects, she responded ordering me to return to Rome as soon as possible. I again consulted Mother Carolina. She sent another telegram: "Take courage. As soon as you are well, go to Rome."

This was the beginning of much suffering. I was troubled, confused and even growing ill over a possible misunderstanding. Fortunately Maria Silvia Abbo, a friend who occasionally was my traveling companion, came to my assistance and invited me to recuperate at her home in Nava (near Genova). I finally did meet with Mother Ninetta in Rome and the matter ended peacefully.

My friendship with Prezzolini continued unabated. I recall that, in 1964, while participating in the NDEA French Institute in Kentucky, I received a letter from him announcing that he had married Gioconda Savini and would soon move from New York to Vietri sul Mare in the Province of Salerno, Italy. Everytime I went to Italy, I was always invited to be their house guest. They loved me dearly and I reciprocated their love by visiting them regularly, and helping with their files and research. In fact, years later, when they moved to Lugano, Switzerland, I published Prezzolini's very controversial booklet, *The Case of the Casa Italiana,* pleasing him immensely. Those visits were delightful for me and we continued to correspond regularly.

After presenting my thesis, *La politica di Girolamo Savonarola,* I received the M.A. degree in February 1949, from Columbia University under the presidency of General Dwight D. Eisenhower. Eleven years later, May 18, 1960, I was awarded a Ph.D.

I have many memories of those years at Columbia University. Sister Mary Paglia, a dear friend had studied with me in the 1940s. When she, too, was assigned teaching duties at Villa Walsh, Mother Carolina Jonata decided to send us to New York on a holiday. She gave us an envelope with money and instructed us to go to a Broadway show—*The Miracle Worker*—and then have dinner.

We could not recall receiving a treat like this. As directed, we took the Lackawanna train in Morristown, went to Hoboken, and proceeded to New York City. Neither one of us had ever been to Times Square. When we attended classes at Columbia University, we passed through by subway but never stopped. Indeed, this midtown area was quite a different world. We were fascinated. At the theater office, when asked what seats, I said, "Oh, the cheapest tickets you have!" We knew nothing about seating arrangements in a theater. Our excitement increased as the usher led us to the last row in the theater balcony. Giggling like two young school girls, we were contented. Yes, this would be a wonderful treat—Helen Keller's story. Soon the actors appeared on the stage, but we could hear very little of the story.

Yet, we were happy and left the theater in search of a restaurant. Walking along the street, we noticed a sign, "Hot Dogs and Beans, $.99." What a bargain! So we decided to have our dinner. When we returned and gave Mother Carolina all our change, she could not understand how it was possible until we explained how we managed to be so economical. Smiling, she thanked us, and remarked that we had been very foolish.

When I resumed studies for the Ph.D. degree, I immediately began working on my dissertation. It was my first book, *L'imagine tesa: la vita e l'opera di Clemente Rebora*, released in Rome, Italy, by Edizioni di Storia e Letteratura (1960). There I joined prestigious scholars—Paul Kristeller, Jean Leclerq, Mario Praz, Louis Ullman, Ernest H. Wilkins—and became one of that publisher's most prolific contributors.

With the publication of *L'imagine tesa*, my account of the poet's 1914-1919 love affair with Lydia Natus, a Russian pianist in Milan, incited a debate in *La Fiera Letteraria,* a literary newspaper, between his brother Piero Rebora, and my mentor, Giuseppe Prezzolini. Piero Rebora threatened to boycott my book because I had not followed his instructions to ignore that interval of his brother's life. Prezzolini came to my defense. The debate continued for several issues.

Critics admired the sensitivity and objectivity of my book, in particular where I straightforwardly stated: "Rebora's love for Lydia Natus cannot be ignored. It is clear that his life changed after his conversion to Catholicism; and if he loved this woman, even beyond the moral and material help they exchanged, if he loved her in the full sense of the word, it did not detract from his future sanctity. The greater the obstacles and the more complicated the ties that bound him to the earth, the stronger and more merciful was the Grace that freed him" (pp. 86-87).

I am quoting from the English adaptation of *L'imagine tesa* that was published in the Twayne's World Author Series as *Clemente Rebora: Quest for the Absolute*, 1979. The book represents Rebora's search for God. Its approach to Rebora's life and its analysis of his poetic works incorporate a historical perspective, recounting links between his lyrics and his prose, his letters, and also to his translations from the Russian of Leonid Andreyev, Leo Tolstoi, and Nikolai Gogol.

Lydia Natus had taught Rebora the Russian language, and it followed that he became greatly interested in Russian literature, especially in those works that exalt the goodness and simplicity of ordinary people who endure anxiety and misery. He believed in the dignity of all mankind, in man's inalienable right to respect, understanding, and love. He understood the tragedy of man, preached the need for soul-searching and simplicity of life, and called for improving contemporary moral and social conditions.

Rebora's life and works represent a searching, independent mind—seeking love, beauty, truth, goodness—that is, the embodiment of God. In a letter to me, Peter Sammartino, then president of Fairleigh Dickinson University, commented after reading *Clemente Rebora*: "America is enriched with the acquaintance of a great intellectual whose voice had been muffled by the more raucous sounds of others.... Not only do you bring out the full spirit of a great man but you translate his poetry so beautifully that you also create."

My research on Clemente Rebora would continue with the publication in two volumes of his correspondence. The *Nuova Antologia* reviewed Volume I in January 1977, as follows: "After twenty years, Rebora still speaks to us. He is fully present, marvelously luminous and tenacious, in a very useful and critically precious work of one of the great protagonists of Italian culture of this century." On the twenty-fifth anniversary of his death, Volume II was also well-received by the critics.

Who actually was Clemente Rebora? He was born in Milan, Italy, on January 6, 1885, the fifth of seven children. His family consisted of freethinking, well educated members of the middle class. He loved solitude but also enjoyed the company of simple folk, in the open air, amid the serene surroundings of nature. Here was a man unimpressed by words that merely produce pleasant sounds or harmonious rhythm, but rather devoted to finding truth and evidence of goodness. He represented a generation of Italian intellectuals who, although born in a country so traditionally Catholic, had departed from the Catholic Church to follow the religious liberalism and political anticlericalism of the Risorgimento and the vague mysticism and idealism of Giuseppe Mazzini. However, after much wandering, he did return to the Church as a Rosmini Father. His writings depict his spiritual struggles as he sought the real meaning of life, a spiritual reason for living in a hopelessly chaotic world.

When I first met Clemente Rebora, the person—the poet I already knew—he lay almost lifeless on his bed in the Stresa convent of the Rosmini Fathers, to whom he belonged. In a letter to me, Prezzolini had written (July 7, 1957): "Clemente Rebora, whom I still see as a most handsome and dear youth, of velvety eyes, frank expression, enchanting words; with his family he seemed to be one of the best products of the country which was then mine."

However, I did not see this "handsome and dear youth." What I saw was a bedridden man wasted by arteriosclerosis, speaking only with difficulty. He remembered the letters I had written him and had been awaiting my visit. I immediately conveyed greetings from Prezzolini, adding that the professor still admired Rebora's work and had suggested that I write about his poetry. I then showed him photostatic copies of letters he had written to Prezzolini from 1909 to 1914 and told him of the wonderful response at Columbia University to my lecture on his poetry. He was delighted.

I was privileged to visit Rebora frequently during my sojourn in Stresa. For three months, rain or shine, I climbed the steep hill that led to the Collegio Rosmini every day that I was there. I would meet with the librarian, Fratello Enzo Gritti, who expected me to accept his personal interpretation of Rebora's poetry. I listened respectfully until, one day, I became exasperated, and said: "Fratello Enzo, I came to Italy to listen to all the critics and hear all the bells ring about Rebora's poetry. (Voglio sentire tutte le campane suonare!) Perhaps, I will accept some of your interpretations later; but, as of now, I refuse to listen to you." My visits to the library ceased.

And regularly I continued my visits to Rebora who was very sick and reported to him about my trips through Italy, the interviews, the letters written, the letters received—all my experiences while searching for information about his past. I told him how everyone was anxious to contribute to my research: friends—Angelo Monteverdi of the University of Rome and Antonio Banfi, a Communist senator; journalists—Enrico Falqui of Rome's *Il Tempo* and Enzo Fabiani of *Il Popolo* of Milan; and artists, professors, writers—Carlo Carrà, Alfredo Galletti, Carlo Saggio, Duke Tommaso Gallarati-Scotti, Rebora's brother Piero—all of Milan. There were others too: Michele Cascella, an artist from Portofino, Gioacchino Volpe, a historian from Naples, Cesare Angelini, a poet from Pavia and countless literary critics.

Duke Gallarati-Scotti figured strongly in the group I approached in my quest for information. Born in Milan to an ancient and noble family, he was a well-known writer and diplomat who participated actively in the Modernist Movement until it was condemned. He was also one of the founders of *Il Rinnovamento*, a literary magazine of the early twentieth-century.

Another source of information was Cesare Angelini who, in a letter to me (December 14, 1956), wrote about Rebora's "theosophic lectures for the *belle signore* (society ladies) creating a suggestive atmosphere by the sudden lowering of his voice and the lights in the lovely rooms (*le sale tiepolesche*) in the home of Tommaso Gallarati Scotti."

"Suggestive atmosphere," indeed—the ceilings and walls of the Gallarati-Scotti "palazzo" had been painted by Giovanni Battista Tiepoli (1696-1770), the greatest representative of the Italian eighteenth century artists.

Copies of Rebora's correspondence were not acquired without a struggle. I had to firm up a great deal of courage to appear boldly before critics, professors, the nobility—with or without appointments. Often, I found myself in a precarious situation. Fortunately, Prezzolini knew about Duke Gallarati-Scotti's friendship with Rebora. So, in 1957, he gave me a letter of recommendation which guaranteed that I would be able to interview him. Other letters in my possession were to give me entry to Rebora's friends and former university classmates.

My first attempt to see the duke in Milan was a failure. When I knocked at the door of his home on Via Manzoni 30, in Milan, the servants thought I was seeking alms and refused to admit me. But I knew he was president of the Banca Ambrosiana, so off I went to speak to his secretary. I presented the letter that Prezzolini had written to the duke and was told I would be contacted. When the duke heard about this incident, he sent me a telegram that very day and generously made amends. He not only invited me to dinner the following day, but insisted that I meet Lavinia Mazzucchetti—one of Rebora's former friends—a classmate of his, an invaluable interpreter of the first young Rebora. She became a treasured friend and I hope and pray she finally understood the new Rebora, the Rebora reborn in Christ.

Thus began a lifelong friendship with Tommaso and Aurelia Gallarati-Scotti, his wife. Our friendship lasted many years. Whenever I visited Professor Prezzolini and his wife Jakie in Lugano, Switzerland, I always arranged a few days at the Gallarati-Scotti summer residence and was always their house guest at Villa Melzi, in

Bellagio. This beautiful historical estate, with its gardens and museum on Lake Como, was built in the seventeenth century by their ancestor, Count Francesco Melzi d'Eril, vice-president of the Republic of Italy in 1802. Such a wonderful experience, including all the pomp and circumstance of living with, perhaps, the best part of the remnants of Italian royalty!

Rebora the poet and Prezzolini my mentor had been separated for forty-five years! I had written to the latter, informing him of Rebora's desire to see him. Prezzolini agreed and traveled to Collegio Rosmini in Stresa. Together we went to Rebora's bedside. The emotional encounter took place on July 20, 1957.

The description of this encounter between Rebora and Prezzolini, as the latter described it in his weekly syndicated column, is memorable: "Rebora did not speak. Suffering had transformed the stupified gaze that came from his black pupils surrounded by blue. I noticed that his eyebrows had grown wild. But he was the same Rebora. I explained I had come to tell him that, if perhaps some of my words in the past or even today might have hurt him because of his Catholic faith, nonetheless I had done something kind, by sending from America a messenger of love and patience who was now at his bedside. The nurses told me that he hears well, but cannot respond, just as Papini could not. Rebora's face became illuminated with a happiness that turned to joy when Sister Margherita helped him raise his arm to bless his incredulous friend."

Before leaving Italy in September of 1957, I returned to Stresa and resumed my daily visits to Rebora's bedside. Each time I had stopped on my way up the hill to pick wild flowers for a little table in his room. This gesture always gave him much pleasure. On this day for my final farewell I found it difficult to leave him. I lingered, consoled by the thought that I had fulfilled the poet's desire to see Prezzolini. Refreshening his pillows, I kissed Rebora on the forehead, reminding him about Prezzolini's visit of July 20. His face brightened; it became radiant. "Father," I then asked, "did you remember Prezzolini after all those years?" "Oh, yes, my dear, we have been closely associated.... I love Prezzolini." Then Rebora blessed me for the last time.

Upon my return home, I continued to correspond with Rebora. During the next few weeks his sufferings became more intense. In a letter dated October 29, Rebora's nurse wrote me: "I cannot tell you how moved Father was on receiving your letter. He became unusually animated whenever he heard your name and there was no need to help him remember, as so often happened."

Soon news arrived in a letter dated, November 1, 1957, from Monsignor Cesare Angelini in Pavia: "Our Rebora, 'your poet,' passed away this morning. I think Don Clemente, among his last thoughts and visions of this earthly life which he was about to leave has had those of a dear little Sister who had come from America to concern herself about him, and to celebrate his memory. The merit is also our dear Prezzolini's, who, as he evaluated his [Rebora's] appearance on the literary scene, so too has assisted him in his departure, entrusting you to speak about him. A work of poetry and, at the same time, of compassion which weaves itself into the mysterious ways of the spirit and is transformed into good for the one who has promoted it and for the one who has fulfilled it."

Perhaps Rebora's spiritual strength may be found in his poem, *Dall'imagine tesa*.

> Tense-faced
> I keep a watchful eye upon each instant
> with imminence of expectancy—
> yet I expect no one:
> in the lighted shadow
> I peer at the doorbell
> that scatters an imperceptible
> pollen of sound—
> yet I expect no one:
> within four walls
> more space-stunned
> than a desert
> I expect no one.
> But come it must,

come it will, if I hold out,
to bloom unseen;
it will come of a sudden
when I am least aware;
it will come as forgiveness
of all that brings on death;
it will come to make me certain
of his treasure and mine;
it will come as balm
for my sorrows and his;
it will come, perhaps already is coming
his whispered word.

This poem is a quiet acknowledgment of the Divine Presence. The poet's journey is nearing its end. This expectation, although it overpowers both his physical and spiritual faculties, is mystical in nature. Of the One who will come, the poet will be aware of a single evidence if any: his senses will merely hear His whisper. But within mind, heart, and soul, the Visitor's action will be most powerful and efficacious. It will mean supreme liberation, it will bring the long-sought *Katharsis*—his purification. It will bring forgiveness, security, relief; the past with its darkness and restlessness and agony will be over forever.

A mystic might comment that in reality the Guest had already entered the house while the poet was waiting for Him, recalling the thought of French philosopher Blaise Pascal in *Le Mystère de Jésus,* "You would not search for me if you had not already found me." He would commend also the description of God, who comes when all is quiet and peaceful and silent: God is the one who blossoms unseen; God is forgiveness of sin—and sin (how sharply defined!) is "that which makes one die"; God will bring awareness of His treasures, but He will also make man aware of his precious soul.

With admirable insight into Christian theology, the poet sees God, in His conquest of the poet's soul, as bringing relief both to Himself and to the poet. Rebora does not say that suffering will be eliminated:

he speaks only of relief. He knows that suffering will go on, but it will no longer be accompanied by despair, but be tempered by faith and hope and charity.

Clemente Rebora is no longer with us. His poem, *Curriculum Vitae*, may be called a poetic autobiography, but it practically overlooks the years prior to his conversion at the age of forty-four. How, then, was I to explain his spiritual development, the joys and anguish of his soul? How could I comprehend his philosophy of life during this period? Only through his correspondence would I be able to probe into his innermost thoughts, his intimate considerations, the turmoil and conflicts of his soul and proceed through such an analysis to an interpretation of his poetry.

So many varied experiences met me as I traveled from place to place, seeking documentation about Clemente Rebora. I learned that Antonietta Poggianella, in Rovereto (who lived several hours away from Milan in the region of the Alps) boasted about the letters in her possession coming from her spiritual director, Father Rebora. From Stresa, I rushed to the train in Milan and headed for Rovereto.

When I arrived, I met the woman, her husband, and eight children between ages one and twelve. We chatted in a friendly manner, but I could not convince her to show me the letters. She insisted that they were her personal treasure and she would not part with them. I turned to her husband for support, assuring him I would send them back special delivery in a few days. But to no avail. The woman would not relent: "No, the letters will not leave this house. If you wish, Sister, you can take my children, but not my letters." By that time I was exasperated and answered: "My dear lady, keep your eight children; I'll do without your letters." And I prepared to leave.

At this point, husband and wife moved away for consultation. They decided to give me the packet of letters for a few days. I rushed to the train station, but I did not dare open the packet. Anxious to read the letters, I began as soon as I arrived in my room in Stresa. Soon I realized that the letters were of no use to me; they were mainly congratulatory notes on the birth of each child or about other periods in their life, or whenever she needed spiritual advice. The letters were promptly returned.

I wrote to all those whom I could not visit. They answered with kindness—Luciano Anceschi, Carlo Betocchi, Francesco Casnati, Emilio Cecchi, Mario Costanzo, Eugenio Montale, Giovanni Titta Rosa, Giuseppe Ungaretti. It was easy to perceive their love and respect and admiration for Clemente Rebora. Moreover, I also noted that even though I was an outsider, indeed, even a timid, just first-time visitor to the "Republic of Letters," always and everywhere, the leading citizens of the country welcomed me, with a sense of fraternity and unselfish generosity, treating me as one of them, aiding me in all possible ways.

Among my twelve books published by Edizioni di Storia e Letteratura are Clemente Rebora's correspondence in two volumes, and that of his contemporary Giovanni Boine in five volumes. Boine played an important part in the literary life of the period although he lived only thirty years before succumbing to tuberculosis. His letters to Prezzolini give us a picture of two men so different in temperament and beliefs, but drawn together in friendship by the desire to seek the truth.

Prezzolini wrote the Preface to Volume I of the series. The book was reviewed by Claudio Marabini in *Il Resto del Carlino*: "Prezzolini's realism clarifies questions over which Boine's ideological involvement lingers and suffers...He is aware that his time is short."

Prezzolini calls Boine a "Christian idealist." Highly sensitive to religious and philosophical problems, Boine believed that a revival of religious sentiment would solve the problems which plagued his age. He stressed the non-rational needs of men which must be satisfied in order to achieve Italy's needed spiritual unity and destroy the unwanted materialism and individualism of the bourgeois age.

According to Carlo Bo, in the Milan newspaper *Corriere della Sera*, Boine's correspondence, from 1908 to his early death in 1917, "is a link that helps unravel the mystery of his life and struggles." In *La Stampa* of Turin, Giovanni Bogliolo states that Giovanni Boine's "...brief life did not allow him to emerge from the tangle of contradictions in which his almost morbid attempt to achieve sincerity involved him. His association with *La Voce*, as well as the *Catholic Modernist Movement*, seems to have been motivated by his own inward struggle rather than by any long-lasting spiritual or intellectual affinity."

Looking back on this part of my life, I sincerely hope that my contributions to the fields of literature and history serve to inspire others by example and love as I have been inspired. "Nobility," a poem by Alice Carey, I believe, best tells my story. It is one of my favorite poems:

> "True worth is in being, not in seeming,
> In doing each day that goes by, some little good,
> Not in dreaming of great things to do by and by.
> For whatever men say in their blindness
> And in spite of the fancies of youth,
> There is nothing so kingly as kindness
> And nothing so royal as truth.

Chapter Six: *Fairleigh Dickinson University*

"Fortiter et Suaviter denotes the spirit of FDU:
to forge ahead bravely and
to enjoy the process along the way."
(Peter and Sally Sammartino:Biographical Notes)

Fairleigh Dickinson University Founders Found Dead! The tragic headlines shocked faculty, students, alumni, friends. Newspapers, radio, and television carried the story. Apparently, Peter Sammartino shot Sally, his wife of almost sixty years who had Alzheimer's disease, and then shot himself on March 29, 1992. When the tragedy was being discovered, I was called by the Bergen County Police. They informed me that I was to be the executrix of their Last Will and Testament.

The truly phenomenal growth of Fairleigh Dickinson University must undoubtedly be attributed to Peter and Sally Sammartino, founders of the University who were my dear friends and mentors. The accomplishments of this couple are unequalled. Their remarkable administrative ability, splendid achievements, and combination of spiritual and intellectual qualities give eloquent testimony to their worth.

In their Last Will and Testament, Peter and Sally Sammartino bequeathed their estate to provide scholarships for students in the School of Education who are interested in the teaching profession. Funds are distributed annually to students with outstanding academic records and strong leadership qualities who will make a significant contribution to the community in all fields of education, including music, art, literature, and nutrition research.

Peter Sammartino also mandated that I "write and publish a book within a three-year period," to include Sally, his wife, who deserves much of the credit for his success. Yes, Sally was the FDU Admissions officer for many years. Students respected her opinion. They loved her. For many she became a substitute mother.

Two years after their tragic death, my book, *Peter and Sally Sammartino (Biographical Notes)*, was published by Associated University Presses (Cornwall Books, Cranbury, NJ, 1994).

On June 3, 1991, George McEvoy, a columnist for *The Palm Beach Post* wrote about his fortieth FDU Class Reunion in Rutherford. "It was surprising how little the old campus had changed. There were a few new buildings, but the dominant structure was still the Castle, a medieval replica where Douglas Fairbanks, Sr., filmed several of his movies back in the 1920s... Mrs. Sammartino was the registrar who enrolled me." Having already lost three years to the Army, he had second thoughts. "I'll be well into my twenties by the time I graduate," he told Sally. She smiled: "You'll be well into your twenties some day, anyway. You may as well have a degree." George McEvoy agrees that hers was the best advice he had ever received.

Peter and Sally were closely associated with kings and queens, presidents and diplomats of various nations, governors and mayors, executives and actors, professors, students, staff, friends. The book is a medley of anecdotes and memories, a portrait of extraordinary dimensions, both colorful and informative. Included in the Appendix are: A Chronology of Fairleigh Dickinson University; Peter Sammartino's Report on national publicity during his presidency; Before and After 1967; and, finally, his answers to the questions "Why did FDU grow?" "What happened after 1967?" "What do we do now?" The book is a testimonial, to their lives and careers.

The story of Peter and Sally can be described in three words—innovation, action, accomplishments. It took them only twenty-five years to make Fairleigh Dickinson University the eighth largest privately supported college in the country with an enrollment of twenty thousand students! Their vision and genius is undeniable. For over half a century they devoted their lives to giving students a dynamic cultural background along with training in a career. Fairleigh Dickinson University stands as a monument to the memory of its founders whose enthusiasm, energy and purpose radiated everywhere and affected many lives.

They certainly affected my life. As directors of the FDU Gallery of Modern Art in New York, in August 1968, they asked me to represent the Gallery in Paris. Student riots had taken place in May. My mission was to collect the French student riot posters for a special fall exhibit. Because they were available at black market prices only, and terribly expensive, I solved the problem in my own fashion. Walking the streets of Paris, I noticed that the remains of some posters that had been burned or torn were still very much in evidence; so I helped clean the billboards by taking pieces here and there. The result of this "collection": a clever collage with the attraction of authenticity later exhibited in New York.

Peter and Sally were unprecedented in meeting educational challenges. Untiring and selfless in their devotion to the academic life of our nation, they never paused to serve the cause of peace and international friendship; they encouraged student exchanges in Europe, Africa and Asia. Not only did Peter organize the International Association of University Presidents, but, along with Sally, he was responsible for initiating the restoration of Ellis Island.

Fannie Hurst wrote (May 15, 1962): "Aside from its functional originality, FDU represents the winged imagination of its founders who first dreamed it into reality."

I was close to Peter and Sally Sammartino for thirty years and, in a sense, "adopted" by them. They followed my activities very carefully and were proud of my successes. Early in my career, I sought their advice, and during their last years I tried to assist them. They knew they could count on me, no matter what their needs. To them I was just plain "Maggie."

How can I forget the Miracle on 72nd Street? That story begins for me as a once-in-a-lifetime experience when Peter Sammartino offered me a choice between a $100,000 gift in his will or his condo in Palm Beach worth $200,000? I accepted the latter.

Among the paintings in the Palm Beach condo, there was one by a Chinese artist, Zhang Daqian, who, during the Tang Dynasty, brought the splash ink technique known as *Pomo* into contemporary art.

"Maggie," Peter stated, "I paid $10,000 for this painting. If you sell it, you can get $20,000; if you go to Hong-Kong to sell it, you will earn $40,000."

Well, I could not go to Hong-Kong, so I went to Sotheby's. However, after our discussion in which I consented to selling the painting, they neglected to list it in the October catalog. When I pointed out the omission, they agreed to include it in their June catalog and assured me I would not be charged insurance fees, photography fees, or commission fees. What they did not realize was the fact that Peter Sammartino's words of long-ago were prophetic. During the auction, I waited patiently for Painting No. 94—and, meanwhile, I prayed. Suddenly there were bids from Hong-Kong, rising from $15,000 to $25,000, then from $50,000 to $90,000, to $125,000, to $175,000, $200,000, $210,000 $220,000, and finally $230,000 before the hammer went down. Peter and his wonderful wife Sally must have smiled in Heaven!

Writing about my determination to celebrate the memory of Peter and Sally, Shirley Horner compared my efforts in *The New York Times* on February 6, 1993, to those of a nun in a recent movie, "Sister Act 2," whose firmness turns around an errant high school. "Sister Whoopi Goldberg, who plays the nun," wrote Ms. Horner, "has nothing on Sister Margherita Marchione of Villa Walsh in Morristown."

Whatever the challenge, I was happy and ready to dedicate myself to it. I recall with pleasure the Fairleigh Dickinson University students who rallied around me on campus for some twenty years; the appreciation of Corfinio College students in the ten years of culture and language study I conducted in Italy; the joy of discovery during my research projects; and, later, when I wrote books, the proofreading of thousands of pages, sometimes, as they came off the press. Those were wonderful times!

I tried always to help young students in need, soliciting the help of my friends. One such "angel" was the manager of Bamberger's in

Morristown, known to everyone as J. P. Meyer. (Only I called him, Jean-Pierre.) For years he tolerated my telephone calls for help to solve problems, e.g., a student at the University wanted a part-time job, or some poor people needed clothing, or I needed an interior decorator to prepare stage settings for a program.

I had succeeded in getting his private phone number at Bamberger's, and whenever I needed help from Jean-Pierre, I would call before 8 a.m. As I would attempt to say, "Good morning, Jean-Pierre," I'd hear a loud voice singing "Helloooo...., Sister!" Immediately there followed a Hebrew song. Only after I would giggle and say, "But, Jean-Pierre, how did you know it was I?" —did he get serious and take care of my problem. This ritual lasted many years. Then, one morning, at 8 a.m. Jean-Pierre, expecting me, picked up the phone, and sang, "Helloooo...., Sister!"

But, this time, his Hebrew tune was interrupted by a man's voice yelling: "This isn't your sister, it's your daddy!" It was his boss, the president of the Bamberger Department Stores. Not that this contretemps affected our friendship. In fact, when Jean-Pierre was transferred to Newark, he voluntarily gave me his private telephone number, because he knew I would manage to get it anyway!

But some memories are not so pleasant. In the Fall of 1966, I became chairperson for the Foreign Language Department of the Madison campus. Since an evaluating team from the Middle States Accreditation Association was due to arrive, I was told to update the files of each member of the faculty. This I did conscientiously. In my examination I soon discovered several deficiencies. Documentation for the credentials of a French professor was missing. Complaints from his students had been pouring into my office that his teaching lacked professionalism. Not only did he insist that the young ladies wishing to learn French must go to Paris and sleep with the opposite sex, but his methodology was unorthodox.

I sought counsel. Chancellor Peter Sammartino advised me to contact the Sorbonne to confirm the "verbal" qualifications of the errant professor. Soon a telegram arrived stating that the professor had never received degrees from the Sorbonne. I submitted this report to

President Osborne Fuller. Of course, no one wanted to rock the boat or incur adverse publicity. The professor was finally granted a sabbatical and advised to attend Rutgers University to complete his studies toward a degree.

Discussion ensued among some faculty members who defended this professor and, dissatisfied with the fact that his records had come under investigation, requested that I resign as chairperson. I refused. The debate continued for several months. I received notice of non-renewal of contract. My fate became a subject of controversy. Students protested in my favor. Their homemade posters read: "Happiness is the warmth of a nun. Save Sister Margherita!" The matter soon became a *cause célèbre* on campus. The outcome: I remained on the faculty.

Chancellor Sammartino had come to my defense and had written a letter to the Board of Trustees: "I am ashamed of the way Fairleigh Dickinson University has treated Professor Margherita Marchione. In my forty years of experience in higher education, I have never seen a miscarriage of justice as in this case. The argument as far as the Board of Trustees is concerned is that we should not be concerned with administrative matters. This is true except in cases of *force majeure*.

"Suppose one faculty member had plunged a knife in another faculty member and through administrative indifference nothing was done about the matter, would it be right for us not to be concerned? Suppose we know that someone had stolen $100,000 and through administrative bungling nothing was ever done, would you feel that you could overlook it? In this case we have a serious example of professional character assassination. ...

"I hope that we are not called upon either by the AAUP where the case is being investigated or by newspapers; but if we are, I would have to state categorically that there has been a grave miscarriage of justice and I would support this professor unqualifiedly."

My recollections of Fairleigh Dickinson University go back also to times in the early sixties when new acquaintances enriched my life. Among the trustees were Leonard and Alice Dreyfuss, whose friendship bears witness to the truth of Sacred Scripture: "He who has found a friend has found a treasure."

I first met Leonard and Alice Dreyfuss during a reception I had arranged, as secretary to Mother Carolina, in honor of Sister Francesca Cominazzi who was visiting us at Villa Walsh. Sister Francesca, who had taught in the United States in the 1920s, worked for more than fifty years in the Vatican. She was revered and loved by everyone—many bishops, priests and members of the Catholic laity from America depended on her during their visits to the Vatican. (One merely mentioned her name and the Swiss Guards were ready to assist you!)

From the moment Sister Francesca arrived at Villa Walsh, telephones were ringing constantly. Friends from all over the United States wanted to speak to her. Several hundred attended the May 27, 1967, afternoon tea commemorating her Golden Jubilee. The next day, *Newark Sunday News* quoted me: "Sister Francesca is a true and understanding friend whose admirable qualities and rare capabilities have won her the esteem of countless persons in every walk of life."

Among the invited guests, were Leonard and Alice Dreyfuss from Roseland and their daughter and son-in-law, Thelma and Billy Dear, the well-known golf player from Morristown, NJ. Sister Francesca had accompanied them during an audience with the Pope. In gratitude they sponsored her trip to the United States, where I first met her. It was the beginning of a long relationship. During all my trips to Italy until the day she passed away at age eighty-eight, still acting as guide to our friends, I would say: "I am here to see the Pope and Sister Francesca!"

Leonard and Alice Dreyfuss had a particular interest in the Fairleigh Dickinson University Florham-Madison Campus. Concerned about educational improvement as well as the continuing development of the campus, they donated funds to build Dreyfuss College. After attending my lecture "Dante and the American Way" at Seton Hall University (May 2, 1965), commemorating the VII Centennial of Dante Alighieri's birth, Leonard Dreyfuss wrote expressing his interest in my scholarship: "I have good news for you! There was a discussion at Fairleigh Dickinson University regarding the teaching of Italian. I am happy to report that you are invited to join the staff…I know you will do a very efficient job."

Leonard Dreyfuss was president of United Advertising Company and taught me an important lesson in efficiency when I asked him to comment on a letter I had written. His advice was: "I once bid $750.00 for a letter of Abraham Lincoln's which was five pages long. I didn't get it! At the end of the letter Lincoln had a P.S. which said, 'I apologize for this letter. I did not have the time to make it short.' So I suggest the attached letter which is one-third the size of yours."

Thanks to Leonard and Alice Dreyfuss, over a period of twenty years, hundreds of students attended my classes in Italian language and culture; the Italian Club activities included field trips, lectures, films, exhibits; the university's Summer Institutes in Italy enabled students to appreciate their Italian heritage.

Having received an M.A. degree at Columbia University, I began teaching Italian Literature in Villa Walsh Junior College, July 1949, and continued teaching each summer. In September 1954, I was assigned the teaching of Italian Language and Literature in Villa Walsh High School. To update my teaching skills, I later applied, in 1962, to a National Defense Education Act Foreign Language Institute for Secondary School Teachers of Italian. To this day I cannot understand why the director sent my application to the University of Kentucky where a French Institute for Secondary School Teachers of French was to be held. Since I had already received my Ph.D. (1960), perhaps he felt I should not be with the Teachers of Italian.

But I had never formally studied French. I knew I could not compete with these qualified teachers. I had acquired some book knowledge of French on my own, preparing for the required French language exam at Columbia. But this was an intensive program aimed at improving French competency and teaching proficiency. It was an awkward situation. However, from June 18 to August 10, 1962, I was speaking French, at least among the professors since most of these teachers were unable to communicate in French.

They were experienced teachers but they knew neither modern teaching techniques nor modern methodology. This was precisely the purpose of the National Defense Education Act. We were deficient in teaching foreign languages and the Language Institutes helped improve competency and teaching proficiency. It was difficult for these teachers to speak fluently. On the other hand, my experience with the Italian language enabled me to communicate with ease. As I learned I immediately put my knowledge into practice. I was not embarrassed to make mistakes and tried to encourage others. In fact, the professors were delighted with my performance. I earned the title of "joie de vivre."

Two years later, encouraged to apply for a Fulbright Scholarship, I participated in the educational exchange program under United States Public Law 256. I was privileged to be considered more a "professor" than a "student," having been already known as a scholar in Italy and in the United States. My doctoral dissertation had been published, and my articles appeared in scholarly magazines: "Ecclesia," "Forum Italicum," "La Fiera Letteraria," "Lingua Nostra," "Nuova Antologia," "Rassegna di Politica e di Storia," "Stagione," and "The Italian Quarterly. The Board of Foreign Scholarships and The American Commission for Cultural Exchange with Italy awarded me a certificate on July 31, 1964.

The history of the FDU Institutes dates back to 1968 when I directed the NDEA Language Institute that prepared forty future teachers of Italian. The Institute was sponsored by the U.S. Office of Education with $64,000 in federal grant money. My associate director was Professor Filomena Peloro, whose experience in foreign languages was exceptional. She was responsible for the introduction of the FLES programs in all the public schools in Hackensack, NJ. Her expertise was crucial to the success of this program. Through the years, she made a valuable contribution to Fairleigh Dickinson University. Her friendship continues to the present. Other professors on the staff were the poet, Joseph Tusiani, and the linguist, Luigi Romeo, as well as several assistant professors and staff members.

Living with the NDEA Italian Institute students on the FDU Madison campus was a special experience. Students came from many colleges and universities. At the end of this summer course, the students presented a plaque:

> To Sister Margherita Marchione
> Whose goodness, silent and active,
> Inimitable and sweet,
> Has kindled in our memory
> The most limpid torch of *Italianità*
> With the command to pass it,
> Equally bright and pure,
> On younger hearts in years to come.

Students from many areas of the United States were grateful for permission to join the Italian Summer Institutes Abroad. I wish I had kept all the wonderful letters I received from these young people. They even became more aware of God's many blessings when they learned from the Italian people that they should not take things for granted.

One student wrote: "It's my belief that we can never fully know who we are or what we have without the aid of comparison. Something that only a course such as yours could possibly fulfill. It strengthened my belief that any true educaton doesn't come only from the classroom. My only wish is to be able to convey to you my true feelings for the six most momentous weeks in my life. What I learned was immeasurable and what I felt was inconceivable. Thank you for making all that happened possible..." Someone even wrote in Italian, "Mi sono innamorato d'Italia!" ("I fell in love with Italy!)"

I agreed with Professor Peloro that language teaching must begin at an early age. Inspired by her example, I prepared a FLES Italian Series for use in the Religious Teachers Filippini elementary schools (*Materials for Teaching Italian—Kindergarten through Grade 4*).

An educator needs stamina. Teachers must be steeped in love for their students and serve them with faith and dedication. They must create a classroom climate where differences are shared with respect and freedom. They must esteem integrity and excellence. This millennium needs pioneers, innovators, men and women of vision who constantly find new approaches to achieve the true purpose of education: strengthening our creativity, dignity, freedom, individuality, thus helping humankind fulfill the ideals of a democratic society. These are times that demand integrity, intellectual competence, and love of God and neighbor.

I was always interested in my students. I thought about the great Italian artist, Michelangelo, walking one day with friends through a back street in Florence, Italy. He noticed a block of marble lying in a yard, half buried with rubbish. Although in holiday attire, he stopped and began clearing away the filth and dirt. His companions asked what he wanted with that worthless chunk of rock. Michelangelo gave his famous answer; "Oh, there's an angel in that stone, and I must let it out." He had the block of marble carried to his studio and, toiling with chisel and mallet, "he let the angel out." What to others was a shapeless mass of stone, was to the master's eye a buried, challenging possibility. That stone might have become part of a wall or a street. But the artist changed it into a work of genius, for ages to come. So, too, every teacher has the privilege to work with students.

It was a pleasure teaching at Fairleigh Dickinson University. In the Fall of 1965, I began with one Italian language class, and by 1968 there were six classes of over one hundred students. As moderator for the Italian Club, I invited lecturers and singers; there were exhibits and films; among the performances, *Orlando Furioso*, by the Manteo family theater company with its collection of unique and charming puppet characters—the famous life-size Sicilian Puppets.

One exhibit in the Madison Campus Friendship Library was a replica of the Cathedral of Milan. The sculptor, Anthony Falcone, was born in Italy in 1915 and came to this country in 1929. He was interested in wood crafts, having been apprenticed to a cabinet maker. Not to be idle during the Depression, he began to build a miniature of the Duomo: 54 inches long, 34 inches wide, and 40 inches high— completed after two years of tedious work.. It was constructed to scale from the original Cathedral plans. However, only when the Italian Club publicized the masterpiece, did he receive recognition for this work.

I enjoyed being with students both in the classroom and as friends. The Italian Club sponsored a series of my lectures: Dante and The American Way; Modern Italian Poets; Poetry in Teaching Italian; Italian Studies in the United States; Stalking the Elusive ALS: Collecting Documents for a Comprehensive Edition; and countless talks on Philip Mazzei, Clemente Rebora, and other writers.

These talks were given in Rome, Salerno, Milan, Lugano, Rovereto, Padova, Imperia, Pescia, Florence, and many cities in the United States. Some hold amusing memories: I gave a talk honoring Giuseppe Prezzolini on his ninetieth birthday at Piazza Venezia in 1972. It was a cold January day and there was no central heating. After the lecture, Letizia, wife of Giovanni Buitoni, the CEO of the U. S. Buitoni Pasta Company, invited me to lunch. I accepted, and the following day was at her apartment on Via Veneto opposite the Hotel Excelsior.

Instead of going directly to a restaurant, Letizia accompanied me to the Luisa Spagnoli Dress Shop. Before I could say "boo," she had three dressmakers fit me into a black skirt and jacket of the finest quality, more suited to the January cold than the habit I had worn the previous evening. Unable to refuse without hurting her feelings, I simply said the outfit was too form fitting for me to wear. But this was no problem. The dressmakers took it apart, and redid it to fit as I thought it should. Years later, when we met in Lugano, Switzerland, in the month of January, Letizia Buitoni felt that my coat was not suitable. This time I inherited one of her black coats!

I have spoken at many universities: Columbia, Duquesne, Fairleigh Dickinson, Georgia State, Georgetown, Harvard, Kentucky, Michigan State, Old Dominion, Rutgers, Seton Hall, University of California, University of Nebraska, University of Steubenville, Wayne State, West Virginia State, Yale. I do not have a complete record of my published articles, or the articles about my work that appeared in periodicals, or reviews of my books. It would be difficult to list the awards received in the United States and in Italy. Suffice it to say that I have been available and will continue to speak especially in defense of Pope Pius XII, my newest mission, be it on TV, radio or any other avenue of communication.

One year, several of my students were on the editorial staff of the FDU Madison Campus school newspaper, *The Metropolitan*. The newspaper kept students informed about my activities. In 1971, when I was to receive the Amita Award (joining women like Opera Singer Licia Albanese, Educator Sally Sammartino, Writer Frances Winwar, Actress Anne Bancroft), the students wrote (April 14, 1971): "The recent announcement that Sister Margherita will receive the national Amita Achievement Award in Education doesn't surprise us at all. Since her appearance on the Madison Campus in 1965, she has been classified as an exceptional teacher, lecturer, scholar. Interested in the life and problems of her students, she knows how to encourage them and captivate them.

"A word of advice—don't miss the experience of being in one of her classes. It's a must. She will shatter every preconceived idea you might have of a nun. Nothing is too difficult for her to accomplish. Do you need a contact? She'll know how to make it. Do you need a job? She'll help you find it. Have you ever been abroad? Well, you will want to make the trip to Italy. In the meantime, when she greets you with "Buon giorno. Come sta?", you will answer in Italian without even realizing that you are no longer in Italian class.

"A chat with her and you are where the action is. Around the world! Things just happen. It's exciting! She doesn't need membership in the Woman's Liberation Movement. She has been free all her life. Her independent spirit is known here and abroad." [See: Shirley Lazarus' fine article *Who's Who in Morris* with the caption, ADMINISTRATOR, AUTHOR, WHIRLWIND (*Daily Record*, June 3, 1970).]

"With the Amita Award, Sister Margherita is being recognized for her dedication to excellence in education. Dean James Griffo has expressed the sentiments of all her students: 'Sister Margherita is a dynamic teacher devoted to her students who have learned *how to learn* under her guidance. For those of us who know her and love her, this national award is most timely in a career that has many more years of innovation and adventure in education in the future.' "

After a detailed listing of awards and accomplishments, students Robert Sternberg, Eliott Kominsky and Michael Bieber ended their lengthy article: "An educator, who is at once a challenge and an inspiration, Sister Margherita inculcates truth and beauty and goodness, thus nourishing her students and accomplishing her mission in life."

I encouraged the students in the Italian Club to participate in the Blood Bank Campaign. They did, and so did I. Soon the newspaper carried a photograph of me (and other professors!) with a Red Cross Nurse taking my pressure and a thermometer in my mouth. Unknown to me, the caption read, "No, I haven't been pregnant during the last six months."

I was usually greeted in the classroom by a group of smiling students. But the day this issue appeared, the students seemed very serious as I entered. The mischievous student who was responsible for the newspaper article told me my photo was in the centerfold. As he opened the newspaper to show it to me, I sensed that the students did not know how to react as they waited for my reaction. I laughed and said, "Oh, thank you. I'm proud of my femininity and I'm happy to know that you have acknowledged it!" Of course, the strain was over. Everyone was at ease, and class began with its usual enthusiasm.

I have always accepted speaking engagements from all groups: male or female, Catholic or non-Catholic. I was the only woman in the room the first time I spoke to members of Unico National. I was so surprised that, before beginning my talk, I said: "There's only one thing that comes to my mind— a motion picture I saw many years ago. I even remember the actress, Deanna Durbin! I think the title was, *One Hundred Men and a Girl*!" I added that if a reporter from a local newspaper would walk into the restaurant, he might improve that title with *Fifty Men and a Nun*! That caption would have been picked up by all possible news media (at least, in those days).

About fifty years ago, I was waiting for the train in a crowded subway station at Columbia University. A little girl walked up to me, looked at my outfit and asked: "Are you a real nun?" I smiled and said: "Why, yes, I am. Can I help you?" Looking at me, the child answered: "Well, how come you have hair?" Things have changed. Today no one is surprised that nuns show their hair. Not much has changed for me, however. I've been wearing this seventeenth century bonnet since 1938.

In 1966 other nuns were able to show their hair for the first time. One nun, delighted with her "red" hair, approached the pastor for the first time, and asked if he had noticed her "red" hair. He looked at her and responded: "Yeah, I did. But I also see your varicose veins!"

As for my skirt, it has now been shortened. Forty years ago, when nuns were changing into less cumbersome outfits, I delayed doing so for want of time. An elderly gentleman of German descent, Mr. Paul F. Freytag, who lived on our property, had been a prisoner of war in England during World War I. He frequently mentioned that he considered himself a guest of the Queen.

As our guest at Villa Walsh, Mr. Freytag came to church services every morning with the nuns. Since I was secretary to Mother Carolina Jonata, Provincial Superior, I had to take care of his needs. I not only did secretarial work for him or accompany him to his attorney or banker but, at times, I would also wash his dishes. Jokingly, I would remind him that not even the Queen of England had a Ph.D. washing her dishes.

In chapel, I sat next to him. This 90-year old gentleman repeated often, "Now, M.M. (as he usually called me), when are you going to change your habit?" I promised to modify it as soon as possible. Months later, I visited him and modelled my new habit. I removed the bolero, turned around, curtsied, and asked Mr. Freytag's opinion. My expectations were that he would say: "It's too long, too short, too tight." Ignoring me completely, he did not utter a word during my performance. Finally, with arms folded as though obliged to make a very important decision, Mr. Freytag turned to the young Sister who had made the outfit and remarked: "Well, M.M. has some good curves!"

I have so many memories of Mr. Freytag whose generosity and

guidance, during the early years that I was Villa Walsh treasurer, were invaluable, especially with regard to maintenance problems. For example, when there was need to paint a building, he would offer to pay part of the bill. During the ten years that he lived in a house on our property, I cared for him personally. We became the beneficiaries of his estate which amounted to about a half-million dollars. Among other recipients were Peter and Paul, his two young grandsons from Colorado; to each he left $100,000. However, I decided that some of Mr. Freytag's personal property should also be given to his grandsons.

After the funeral, I invited them to choose various items that belonged to their grandparents: crystal vases, seventeenth-century sterling silver teapots and other silver pieces, a 24-piece set of silverware crested with the family seal, valuable watches, jewelry. I explained the procedure: the older brother would choose first and they would continue taking turns to select what they preferred. Everything went smoothly as we divided these items. Then I showed them a large diamond pin in the shape of a butterfly. They began to argue about it. I could not pacify them. They became violent and would not come to an agreement. When we could no longer negotiate the diamond pin, I reminded the boys of the conditions I had laid down at the beginning of this selection process and declared that my offer was now terminated.

Soon after, the diamond butterfly pin was appraised at over $3,000, and remained with the estate. Later, young Peter and Paul attempted to contest their grandfather's will. But Mr. Freytag had carefully stipulated that whoever contested his last will and testament would be automatically eliminated and their portion would revert to the estate.

Several years earlier, according to Mr. Freytag's wishes, the remains of his wife Evelyn and his only son Peter, who was killed in World War II, had been transferred to the Villa Walsh Cemetery. It was his wish to be buried with them. In gratitude for his munificence, the infirmary building at Villa Walsh was named Freytag Hall in his memory.

It is sad for me to remember how two months before they died, Peter and Sally Sammartino made their last public appearance during the Snow Ball Dinner-Dance on January 18, 1992. As founding members of Opera at Florham, they were honored during the first of FDU's Golden Jubilee Anniversary celebrations. Theirs was a precious legacy of fifty years of dedicated and personal involvement with the experimentation, philosophy, and administration of Fairleigh Dickinson University. As a member of the Board of Trustees of Opera at Florham, I prepared the following citation in gratitude for their contributions to education and to the arts:

Peter and Sally Sammartino
—educators and administrators—
you founded Fairleigh Dickinson University in 1942,
in the Castle, Rutherford, NJ.
You worked hard to encourage in the community
a love of opera
and arranged with Estelle Liebling,
Metropolitan Opera star,
to have her pupils present opera scenes four times a year.
Beverly Sills was among them.
Peter and Sally, you accompanied FDU students
to the Metropolitan Opera and invited them backstage
to meet some of the stars.
Students at Edward Williams College received free tickets
for opera, symphony, ballet and theater.
Peter, in 1929, you organized the
Verdi Choral Society in New York City
which exists today as the Coro d'Italia.
Sally, you were president of the
Garden State Ballet and one of the founders
of the Williams Center in Rutherford
where the Sammartino Theater is located.
Peter and Sally Sammartino,
when you retired in 1967, FDU had 52 buildings

and seven campuses valued at $250,000,000,
with an endowment of $62,000,000 consisting of
stocks, bonds, and real estate.
In recognition of your outstanding contribution
to higher education and, in particular, to the music world,
the Board of Trustees of Opera at Florham
commends you and expresses sincere appreciation.

Even in the late sixties, my friendship with Giuseppe Prezzolini continued to add drama to my life. At one time, April 18, 1969, I received an invitation to a reception at the Cultural Institute of the Italian Consulate General on Park Avenue in honor of Giuseppe Ungaretti, the Nobel Prize-winning poet. How could I not attend! Prezzolini had even written a personal letter to the poet alerting him that I would be present and I had written for permission to include several of his poems I had translated in my anthology, *Twentieth Century Italian Poetry*.

When I arrived at 5:30 p.m., hundreds of guests were already gathered on the steps to greet Ungaretti. I waited in a corner so that I would not be in the way. Surrounded by dignitaries, the poet slowly ascended the steps, looked around, spotted me and said, as he made his way directly toward me, "Ecco la sorellina di Prezzolini!" ("There's Prezzolini's little nun!"). Not only did he embrace me, but he instructed me to stay next to him. In fact, I was seated with him all evening as the guests approached to greet him and he introduced me. Before I left, he inscribed a book he gave me: "Per la suorina che amo senza commettere sacrilegi, perché è purezza che rende puri. Giuseppe Ungaretti." ("For the little nun whom I love without committing a sacrilege, because it is purity that renders one pure. Giuseppe Ungaretti.") Since we could not discuss his poetry during the reception, Ungaretti invited me to visit him the following day in his Manhattan hotel. [*Lettere a Suor Margherita*, p. 203].

Chapter Seven: Giuseppe Prezzolini

"Prezzolini's chief distinction is to have 'discovered'
and forced upon public attention the works of
Croce and Gentile, of Papini and Soffici...."
(New York Times, July 1, 1923)

Giuseppe Prezzolini—Columbia University Professor Emeritus—was a clear thinker, a great Italian writer, a fearless critic. He was born in Perugia on January 27, 1882, into a family of cultural and literary interests.

Prezzolini, prolific writer,was also a journalist and philosopher. Columbia thought so highly of him that in 1923 they called him to teach when he was serving in France as literary secretary with the League of Nations. He became professor emeritus without ever having received a degree. He was a self-taught man of untiring energy.

As a high school student, I met Giuseppe Prezzolini during a scholastic performance on the stage of Casa Italiana. In the presence of church and university dignitaries, I recited a poem, "La Violetta" by Gabriele Chiabrera. After the performance, all the students posed for a photograph with Prezzolini.

That meeting changed the course of my life. I certainly did not renounce my vocation, nor did Prezzolini ever advise me to do so. But all I have accomplished as a scholar I owe to him. I blush when I recall how this noted author and journalist described me as a "brava insegnante, grande organizzatrice, fedelissima amica, piena di spirito di sacrificio e animatrice di ogni gruppo con il quale veniva in relazione." ("An excellent teacher, a great organizer, a most faithful friend, full of the spirit of sacrifice, an animator of every group she encountered.")

Although it was unusual for a nun to attend a secular university in the 1940s, I thrived there and was encouraged to pursue scholarship. My accomplishments must be attributed to Prezzolini's guidance.

Early on, he had said clearly: "You are not a genius, but you have the potentiality for good work." His words inspired me and contributed to the fabric of my life.

In a Contemporary Italian Culture course some sixty years ago, Prezzolini distributed magazines to the class. When he came to me, he removed certain pages that contained scandalous and pornographic photographs. Apparently he felt it was not necessary for me, as a young nun, to be exposed to this material.

Giuseppe Prezzolini later became my mentor for my M.A. thesis on *The Politics of Girolamo Savonarola.* My lifelong association with him was the driving force behind my love of Italian and the spreading of Italian culture. His son Giuliano and I are directors of a collection of his correspondence (published by Edizioni di Storia e Letteratura, Rome) with many internationally-known literary and philosophical writers and leaders of the twentieth-century, such as Benedetto Croce, Giovanni Papini, Aldo Palazzeschi, and scores of other personalities.

Nuccia De Luca, director of the publishing house, introduced me to many interesting people in Rome. Among them was the Italian sculptor Giacomo Manzù who, at that time, had just completed his bronze masterpiece, *Porta della morte*, for Saint Peter's Basilica. One day, Nuccia and I were driving along the Appian Way. She stopped the car to deliver a package to Manzù, who lived on the top of a circular Roman fortress in an apartment surrounded by a beautiful roof garden.

At that time I was still wearing the original long, black religious habit. Knowing that the sculptor was anticlerical, Nuccia said, "Manzù does not like black clothing." He extended his hand and frowned disparagingly. Smiling at him, I responded to Nuccia's statement: "Oh, my dear, the next time I visit, I'll wear my bathing suit." Manzù's attitude changed completely. We became friends.

In the convent I learned about both human and supernatural virtues. Through my friendship with Prezzolini I again saw examples of human virtues: loyalty during good and bad times, fidelity to one's word, commitment in work, respect for the ideas of others, the cult of personal dignity; an openness toward the most diverse currents of

(Above) Early family photograph of grandparents, Luigi and Rosa Marchione, and my father, mother with baby Jean in her arms, sister Rose and uncle Pietro in center.

(Below) Crescenzo and Felicia Marchione holding Pope Pius XII's blessing on their golden jubilee of matrimony.

**(Above) Mamma with her brother Michael and sister Alfonsina.
(Below) Photos of Mamma and Papa.**

(Above) Papa interrupts work to play with Margherita, Ceil and Louis.
(Below) Margherita, dressed as an angel with wings, accompanied First
Communicants to the altar of St. Margaret's Church in Little Ferry.
Graduation Day: St. Mary's Elementary School, Hackensack, NJ.

(Above) Sister Margherita was baptismal sponsor for George Gallis' children: Michael, Julie Ann and Alicia.

(Below) Papa with grandchildren: Louis, Jr. and Dolores Marchione (twins) and Joan Messner (center).

(Above) Sister Margherita on her Investiture Day, June 12, 1938, with
    Mamma and Papa.
(Below) Sister Margherita on her Profession Day, August 31, 1941, with family
    and relatives.

(Above) Profession Day, August 31, 1941, with family and relatives.
(Below) Sister Margherita with sisters Rose and Marie.

(Above) Ceil leaving the house in Little Ferry accompanied by Papa.
(Below) Bridal Party: Marie, Ceil, Nick, Louis.

(Above) John Schettino, Palmina Pirro, Mrs. Gallis, Harry Gallis, Mamma
and Papa.
(Below) George and Mildred Constantine, Harold and Jean Messner, Tom
and Rose Pirro, Bob and Kay Messner.

thought, a passion for research of the beautiful and good no matter where; the rejection of laziness, imprecision, artificiality or mediocrity; the love of freedom even if within the discipline imposed by the dictates of one's conscience.

All this Giuseppe Prezzolini reinforced for me with the example of his incorruptibility and righteousness. In *Lettere a Suor Margherita* (Edizioni di Storia e Letteratura, Rome, 1992), these sentiments are revealed in his correspondence with me over a period of 25 years. His letters are delightful reading. Published on the occasion of the 10th anniversary of his death, they cover the years when he was my mentor at Columbia University to his death (1957-1982).

When I arrived in Lugano, Switzerland, on May 23, 1981, Prezzolini wrote an article in *Gazzetta Ticinese*: "Sister Margherita is one of my little plants, many of which did not take root; but she did and, contrary to my expectations, produced good fruit. I had taught her Machiavelli and Guicciardini. She surpassed me with Philip Mazzei, a Tuscan who wrote well and had spirit and, above all, courage. It seemed to me when I saw her that she was the sign of an alliance between the United States and Italy. In fact, with Europe, because Mazzei was one of those Italians who knew how to speak several languages and, as he visited each country, he always brought something new." In fact, it was my research on Mazzei during a sabbatical that offered me the opportunity to be present for Prezzolini's 100th birthday celebration on January 27, 1982.

Critics have considered 1903 to 1907 as a period of transition from positivism to idealism when Prezzolini collaborated with Giovanni Papini on the *Leonardo,* one of the more important literary and philosophical periodicals of the century. During this time he began his quest for God by studying mysticism under the influence of the French philosopher Henri Bergson (1859-1941), Henry James (1843-1916), and Saint Augustine (354-430). This was a quest that never ended, as can be seen in his book, *Dio è un rischio*, published in 1969. Prezzolini sent me a copy, which he autographed: "To Margherita Marchione, known to me as a child, recognized by me as a professor, what will she become when I am deceased?"

A few years later, in the article "La Suora letterata" (*Resto del Carlino*, January 6, 1972), Prezzolini tells the story that one day Nuccia De Luca, my publisher in Rome, telephoned him. "This nun has too many ideas," she lamented. His response was: "Thank God! There are too many people who have too few ideas."

Prezzolini has a place in the history of Italian literature of this century as the founder and first editor of *La Voce* (1908-1914), a periodical dedicated to the moral, social, and intellectual regeneration of Italy. He was the moving spirit behind a whole generation of writers known as "vociani." *La Voce* became the rallying point of many of the best minds of Italy—minds of all shades of political thought and religious belief (including agnosticism), united only by their common desire to promote a spiritual regeneration.

The credo of the "vociani" was action. They had an awareness of social and spiritual issues that enlisted the support of men who differed not only in character but in political and philosophical thought. Among its contributors were Benedetto Croce and Giovanni Gentile, Giovanni Papini and Ardengo Soffici, the young Benito Mussolini and Giovanni Amendola, Dino Campana and Umberto Saba, Scipio Slataper and Renato Serra, Aldo Palazzeschi and Clemente Rebora, Giovanni Boine and Piero Jahier, Gaetano Salvemini and Romolo Murri—all leading figures in the Italy of that day and later.

The effect that *La Voce* had on Italian culture was felt in literature, music, art, philosophy, and politics. Thus was Italian culture integrated into the life of the nation. It assumed a true significance not only in relation to the arts and literature, but on a moral plane as well.

When Italy entered World War I, Prezzolini enlisted, and had ample opportunity to witness the ineptitude of old generals and the ill-preparedness of the troops. In his writings he criticized his country, whose government was responsible for the defeat of Caporetto. In 1925 he went to Paris to direct the Literary and Information Department of the Bureau for Intellectual Cooperation founded by the League of Nations. He left it in 1930 to come to Columbia University, where he was director of its Casa Italiana (1930-1940), and professor of Italian for over twenty years, until his retirement.

Casa Italiana was a seven-story building in Florentine Renaissance style, that was inaugurated in 1927 on Columbus Day. At the ceremony, the Italian government was represented by Guglielmo Marconi (1874-1937), inventor of wireless telegraphy and Nobel Prize-winner for physics in 1909. Its library housed a first-rate collection devoted to contemporary Italian literature and history, and was rich in reference works, periodicals and bibliographical tools.

Here from 1937 to 1948 Prezzolini and his students produced research projects and dissertations, as well as a four-volume *Repertorio bibliografico della storia e della critica della Letteratura Italiana dal 1902 al 1942* and the *Columbia Dictionary of Modern European Literature* (1947). Other publications he directed were: *Casa Italiana Monthly, Il Giornalino, The Italian Book of the Month Club, Newspaper and Periodical Information Clipping Bureau.*

An extraordinary exponent of Italy's cultural legacy, Prezzolini guided and nurtured innumerable young men and women. His correspondence with them was an extension of his fascinating *Diario*. In a special way, he loved his Columbia University students. By his example of moral integrity, he taught them to appreciate spiritual values. He guided them during the research on their books, counseled them in the publication stage, and even assisted them in the correction of proofs. Indeed, he was the catalyst who skillfully blended literary and philosophical developments with Italian genius and brought forth a new generation of distinguished teachers and a twentieth-century Italian Renaissance.

In 1922, Prezzolini wrote a remarkable self-portrait in his book, *Amici* (Vallecchi, Firenze): "I possess a certain clarity of ideas, the capacity to grasp the character of a man or of a movement, the strength of soul to refuse to be seduced by friendships or to be upset by hatreds in evaluating merits and in measuring defects. At a certain point in my life, having buried the romantic turmoils and aspirations, I decided to become the 'useful man' for others; to clarify certain ideas to Italians, to indicate their inferiorities in order to overcome them, to characterize foreign people and foreign movements, to translate from different languages, to reveal promising young men, to point out hidden greatness; that is what one calls work of culture. It is very much like building ditches, plowing the soil, planting trees, pruning, sowing, weeding, trimming, and all the operations of a good agriculturist.

"Yes, I have always wanted to be useful. I don't say I have always succeeded, but that was my intention. I have always put myself at the service of a man who needed to be known, of an idea that needed conquering, of a propaganda that needed dissemination. This was the principal character of all my works."

Albert Schweitzer once said: "I don't know what your destiny will be, but one thing I know—the only ones among you who will be really happy are those who have sought and found how to serve." I believe that he was describing the people God holds in the "palm of His hand."

Prezzolini knew how to serve his students. A born educator, his writings exemplify intellectual stimulation, moral integrity and spiritual values. They are delightful reading because of his clear, well-balanced style. His pen ranges from German mysticism to an erudite history of spaghetti, with scholarship, reportage, allegory, religion, biography, criticism, philosophy, and psychology filling the gap.

Undoubtedly, Giuseppe Prezzolini was a very controversial contemporary Italian writer. He once defined himself as "the traveling salesman of Italian culture." He was convinced, as he wrote in *The Modern Language Journal* (February, 1939): "Modern civilization cannot be thoroughly appreciated without a study of its lasting spiritual qualities; and the study of Italian, heir to the humanistic culture of ancient Greece and Rome, should be given primary consideration because of its achievements in art, letters, music, science and human thought."

On its thirty-fifth anniversary, Casa Italiana issued a souvenir booklet stating: "A tireless and intrepid exponent of Italy's cultural legacy, Prezzolini made the Casa a veritable beehive of scholarly and educational activity. He set a pace too blistering for us, his successors, to follow. Have you ever stopped to think of the number of books he has written? His bibliography alone could fill a tome."

This prophetic statement was realized in 1982, in one of my books entitled *Prezzolini: un secolo di attività* (Rusconi, Milan, 1982), published on the occasion of his 100th birthday. It contains an annotated bibliography of his 58 books and the names of 136 magazines and newspapers throughout the world where his weekly articles have appeared. It includes his 22 anthologies; 9 books in translation; 47 new editions of his books.

Listed also are 28 Prefaces written by Prezzolini for books by others, including four of mine on Clemente Rebora, Giovanni Boine, Cesare Angelini, and Philip Mazzei. Recorded in the bibliography are: 27 translations of Prezzolini's books; 22 of his literary contributions form part of miscellaneous volumes, as well as many contained in four encyclopedias. The number of volumes of his correspondence total 25. The number of new editions and his correspondence have been increasing since 1982. In fact, as mentioned, Giuliano Prezzolini and I have been directors of this series.

In 1971, Giuseppe Longo asked me to contact former students for their testimonials honoring Prezzolini on his ninetieth birthday. These tributes became part of the book *Prezzolini 90* of the *Quaderni dell'Osservatore*, N. 13. Prezzolini wrote to me (December 10, 1971): "You know that I am contrary to what you want to do, as though my ninetieth birthday were through my merits, instead of my ancestors' merits. The letters you cite…are words of a friend, of no importance. And many will ask: If this is Prezzolini, I don't know why you would remember his ninetieth birthday; it would be better to wait for his death, at least we would be sure he could not add other senseless phrases."

Nontheless, Prezzolini was thrilled with the book, especially because of the expressions of gratitude on the part of students. I've selected a few excerpts: "Our classroom was, in a certain sense, like an Italian or French Café, where friends would congregate for literary discussions. … 'Prezzy' was for us a dear friend during those years, yet he was never 'one of us.' … Later he became a personal friend" (Anne Paolucci).

"In a *Contemporary Culture* course, Prezzolini often succeeded in making statistics interesting. While our admiration grew with each lesson, fear disappeared because he treated us with courtesy and patience even when our answers were superficial" (Elsa Picone).

"No professor was more a 'teacher' than Prezzolini. For him, clarity and understanding, as well as compassion, were important. It was not possible to find a better friend" (Daisy Fornacca).

"Prezzolini was a true apostle of Italian culture. He was not an orator; he was a thinker, a conversationalist, a self-taught professor who prepared his lessons scrupulously. He not only lectured; he interacted with the students" (S. Eugene Scalia).

"Prezzolini's intense activity signaled 'the golden age' of Casa Italiana" (Joseph DeSimone).

Among colleagues who also expressed their admiration was the Columbia University Dante scholar, Professor Dino Bigongiari: "Prezzolini's conferences, although brilliant, were the least important part of his teaching. He guided students in their research, assisted them with their difficulties, unveiled new panoramas. A whole generation of young teachers can testify that all this is true, but it is also true that Prezzolini knows how to think, how to write, how to work; and, above all, he knows how to be a gentleman."

Whoever had the privilege of enjoying Prezzolini's lectures or hospitality will remember his physical appearance: blue eyes, quick movements, erect; he was totally independent (Woe to you if you tried to help him!); he was full of life, and elegant at all times; his discussions were spontaneous, witty, interesting; his words were simple, provoking, philosophical.

As a guest in Casa Prezzolini, whether in New York, Vietri sul Mare or Lugano, I always found a warm, comfortable atmosphere. His many guests were captivated by his voice, his eyes, his amiability. We would discuss everything: politics, literature, music, history, religion.

Walking with him and Jakie was an unforgettable experience: communing with nature and humanity—everything interested him: the mountains, flowers, birds, children, everyone. And it was Prezzolini who gently proposed the day's schedule, the division of labor, or the "passeggiata." This was the self-sufficient, free-spirited "maestro" I have had the privilege of knowing and honoring as a friend and benefactor.

In June 1981, I went to Lugano to visit Prezzolini and his wife, Jakie (the former Gioconda Savini who, as secretary of Casa Italiana, had helped so many students). During my visit, I noticed a terrible deterioration in both Prezzolini and Jakie. He would soon be one hundred and she was already eighty.

Since I had been invited to speak on the occasion of his 100th birthday on January 27, 1982, I calculated that, during my coming sabbatical, I could stay with them for three months while continuing my research on Philip Mazzei. A month after my arrival in December, Jakie, as everyone endearingly called her, was rushed to the hospital. She died soon after.

It was during my June visit that the civic authorities in Lugano were making plans to celebrate Prezzolini's 100th birthday. Not only was I aware of Prezzolini's dislike for celebrations, but I also realized he could not cope with the situation. So, before my departure I said rather timidly, "Professor, may I have your permission to return in the fall to participate in the January festivities?"

With a twinkle in his eyes, he responded: "If I were to say no, you would come just the same!" (E se dicessi di no, verresti lo stesso!) No doubt he remembered that, while I was a Casa Italiana student, he had described me as, "...a mixture of Catholicism and American independence!"

In preparation for the ceremonies honoring Prezzolini in Lugano, I requested that the Postal Ministry of the Republic of Italy issue a first-day cover, with a sketch of Prezzolini by the Florentine artist, Luciano Guarnieri. I arranged for the covers to be flown in and exhibited on Prezzolini's birthday—much to his amazement. On one of the envelopes Prezzolini wrote the following dedication: "To thank you, my dear, one would need the pen of an angel, not that of a domestic demon, like me, Giuseppe Prezzolini."

Still writing eight articles a month when he turned 100 years old (January 27, 1982), Prezzolini, who was intellectually alert, had a wonderful sense of humor, and was proud of both his Italian and his American citizenship. I was with him when he answered a telephone call from Ed McDowell of *The New York Times.*

He laughed: "My name is no longer Mr. Prezzolini; today it is Mr. Cent'anni—Italian for 100 years." After assuring the interviewer that he was "still in pretty good health," Prezzolini extended his good wishes to his "second fatherland," adding: "I am an American citizen, you know."

Ed McDowell was surprised at Prezzolini's keenness of mind. So were all newspaper and magazine interviewers and the numerous radio and TV program directors when he appeared in their studios during the celebrations.

I remained with Prezzolini for the next six months, except for a few weeks in February when I traveled for a speaking tour first on Prezzolini in Italy, and then on Mazzei in the United States. I kept in touch by telephone and mail. His letters revealed that he was not happy during my absence. He complained that the "captain" of the ship was gone (meaning me) and, although he appreciated Esther and Erica who cared for his daily needs, things were not going well. I returned as soon as possible with more material for the Mazzei project, and life in Lugano resumed normally.

In June, however, I was obliged to leave Prezzolini again for several weeks. I arranged for his care with Dr. Elvezio Minotti who expressed concern for his health. I said goodbye to Prezzolini, assuring him I would return. He insisted on walking with me to the door saying, "I will not see you again." Kissing him I responded, "You know I'm coming back. You saw my ticket." (The Italian Consul General in Lugano had provided my round-trip ticket to make sure I would return!)

Prezzolini had been an agnostic for many years. I was praying God would give him the gift of faith. I telephoned him from the United States to encourage him. In my heart I felt he would not last much longer. Within a few days after my departure, he was rushed to the hospital. He continued to write me from his hospital bed. Several days before he passed away, he sent me his last letter before ending his spiritual quest. His handwriting was barely legible but his words were clear: "I am arriving at a clarification that I would like to study....I am convinced I shall succeed ...I am searching, though I feel lost....Don't worry about me and don't deny me a brief visit."

When he died, I was not at his side. Providentially a nun was passing by and noticed his name on the hospital-room door. She entered and, while she prayed the rosary, Giuseppe Prezzolini died of bronchial complications on July 14, 1982.

There are so many memories of my visits. One day Dr. Minotti was talking about Prezzolini's physical condition and emphasized that he was still "lucido." Present was the doctor's granddaughter who attended the kindergarten. She understood the word "lucido" to be the same as "luce," which means "light." The next day the teacher explained to the children that all the festivities in Lugano were in honor of Giuseppe Prezzolini on his one-hundredth birthday. The little girl interrupted the teacher and, with a symbolic gesture representing light in a semi-circle, exclaimed: "E Prezzolini è tutto lucido!" ("And Prezzolini is all illuminated!").

Prezzolini has indeed "enlightened" many people throughout the twentieth-century. His contribution to the intellectual growth of countless students at Columbia University's Casa Italiana, and to the development of Italian thought and literature is invaluable. He used to say: "I'm not a professor. I'm just an older student who, having made many mistakes, would like you to avoid the ones I made. You will make mistakes, but they will be new ones." (October 10, 1971)

During the last months of his life I contacted literary critics, writers, and friends of Giuseppe Prezzolini asking them to send me a personal tribute to him on his 100th birthday. The response, singly and collaboratively, around the world—Italy, Switzerland, United States, Finland, etc.—was staggering. People from all walks of life sent me their contributions: philosophers and journalists, clerics and anarchists, presidents and professors. The tributes were in the form of letters, poems, studies, recollections, testimonials of all kinds. *Ricordi, Saggi e Testimonianze* (Memoirs, Essays and Testimonials) was published by Edizioni del Palazzo, Prato, in 1983. As I received the contributions, I showed them to Prezzolini who was very pleased. Although published after his death, Prezzolini was able to enjoy and appreciate the sentiments of his friends and colleagues. This book too is my lasting tribute to a great educator and writer.

Yes, I was privileged to assist Prezzolini as he continued writing articles. To express his gratitude to the people of Lugano for the wonderful hospitality he received, in early 1982 he was busy correcting proofs of a collection of articles published in Lugano's *Gazzetta Ticinese* from February 11, 1978 to September 19, 1981. *Bruschette "ticinesi"* was finally published in Switzerland in 1983, in the series "Tempi Moderni" by Edizioni Gottardo, with a preface by Indro Montanelli. According to Prezzolini, the word "bruschetta" is a Tuscan snack, similar to our "garlic bread." Rustic, healthy, and genuine, it is eaten at any time of the day with a glass of wine. Because of its bitter, pungent garlic taste and the delicacy of good olive oil, it has become the symbol of wisdom and good humor, just like his articles.

A TV interview on Prezzolini's one-hundredth birthday, filmed in Comano, Switzerland, is found in the Appendix. I accompanied him for that taping. The two reporters, Claudio Pozzoli and Cesare Chiericati, could not keep up with him. Prezzolini's responses— intelligent, witty, unexpected—could not be matched. Since I had convinced him to accept this invitation and I had also made arrangements for the program, the reporters sent me a personal copy of the transcript transmitted on TSI (Swiss Italian Television).

During this period, I suggested that Prezzolini do a special book —an anthology of his articles on religion and the church in today's world. It would be a sequel to his best seller *Dio è un rischio* (God Is a Risk), showing the development of his ideas on religion from his 1903 writings to the present. I convinced him, and together we selected articles. Rusconi was willing to publish the manuscript.

One day, Prezzolini noticed the shadow that kept following us during a "passeggiata" on the terrace. He remarked that it was *L'ombra di Dio* ("God's shadow"). We agreed that *L'ombra di Dio* should be the title of the new book. The introductory chapter caused him extreme anguish and spiritual torment. Day in and day out he would destroy his drafts.

Finally, after much meditation, Prezzolini completed it, stating: "This is my chapter; I have never been a hypocrite; these are my sentiments; it is the truth." Having received the key to the book, I completed preparation of the manuscript and sent it to press several weeks before his death. It was published by Rusconi (Milan, 1984). *L'ombra di Dio* is Prezzolini's spiritual testament.

Prezzolini's respect and love for his students is documented in *The Case of the Casa Italiana* that I published (American Institute of Italian Studies, 1976). Here he acknowledges that, immediately following World War I, "a group of young students of Italian extraction (who could not have bought a little hut even if they had pooled all their funds), was the promoter of the tallest, most artistic, most original house on Columbia University's new campus." As visiting professor, these were the students taught in 1923, 1927, and 1929 by Prezzolini who was still associated with the League of Nations in Paris. He returned to Columbia permanently in 1930.

During a period of anti-clericalism in Italy, Prezzolini was educating Italian-American students. Many came from Catholic Institutions; some came from Italy; others were first generation children of Italian immigrants: Professor Peter M. Riccio, Sister Serafina Mazza (a member of the Mother Seton Sisters), Monsignor William Granger Ryan, Professor Armando DeGaetano, Diplomat Federico Mascioli, Poet Joseph Tuccio, and Professor Arnold Del Greco, about whom Prezzolini writes in his *Diario II*. Very dear to Prezzolini was Professor S. Eugene Scalia (the father of Antonin Scalia, U.S. Associate Justice of the Supreme Court).

Prezzolini suggested that I engage S. Eugene Scalia as my associate editor for the Bicentennial Philip Mazzei project. Scalia, a retired professor from Brooklyn College, added greatly to the success of the work I had begun. For several years during his retirement he traveled weekly from Trenton to Morristown, and even worked faithfully at home.

Whenever Professor Scalia arrived in the office with news that he had a new grandchild, he would remark, "But how can Antonin expect to send so many children to college while earning a professor's salary?" His son had nine children. Little did his father dream that Antonin would become an Associate Justice of the United States Supreme Court!

Perhaps *Lettere a Suor Margherita* (Edizioni di Storia e Letteratura, 1992), one of the latest books concerning him, fills certain gaps in the biography of Giuseppe Prezzolini. A publication of 375 letters to a student (I am the recipient), it also includes an Appendix with unpublished letters to other correspondents (clergy, critics, editors, friends), a Chronology, 26 Illustrations, Preface and Introduction. There are also reprints of three publications about me: Preface to *L'imagine tesa* (1960); *La suora letteraria* ("Resto del carlino," January 6, 1972); *Suora Margherita* ("Gazzetta ticinese," May 23, 1981).

My own letters to Prezzoini are missing because, whenever I helped arrange his files during my visits, I discarded those letters I had written as being of no importance. Covering more than a quarter of a century, Giuseppe Prezzolini's extraordinary and delightful letters are complicated by the fact that, while I was assuring him of my prayers and asking God to bless him, he was desperately searching to find God.

These letters do not have all the universal themes one finds in the other volumes of his correspondence. Rather they are personal and contain concern for my health, interest in my activities, books for me to consult, methodology, advice, and assistance in my research. This dramatic, spiritual dialogue between student and teacher is intense. His advice was always practical; e.g., he suggested that I read a German Bible in preparation for the reading test at Columbia. Meanwhile he wrote to me in German. I answered his letter in German. I was ready for the exam.

Edited by Claudio Quarantotto, the Preface in *Lettere a Suor Margherita* assures us that these letters "clarify a particular aspect of Prezzolini's personality. For the first time, that is, we now see the 'professor' Prezzolini in action, as he guides a very special student and puts into practice his ideas and theories on education."

In fact, Quarantotto wrote that Sister Margherita accepts the challenging topics suggested by her professor and becomes his colleague, friend and confidante. "The letters in this collection are unique," Quarantotto continued, "since they contain information and confessions on the private and, at times, intimate life of the writer which one would search for in vain elsewhere among the more 'important' letters written by Prezzolini. Indeed, the letters to Sister Margherita may be compared only with some of the more uninhibited pages of his *Diario*."

The publication, *Lettere a Suor Margherita*, begins the series of "Quaderni" of Prezzolini's correspondence with "minor" persons who are still alive. In these letters, Prezzolini, who usually writes about practical topics or is engaged in polemics, abandons himself and reminisces on past events and relationships. His letters reveal a period of forty years of friendship and is the story of his association with twentieth-century Italian culture. Prezzolini not only appreciated my work, but also admired and respected my faith and mission as a member of the Religious Teachers Filippini.

It suffices to quote from several of these letters: "Do not forget me in your prayers; I believe that they always do good, even if one does not believe" (February 2, 1959); "I hope you will be able to bear all adversities and that you will act with honor: this is the most important thing in life, for one who does not have the Grace of God, which is more important than honor" (December 28, 1960); "My dearest little Sister, we are concerned about your health. ... We wish you would take better care of yourself. A healthy sinner can do more than a sick saint" (October 19, 1974).

Writing to me only a few days before he died (July 2, 1982), Prezzolini expressed his final thoughts: "Do not deprive me of a brief visit... ." Our visits continue in the realms of the spirit. I recall Cesare Angelini's words when I asked him to comment on *Dio è un rischio* (May 10, 1969): "It is the strange book of a man who calls himself an atheist, a book which turns out to be an act of faith. There are in it forceful pages like the complaint Job invokes against God; but Job raises it because he has faith. Prezzolini, the dear man! Irreligious out of a demand for fresher religiosity. ...

"When a man has no use for someone, he lets him go on his way and speaks no more of him. Prezzolini is still talking about Him, is always talking about Him, disconsolately. Like someone that is seeking; but in the ways of the spirit, anyone who seeks has already found." The philosophical aim of *Dio è un rischio* was to show that man is not motivated by reason, but rather by faith. It is Prezzolini's sincere, personal confession—his spiritual itinerary, written with diligence, clarity, sincerity.

Prezzolini personified the crisis of the modern man. He experienced the drama of our times in the demanding context of spirituality and search for God. Until his final days, Prezzolini's destiny was an ambivalence between his sincere recognition of the validity of Catholicism, and his personal inablitiy to espouse its norms. He was humble, sincere, and consistent, despite the apparent contradictions in his temperament.

After Pope Paul VI spoke about him from the balcony of St. Peter's Square in 1974, Prezzolini stated: "One point seems certain inside me. If I were to be converted by divine grace, I would hide myself well, not out of shame, but out of fear that it might seem like an inconvenient publicity."

Among the first publications of the series of "Carteggi" (Edizioni di Storia e letteratura) was *Giovanni Boine-Giuseppe Prezzolini (1908-1917)*. Prezzolini wrote the Preface for this book, as well as for *Cesare Angelini-Giuseppe Prezzolini (1919-1976)*. Since Prezzolini's death in 1982, the complete series of "Carteggi" is being sponsored by the Department of Public Instruction of the Canton Ticino, the Biblioteca Cantonale di Lugano, and the Prezzolini Archives. The protagonists of the published volumes are writers, politicians, philosophers—Soffici, Angelini, Palazzeschi, Croce, Casati, Missiroli, Baldini. They are "major" personalities who discuss universal themes and literary, philosophical and religious concepts.

In my most recent book, *Carteggio Giovanni Abbo-Giuseppe Prezzolini*, released by Edizioni di Storia e Letteratura (Rome, 2000), Prezzolini again reveals his spiritual itinerary to a mutual friend, Monsignor John A. Abbo. The book is dedicated to Graziano Bianchi, an attorney, because of his long friendship with both Abbo and Prezzolini.

This friendship began one evening in 1957, after Prezzolini's lecture on Giovanni Papini in Columbia's Casa Italiana. I introduced him to Abbo, a poet and author, as well as chaplain at Villa Walsh. Monsignor Abbo was interested in my studies. Thanks to his insistence, I did not destroy Prezzolini's letters to me, and the book, *Lettere a Suor Margherita,* was eventually published in 1992.

But the idea to publish the book began years earlier at a dinner table in Florence, Italy, in 1980. Abbo was describing the importance of these letters to his friend, Graziano Bianchi, who immediately declared: "The title must be *Lettere a Suor Margherita.*" I was present for this conversation and agreed with the title.

These letters reveal Prezzolini's constant search for Truth. His quest for God continued to the very end of his life. His spirit did not die. Although he always felt unworthy of the marvelous gift of faith, I am confident that God, who is "Love," reached Giuseppe Prezzolini.

Archbishop Peter L. Gerety wrote a discerning statement of my friendship with Giuseppe Prezzolini (October 28, 1991): "Prezzolini thought he was an atheist, but you saw in him wonderful qualities of goodness that were a reflection of our good God. How truly Christian are your sentiments! Perhaps he was one of those with an *anima naturaliter christiana* [a naturally Christian soul]."

Chapter Eight: Philip Mazzei

**"We admire the Bill of Rights, as truly a masterpiece.
There is in few words, according to our opinion,
everything comprehended for instituting the most free,
and of consequence the most perfect Government..."**
(Mazzei to the Delegates in Convention, May 16, 1776)

"Who is Philip Mazzei?" I asked Dr. Peter Sammartino when he suggested that I translate a book by this little-known patriot.

Although teaching and research were part of my life and mission, my expertise was now challenged by Philip Mazzei (1730-1816). I submitted a proposal to the New Jersey Bicentennial Commission and received a $3,500 grant. This work was to be completed for the Bicentennial. I translated the first volume of Mazzei's four-volume history of the American colonies, *Recherches historiques et politiques sur les États-Unis de l'Amérique septentrionale*, printed in French (Paris, 1788). Mazzei's aim was to clarify misrepresentations about America. I dedicated the book to "Peter Sammartino and Sally, his charming wife."

When my manuscript was ready, I presented it to Mario DeVita, a printer in New York, offering him the grant money. He laughed, and said that the grant money would not even pay for the paper. He then asked me how many copies. Having had no experience as a publisher, with great confidence, I said: "Well, I'd like to have 12,000 copies of this book!" He was shocked, but I assured him I would sell them and then pay him. I immediately appealed to several friends, including Frank Sinatra. When the bill arrived, the cost was $30,000! Yes, I was able to finance this project about an unsung hero whose agricultural talents retreated as he accepted the challenges of his day, becoming a writer, diplomat, philosopher and friend of the American Revolution.

This book, *Philip Mazzei: Jefferson's "Zealous Whig"* served as my "visiting card." I applied for future grants.

The Public Relations Office of Fairleigh Dickinson University sent an article about this book, "Special to *The New York Times*," with a photograph. Interestingly, both were accepted. Mazzei's relationship with some of the leaders of the American Revolution attracted attention and the FDU interview was published in the Sunday edition, December 7, 1975.

This was the beginning of nationwide publicity. The article noted that John Adams wrote to Jefferson in 1780, stating that Mazzei was "a zealous defender of our affairs." In Italy in 1800, newspapers labeled him "one of the most zealous actors in the American Revolution." After Mazzei's death in 1816, Jefferson wrote: "An intimacy of 40 years has proven to me his great worth...his early and zealous cooperation in the establishment of our independence having acquired for him a great degree of favor."

Jeffersonian scholar Dumas Malone wrote to me (April 14, 1976): "Philip Mazzei's work on the United States, published in French while his friend Jefferson was minister to France, was one of the best of its time on its subject. By translating and editing it you have rendered valuable service to historical scholarship and made a significant contribution to the literature of the Bicentennial."

In the May 30, 1976 Sunday issue of *The New York Times*, Fred Ferretti wrote: *Philip Mazzei: Jefferson's "Zealous Whig"* is not only a biography of one of the relatively unknown protagonists of the American Revolution. It also is a highly literate translation of the works of the pamphleteer who, writing under the name of *Furioso* exhorted the Colonies early on to sever their ties with England....The book is a fascinating compendium of little-known facts and highly opinionated tracts."

Grants from the National Historical Publications and Records Commission, National Endowment for the Humanities and other foundations followed, as I dedicated ten years to researching and writing about Mazzei's contributions to the creation of the United States. Besides *Philip Mazzei: Jefferson's "Zealous Whig"* (1975), I published *Philip Mazzei: My Life and Wanderings* (1980); *The Comprehensive Microform Edition of His Papers, 1730-1816, with Guide and Index*, 9 reels (1982); *Selected Writings and Correspondence*, 3 vols. (1983, English edition; 1984, Italian edition); *The Constitutional Society of 1784* (1984); *Philip Mazzei: World Citizen* (1994); and a bilingual book, *The Adventurous Life of Philip Mazzei* (1995). This world-wide research project resulted in the collection of over 3,000 documents, now preserved at the Salvatori Center for Mazzei Studies in Morristown, NJ, and at the American Philosophical Society Library in Philadelphia.

When U.S. President Jimmy Carter received Prime Minister Francesco Cossiga of Italy at the White House on January 24, 1980, he made a surprise announcement—the United States would issue an international airmail stamp during the 250th anniversary of Philip Mazzei's birth. Ken Lawrence in the February 1995 issue of *The American Philatelist* magazine carried the story: "Underlying the successful lobbying drive was a five-year promotion by Sister Margherita Marchione, a professor of Italian who was administrator of the *Philip Mazzei Papers* at Fairleigh Dickinson University in New Jersey. On a research trip to Florence, she unearthed the 1790 miniature portrait of Mazzei that became the basis for both U.S. and Italy postage stamp designs and for the pictorial first-day cancellation applied to the Italian stamp. ... The Postal Service's original offer to her congressional patrons was a commemorative postal card, but she persuaded them to reject that and to hold out for a stamp."

In fact, I was sitting in a wheelchair with my right leg in a cast—owing to a fall a few weeks before at Harvard University—during a breakfast reunion of senators and congressmen representing the Italian delegation in Washington, DC. When the offer of a postal card instead of a commemorative stamp was made, I spontaneously blurted out: "Apparently the Postmaster General does not deem Philip Mazzei worthy of a stamp. I think we should refuse anything less than a commemorative stamp!" Everyone applauded and the proposal was rejected. We succeeded in obtaining an international commemorative airmail stamp.

The design for the stamp was unveiled at the April 18, 1980 annual dinner-dance in the Washington Hilton sponsored by the National Italian American Foundation. Also unveiled was a bronze bust sculpted, at my request, by Joseph Amelio Finelli. The bust, now in Monticello, became part of the official First Day Cover with Philip Mazzei's words: "If we could have but one & the same constitution for all the united colonies our union would be infinitely stronger (May 11, 1776)." According to a UPS news release, Columbus Day, October 13, 1980 was selected "because of the significance of the holiday to Italian-Americans." The 40-cent United States international airmail stamp, designed by Sante Graziani of Massachusetts, appeared with the words "Philip Mazzei, Patriot Remembered." The ceremony was sponsored by the Daughters of the American Revolution in Washington, DC.

I had been invited to speak throughout the United States, e.g., October 10, 1980 I was at the European Studies Conference at the University of Nebraska at Omaha and, upon my return from Italy, I addressed the Italian Community of Los Angeles and was honored at a dinner-dance, December 6, 1980.

Meanwhile, on October 6, 1980, the 250th anniversary of Mazzei's birth was commemorated during ceremonies held at the Center for Mazzei Studies, presided by Dr. Peter Sammartino, FDU Chancellor. Donald McDowell, General Manager of the U.S. Postal Service, presented the original artwork to me, and I responded with *A Tribute to Philip Mazzei.*

The ceremony was enhanced by the presence of the local postmaster, J. Robert Tracey, representatives of church and state, as well as of the Italian Embassy and other Italian American organizations. Sally Sammartino read Governor Brendan Byrne's *Proclamation* declaring *Philip Mazzei Day in New Jersey,* "in recognition of Mazzei's unique contributions to the cause of American independence as a political philosopher and propagandist." A medley of patriotic songs by the Villa Walsh Academy Choir closed the program which was followed with a formal reception by the New Jersey Italian American Professional Women.

Dr. Sammartino and I arranged to have a Conference in Rome, October 15, 1980, to celebrate Philip Mazzei's 250th anniversary of birth and the issuance of a stamp by the Republic of Italy. It was sponsored by the National Italian American Foundation, the American Ambassador to Italy, Richard Gardner, and associated organizations.

From Washington, DC, a group of Americans traveled by plane for the Conference. We had accommodations at the Excelsior Hotel on Via Veneto in Rome where representatives of the academic world and civil authorities attended a Gala Dinner. The following morning the Conference took place on Piazza San Marco in Rome's center where a hall had been reserved for us.

During the panel discussion, Peter Sammartino received a telegram and passed it to me. It stated that Senator Amintore Fanfani, the Prime Minister, was no longer able to attend because he was busy with Queen Elizabeth from England who had arrived that morning and was being officially honored at Piazza Venezia. Protocol required his presence. This caused much concern to both of us. The audience was unaware of the difficulty.

Sammartino's plan was to honor Fanfani who had received an honorary degree from Fairleigh Dickinson University during one of his official visits to the United States. He wished to honor his friend again as an Indian Chief. The Shinnecock Indians, who lived on the Southhampton Reservation on the south shore of Long Island, had prepared a beautiful headdress for him. Sammartino turned to me to help solve the problem. I suggested he substitute Giulio Andreotti who was seated in the front row with other Italian dignitaries.

Without batting an eyelash, Sammartino invited Giulio Andreotti to come to the podium. You can imagine his amazement when he learned that he was to become an Indian Chief with all the pomp and ceremony and headgear. Little did he realize, nor did anyone else, that he was filling in for Prime Minister Fanfani! He accepted graciously and the newspapers had a ball, showing Andreotti as an Indian Chief.

Incidentally, several years before this incident, when Fanfani received a FDU honorary degree, I was introduced to him during the reception. Soon after, before leaving for Italy, Peter Sammartino asked me to contact him. Having arrived early for the appointment, I was prepared to wait. Instead I was ushered immediately into his office. We chatted and reminisced about his long friendship with the Sammartinos. Fanfani was also interested in my books and research in Italy.

As I left Fanfani's office I was smiling until I noticed one person glaring at me and complaining to the receptionist about the delay. I did not know who she was until that evening when I recognized her on the TV news. She was wearing the same outfit and was being interviewed after her encounter with Fanfani. Her name—Leonilde Iotti, wife of Palmiro Togliatti, head of the Italian Communist Party and first woman president of Italy's lower house of parliament in 1979. She served thirteen years in the post, which is equivalent to the speaker of the U.S. House of Representatives. She served a total of fifty-three years in the Chamber of Deputies and was also on the foreign affairs committee of the European Parliament. Little did I realize who she was when I left Fanfani's office. No wonder she was fuming!

There were so many adventures in the life of Peter and Sally. They had deep faith in God, as well as in the ability to adapt to new situations. Their activities and mine were often intertwined. For example, during the Philip Mazzei Conference, Ambassador Gardner invited the entire group for a reception at his home in Rome. It was here that the idea of Corfinio College was conceived during a discussion with Henry Tessicini, a philanthropist, who was interested in promoting the teaching of Italian culture. His friendship with Peter Sammartino inspired him to donate funds for young American students to study in Italy. The project to develop and implement plans was then placed in my hands. For ten summers it was a College-on-wheels, based in Corfinio. Approximately five hundred college students were introduced to the Italian language and its culture. It was a successful enterprise.

I will write more of Corfinio College later. But as further illustration of the cross-currents of life, I want to include here how my work on Philip Mazzei was especially rewarded when his grave was unexpectedly located.

The discovery was made one summer by the Corfinio College students. We were passing through Pisa when I noticed a sign indicating the local cemetery where Philip Mazzei was said to be buried. We decided to visit his grave, but soon learned that the custodian had never heard of him. There was no such grave listed in the records. But, I knew he was buried there and I challenged the students to search for his grave. We divided into groups. Finally one group visited a small chapel and as they stepped on a large marble slab they read Mazzei's name. The epitaph was in Latin, written by Giovanni Carmignani, a professor at the University of Pisa:

To Philip Mazzei of Poggio a Caiano
A high-minded and most incorruptible man
The best of citizens even in evil times
Who saw the ways of many peoples and cities.
Granted citizenship in the united colonies
Of North America, he carried out for them
A diplomatic mission in France and throughout Europe
And wrote excellent commentaries on their bodies politic.
He accepted a diplomatic mission in France
From the most humane of Polish Kings,
Stanislaus Poniatowski
Who was one of his more intimate friends.
He died in Pisa on March 19, 1916
At the age of 86.
Wherefore Antonia, his wife, and Elizabeth, his daughter,
Gratefully placed this memorial.

To return to the Mazzei Conference group, while they proceeded to Sardinia for a tour of the Island, I remained in Italy with three of my sisters (Jean, Marie, and Ceil), who were with me at the Conference and would accompany me for the October 18 Italian stamp ceremony in Poggio a Caiano, where Mazzei was born.

We decided to fly to Venice. We settled for the only available room with four beds and a bath on Piazza San Marco. The next morning the guide would accompany us to the train. Hours passed before he arrived announcing that Piazza San Marco was flooded. Planks had been placed above the water to make walking possible. Our guide was very tall and wore boots up to his thighs, but we were not prepared for this weather. Without giving me a chance to react, he picked me up, placed me piggy-back on his shoulders, and told the others to wait for his return. He followed the same procedure for each of my sisters, then went for our luggage. A boat was waiting for us; and, soon after, we arrived at the train station. We stopped in Padova for a pre-arranged interview with Giovanni Lugaresi, an Italian reporter for *Il Gazzettino* of Venice.

We then took a train to Florence, where we were greeted with fanfare and affection by Mayor Sergio Pezzati and by the townsfolk of Poggio a Caiano. The stamp ceremony honoring Philip Mazzei, amidst the splendor of Villa Medici, was glorious. We later joined the American group in Sardinia.

Also, my sisters and I were part of the Giuseppe Garibaldi Centennial Committee organized by Peter Sammartino under the aegis of the National Italian American Foundation. I was an honorary member. We joined the Italian Americans to commemorate the 100th anniversary of Garibaldi's death (June 2), and also the anniversary of the establishment of the present Republic of Italy in 1946. The Philip Mazzei international conference would close with a sentimental trip to the Island of Caprera, off the coast of Sardinia. The final ceremony of our trip ended there, as I placed flowers on Garibaldi's tomb.

I was included as No. 144 of the Women's History Series of First Day Covers by the National Organization of Women, perhaps because I spearheaded a campaign that succeeded in obtaining the international airmail stamp for the 250th anniversary (1980) of Mazzei's birth. During the celebrations, an article by Shirley Horner in the *New York Times* stated: "Although Mazzei seems to have had a good life, his real luck was falling into Sister Margherita's lap. Wherever she goes on his behalf, the doors spring open, too." My reply: "Not only did he fall into my lap, but I have been living with him for many years!"

Cosponsored by Fairleigh Dickinson University and The New Jersey Historical Commission and funded by The New Jersey Committee for the Humanities, a Symposium, entitled *Philip Mazzei's Role: Age of the Enlightenment*, was held on April 25, 1981, to honor Philip Mazzei. The morning session was held in Lenfell Hall of the FDU Madison campus, followed by a luncheon in the Mansion Lobby. Speakers were Senator Laurence S. Weiss, a member of the NJ Historical Commission and Senate President Joseph P. Merlino, representing Governor Brendan Byrne. My talk was "Virginia Politics: Mazzei's Role," while historian Stanley Idzerda delivered his presentation on "The Age of the Enlightenment," followed by a discussion with Peter Sammartino as moderator.

A copy of the microfilm edition of *The Papers of Philip Mazzei* was presented to the provost, Dr. James V. Griffo. There was also a presentation of *Philip Mazzei: My Life and Wanderings* to Vincent Visceglia, a patron of Italian culture and President of Summit Associates Corporation. Several days before this Symposium, Shirley Horner's review in the *New York Times* explained that "the book provides an often-uninhibited account of life over two centuries ago, including the tastes of Virginia, the terror of the French Revolution and the tragedy of Louis XVI, who, unlike his predecessors, never had any desire for any woman other than his wife [Marie Antoinette], who never had any for him."

The afternoon session was held in Friendship Library with a large exhibit (April 10 to May 15) of Mazzei's books and memorabilia, which included Mazzei's ivory letter opener, copper candlestick, and ivory necktie pin, courtesy of Mario Giani, his closest living descendant. Frank Raciti, formerly a civil engineer, who now devotes his time to philately and to the new 40-cent Mazzei postage stamp, said, "It is significant as the first U.S. airmail to feature a person of foreign birth." Incidentally, soon after, Mr. Raciti donated his unique collection of First Day Covers to the Mazzei Center. The program ended with Italian songs and dances, directed by Professor Filomena Peloro.

At a conference on Prezzolini (January 1982), in Pescia, near Florence, Italy, I concluded my talk by mentioning the need for funding the Mazzei Project. Mr. Italo Inverni, an elderly local businessman, suggested I meet the president of the Cassa di Risparmi e Depositi di Prato. Dr. Silvano Bambagioni, according to Mr. Inverni, might be interested in the project because his bank had a branch in Poggio a Caiano, the birthplace of Philip Mazzei. Mr. Inverni tried to contact Bambagioni to discuss my research on Philip Mazzei. He was not available.

Only a few hours remained. I could not change my plans and I had to return to Switzerland the next morning. The only appointment Italo Inverni could arrange was for 10:00 p.m. We agreed to meet at Bambagioni's home in Prato. After a brief discussion, I presented my manuscripts for three volumes of Philip Mazzei's documents in the English language as required by the National Endowment for the Humanities Grant. The president of the bank was pleased. He sent for his administrator who rushed to meet us. They agreed that this would be a worthy project for their bank to sponsor. However, I had to make a commitment to produce these same three volumes in an Italian and French edition. Shortly after this meeting, I signed the contract, accepting this enormous task.

The six volumes entitled *Selected Writings and Correspondence* in English, French and Italian were published in an elegantly-boxed edition by Edizioni del Palazzo (1984), each volume containing forty-eight colored photographs, including excerpts of letters to and from the first five presidents of the United States.

The official presentation of the six volumes took place on January 11, 1984, at a dinner in the New York Waldorf-Astoria. Present were Giulio Andreotti, the Republic of Italy's Foreign Minister; Rinaldo Petrignani, the Ambassador of Italy to the U. S.; Maxwell Rabb, the U. S. Ambassador to Italy; other ambassadors and ministers from Italy, presidents of banks and industry, professors and other prestigious professionals, as well as members of my family and friends. Sitting on the dais next to Minister Andreotti, who had written the preface to the Italian edition, I asked him which of his many titles he preferred that I use. His answer was, "Call me Giulio!" This was the beginning of our friendship.

The media had described me as "a whirlwind of exceptional deeds, a caring person with the kind of warm personality that immediately makes one feel she has been a friend for years."

I must admit my pleasure in reading how I am described by the inscription on the Christopher Columbus "Woman of the Year" award presented on October 11, 1987: "Sister Margherita Marchione— whose indispensable contributions as a great woman of God, educator and historian, whose scholarly life will stand forever as a symbol of the bond of sentiment between Italy and America, a molder of men and women in her exemplary life who has dictated exceptional awareness to the minds of our young leaders of tomorrow, we honor her, a true daughter of Columbus."

New Jersey is proud to have been the first state to ratify the 10 amendments which constitute the Bill of Rights. And in Morristown, NJ—the military capital of the American Revolution—there is another "first": The Center for Mazzei Studies was established in 1976 at Villa Walsh in honor of Grace and Henry Salvatori. Here documents are examined and scholars inspired to study the life and times of Philip Mazzei.

For this project, I solicited funds from friends, among them Henry Salvatori, from Los Angeles, CA., an Italian-born geophysicist who founded an international oil exploration company. Born in Rome, he came to the United States as a child and grew up on a farm in Southern New Jersey. He was graduated from the University of Pennsylvania and earned a master's degree at Columbia University, becoming an expert in the new science of finding oil by seismic technology. In 1933 he founded the Western Geophysical Corporation which became the world's foremost off-shore seismic contractor. Not only did he use his wealth to encourage young students, but he also used his influence as a Republican presidential adviser.

Henry Salvatori's letters to me began when I requested funding for the Mazzei Center. During the next few years, his donations totaled $100,000. Interested in promoting Italian culture, Henry

Salvatori also sponsored the publication of several of my books. I kept him informed of my activities by phone and we corresponded frequently. If I requested a check for $1,000, his check would be $5,000 or $10,000. Grace and Henry Salvatori visited the Mazzei Center and were very pleased with my scholarly research projects. She passed away in 1990. Seven years later, he, too, passed away at the age of 96.

The Salvatori Center for Mazzei Studies not only houses over 3,000 copies of Mazzei documents, but has served for many other activities. Here many of my books were written, and much of my work as treasurer of the Religious Teachers Filippini was done. Here meetings were held with bankers and contractors, and friendships flourished. For many years, a group of men and women of the AA have had access to the Mazzei Center for their weekly Sunday morning meetings.

As editor of the Mazzei microfilm project on *The Papers of Philip Mazzei* and the six volumes of *Selected Writings and Correspondence* in English, French and Italian, I received close to a half million dollars in grants from several national and private foundations. The project made requisite the talents of a wonderful team of associate editors: Dr. S. Eugene Scalia, father of Antonin Scalia, an associate justice of the United States Supreme Court; Dr. Stanley Idzerda, Director of the Papers of Lafayette, Cornell University; Dr. Barbara Oberg, who later became Director of the Papers of Thomas Jefferson, Princeton University. We dedicated several years to researching and writing about Philip Mazzei's contributions to the creation of the United States.

A native of Tuscany, Italy, Philip Mazzei was colonial Virginia's agent in Europe and an active propagandist in the American Revolution. He was born in Poggio-a-Caiano, December 25, 1730. He lived in England for 18 years before coming to Virginia in 1773. His political influence predates the Revolution. A compelling figure of the Enlightenment, Mazzei was versatile, enterprising, articulate, and perceptive. He was a surgeon in Italy and Turkey; a merchant and language teacher in England; an agriculturist and zealous Whig in

Virginia; a writer and diplomat in France; a royal chamberlain and privy councillor in Poland.

With his immigration to the colonies, Philip Mazzei began a 43-year fascination with America wherein he befriended and influenced our Founding Fathers, contributed to the commerce of the colonies, and added a fiery voice to Virginia's political stage. His intellectual and philosophical ideas—especially concerning the separation of Church and State, and the recognition of the equality of all men—were as much a part of the American Revolution as was any sea battle or military campaign.

When Mazzei moved to London in 1756, he met Thomas Adams and Benjamin Franklin who urged him to introduce his Italian products and culture to the colonies. He set sail for Virginia in 1773 and settled on land in Charlottesville adjoining the estate of Thomas Jefferson. Ideas of farming were soon put aside when he became caught up in the growing political tensions of his adopted country.

Mazzei encouraged the Virginians in their zeal for rebellion based on natural rights and helped them prepare a new system of government. He was welcomed warmly by George Washington and others in Williamsburg, and shared with them the vital political information he had acquired within professional and social circles during eighteen years of residence in England.

In 1774, when Mazzei formed his Wine Company, Thomas Jefferson, the most influential wine connoisseur of his time, joined and undoubtedly encouraged other famous figures of the day to become investors. The names of the 37 investors read like a list of Virginia's 18th century *Who's Who*. Among the members were Peyton Randolph, first President of the Continental Congress; Robert Carter Nicholas, Treasurer of the colony; Benjamin Harrison, who would be a Signer of the Declaration of Independence; John Blair, President of the *Constitutional Society*; Lord Dunmore, Governor of Virginia; and, of course, George Washington.

Mazzei brought with him Antonio Giannini, his wife and child, four other peasants and a tailor, as well as his former partner's wife, Madame Marie Petronille Hautefeuille Martin who had become his associate and mistress in London, and her daughter Margherita. In Virginia, his friend Thomas Adams persuaded Philip Mazzei to marry the French widow lest he be thought to be cohabiting with her. Unfortunately, the marriage proved an unhappy one for Mazzei.

In 1779, Mazzei was appointed Virginia's Agent in Europe. This gave him a rare chance to support the colonies overseas, as well as the opportunity to be separated from Petronille.

In a letter to Mazzei, who was about to depart for Europe as Virginia's agent, Washington wrote from Windsor, CT (July 1, 1779): "I thank you for your obliging account of the culture of the vine.... I have long been of opinion...that wine sooner or later would become a valuable article of produce. The relation of your experiments convince me I was right." Unfortunately, while Mazzei was abroad, the British prisoners of war living on his estate destroyed his cherished vineyards. Jefferson informed him (April 4, 1780): "Your vines and trees at Colle have suffered extremely from their horses, cattle, and carelessness."

Mazzei relates that while Jefferson was in Boston en route to France as a replacement for Benjamin Franklin, United States Minister Plenipotentiary, some members of the Assembly "proposed a revision of the government, while others feared they would run into Scylla in trying to avoid Charybdis." Mazzei proposed they organize a private club to be called *Constitutional Society* in order to discuss privately all that was to be discussed publicly and passed upon by the Assembly.

Upon Mazzei's return to Virginia in 1783, various factors conspired to make him decide to return to Europe, the main one being the arrival in America of his wife, the woman he had married for the sake of convenience. He permitted her to reside at Colle and bought land in Richmond for himself. He then decided to join Jefferson in France. Mazzei wrote in his *Memorie* that in 1788 he received a letter from Mr. Blair advising him of his wife's death, adding that he—Blair—was very sorry he was unable to send a "white kerchief." On reading the letter that remark moved Jefferson to say: "That would be enough to show how hateful that bitch had made herself, since a man [Blair] made up of sweetness and humanity was able to joke on such an occasion."

Philip Mazzei was a "founding father"of American democracy and a "citizen of the world," serving the cause of freedom everywhere. He was an active participant in the three great national upheavals of the eighteenth-century: the American and the French Revolutions, and the events which led to the second partition of Poland. Indeed, as agent for Virginia, Mazzei had hobnobbed too long with ministers and diplomats to feel satisfied with the life of an agriculturist or merchant.

In a lengthy letter (September 27, 1785), Mazzei describes the purposes of *The Constitutional Society* to the second president of the United States, John Adams, who was representing the United States in England. In his *Memorie* (translated into English as *My Life and Wanderings*, 1980), Mazzei speaks about the Society and about his friendship with Jefferson's successors to the presidency—James Madison and James Monroe.

The friendship with Madison continued even while Mazzei was in Paris, serving as chargé d'affaires for the King of Poland. At Madison's request, Mazzei wrote his letters only in Italian. In 1785 Monroe sent Madison a treatise by Mazzei, written in Italian, in support of national control of seaports.

Confessing to his inadequacy in the Italian language, Monroe told Madison (July 26, 1785): "By committing it to you, I trust I promote his [Mazzei's] views more than I shall otherwise have it in my power to do." The difference in their native languages was more than compensated for by the similarity of their political principles and ideals and Mazzei's correspondence with Monroe was still another means of keeping himself informed of what was happening in his beloved adoptive country; in return, he helped keep Monroe abreast of the events of a turbulent period of European history.

Before joining Jefferson in Paris, Mazzei conceived and organized the *Constitutional Society of 1784* where many of the ideas discussed during the Constitutional Convention were first voiced. Its purpose was to preserve the "pure and sacred principles of Liberty" by organizing discussions of important issues previous to legislative decisions. Its members also took it upon themselves to debate public issues and instruct voters.

In 1937, A. Valta Parma, curator of the Rare Book Collection of the Library of Congress, came across a folded-in leaflet among the bound political pamphlets from Thomas Jefferson's library. Convinced of the importance of these *Minutes of the Constitutional Society*, the curator stated: "There was no other group of men anywhere in the country with the prestige and power of that group of Virginians. There is no question but that the thought of the necessity of a Constitution received its first impulse from them and that here was a definite organization to set about solving many of the problems that would come up in framing a federal constitution."

Besides giving the new society its name, in a letter of May 12, 1785, Mazzei expressed to Blair his thoughts and aspirations concening the new venture. Always the cosmopolitan and the eclectic, Mazzei suggested as members not only eminent Virginians such as James Madison, James Monroe, and John Marshall, but also representatives from other states—Dr. Way of Wilmington, and Elias Boudinot of New Jersey. He even suggested having foreign honorary members—Duke de la Rochefoucauld in Paris, Jurist Cesare Beccaria in Milan, Philosopher Felice Fontana in Florence, Biologist Lazzaro Spallanzani in Bologna.

As evidenced by the documents found some 70 years ago, the *Constitutional Society* was founded three years before the organization of the *Constitutional Convention*. These documents have been called "a true embryo of our Constitution."

John Blair, a member of the Federal Convention, who had been nominated by Philip Mazzei as president of the Society, remained a friend and correspondent. Mazzei had to be content to read about the organization he had founded, rather than be an active participant because, before its activities ever took place, he had departed for good from his beloved adopted country.

Mazzei published his four-volume history of the United States, *Recherches historiques et politiques sur les États-Unis de l'Amérique septentrionale* in 1788. In a glowing two-installment review, the Marquis de Condorcet praised Mazzei's *Recherches*: "Each page of his work bears the stamp of the right spirit and sure tact which meditation and experience give. It shows a writer full of the knowledge of the times, practiced in the study of men and things, animated by respect for the rights of humanity and by zeal for the progress of reason."

Condorcet was one of the most famous mathematicians, philosophers, and political thinkers of eighteenth century France. Speaking of a man he had known intimately for years, Condorcet closed his review by saying, "It is easy to recognize, through the veil that shrouds the author, an illustrious philosopher, worthy for genius and loftiness of character, to enlighten men and defend their rights, and destined through the power of his thought to exert influence on the happiness of his century and posterity."

Mazzei yearned for a diplomatic appointment from his beloved United States, but none came. After consulting his friend Jefferson, he became Poland's first diplomatic representative in Paris and succeeded in re-establishing relations between France and Poland

As chargé d'affaires for Stanislaus, King of Poland, he lived in Paris during the political events leading to the French Revolution and through its turbulent unfolding, its aftermath of unbridled terror and up to the fall of the monarchy. His voluminous correspondence with the king as well as with leading French and American and Polish statesmen of the time provides a multi-colored and multi-faceted portrayal of that most critical period of upheaval in Europe. At the same time, he provided the King and the leading political and literary figures he associated with and admired, with an insight into the issues, the events and the people of moment in America.

Whether he was in Paris or Versailles, Warsaw or Pisa; whether in the company of the *literati*, the nobles or the rising and assertive bourgeois, Mazzei never failed to sing the praises of American patriots and people, and to familiarize his European contacts with the promise and the accomplishment of a nation in progress. Never did he voice regret for the period of his life spent in Virginia, when he relinquished his plans for experimental agriculture to his dream of participating in the founding moments of a democracy. To his dying day the fact that he was an American citizen was a recurrent boast of heraldry for this "zealous whig" from Tuscany.

It is always refreshing and reassuring to consider our origins, our fundamental values at a time when Americans are questioning the very meaning of our nation's basic beliefs. The 1776 Declaration of Rights, adopted by the Virginia Convention, emphasized the priority of the rights of the individual over the powers of the state. Philip Mazzei, Jefferson's friend and neighbor, referred to this document as the Bill of Rights in his 42-page "Instructions."

Writing for the Freeholders of Albemarle County, Mazzei states: "We admire the Bill of Rights, as truly a masterpiece. There is, in a few words, according to our opinion, everything comprehended for instituting the most free, and of consequence the most perfect Government: such as was ever wished, and never obtained on Earth...." These "Instructions" link Philip Mazzei to the group of Virginia statesmen whose ideas on the theory and form of government were incorporated into the major political writings of the period. Mazzei's words (May 11, 1776) were significant: "If we could have but one and the same Constitution for all the united colonies, our union would be infinitely stronger." Those who drew upon his insights and political acumen were the writers associated with the Charters of Freedom: Thomas Jefferson (the Declaration of Independence); James Madison (the Constitution of the United States); and George Mason (the Bill of Rights).

Years later there were indications that Mazzei's efforts had not been in vain, even in matters horticultural. The foremost architect of the time, Benjamin Henry Latrobe, wrote to him, March 6, 1805: "The time is already approaching when our vines & our olives will spread your name & our gratitude over a great portion of our country. Let us also owe to your kindness the introduction of excellence in the most fascinating branch of the Arts."

A shared interest and appreciation of architecture, which Latrobe alluded to, was yet another link to Mazzei's association with Jefferson. The latter had engaged him to provide four plaster of Paris statues to be placed in four niches at Monticello. Later, when Jefferson decided that the country should no longer be without portraits of its first discoverers, Mazzei arranged to have portraits of Columbus, Magellan, Cortes, and Vespucci reproduced from paintings in the Uffizi Gallery in Florence.

Mazzei was seventy-five years old when Jefferson (July 22, 1805) asked him to send two sculptors to work in the nation's capitol in Washington, DC. He immediately set out for Rome to see whether the great neo-classical sculptor, Antonio Canova, would undertake to make a Statue of Liberty. Canova could not take on any more work, but Mazzei was able to find the desired two Italian sculptors in Carrara. He hired Giovanni Andrei and Giuseppe Franzoni to bring their artistic talents to the United States. The former, a well-known architectural sculptor whose work is still admired in Santa Maria Novella Church in Florence, Italy, taught his brother-in-law Franzoni who soon developed his talents as a figure sculptor. Two years after their arrival, Jefferson wrote to Mazzei that the pair were "greatly esteemed" in America.

Latrobe wrote to President Jefferson (August 27, 1806): "I will venture to say that there is not in ancient or modern sculpture an Eagle's head which is in digniity and spirit and drawing superior to Franzoni's." In his November 30, 1807 response to *The Intelligencer*, Washington, DC, Latrobe describes the new hall of the House of Representatives with details of Franzoni's *Liberty and the Eagle*: "The frieze opposite to the entrance is occupied by a colossal eagle in the act of rising, with wings spread for flight... The opposite frieze is ornamented by four larger than life figures, being personifications of agriculture, art, science, and commerce. They are carved in *alto rilievo* in the solid stone of the frieze.

"Between the two columns opposite to the entrance, behind the Speaker's Chair, sits on a pedestal a colossal figure of Liberty... . The figure, sitting, is 8 ft. 6 in. in height. By her stands the American eagle, supporting her left hand, in which is the cap of liberty, her right presents a scroll, the Constitution of the United States. Her foot treads upon a reversed crown as a footstool and upon other emblems of monarchy and bondage."

Seven years later, during the War of 1812, the British entered Washington, DC, and burned the capitol. On August 24, 1814, pieces of furniture, books from the Library of Congress, paintings, portraits and sculptures were piled in the House and Senate Chambers and then put "to the torch." The intense heat destroyed all Franzoni's relief work, including his immense eagle with its outstretched wings, his four figures occupying 25 feet on the frieze, and his Statue of Liberty holding in her right hand the Constitution of the United States.

The tragic loss of the "Lady of Liberty" took its toll. Giuseppe Franzoni died April 6, 1815, leaving Camilla his widow and six children. Soon after Giovanni Andrei was sent to Italy by the Government to procure the carving of the Corinthian capitals now in the statuary hall section of the Capitol. He returned in 1816 with Franzoni's younger brother Carlo and Francesco Iardella, a cousin who married Giuseppe's widow. She had been his former sweetheart in Carrara and now blessed their marriage by the addition of a daughter and six sons.

Iardella's tobacco capitals are in the small rotunda just north of the main rotunda of the Capitol. In the Hall below is Carlo Franzoni's "Car of History Clock," with the Goddess of History standing in the chariot of time recording the legislators on the tablets. His plaster relief of "Justice" is located in the old Supreme Court Chamber. His deceased brother's masterpiece of the "Lady of Liberty" must have inspired him. Besides other elements, the relief contains the figure of a woman seated on a pedestal, an eagle, and the Constitution of the United States—the same elements used in the original "Liberty and the Eagle" sculpture destroyed by the British.

While the Declaration of Independence was a stirring assertion of human rights and, indeed, gave justification for rejecting the former government, it provided no formulas. The Constitution finally gave the nation its strong and subtle governmental form, but it did not give individual liberty. Only the Bill of Rights represented the inalienable value of individuality. It redefined the meaning of hope and freedom.

Italian-Americans are proud of their heritage. Mazzei now has a place of prominence in the history of the birth of our nation. My research took me to embassies and libraries in France, Italy, Poland, Austria, Switzerland, Spain and Czechoslovakia. I experienced both difficult and pleasant moments as I sought visas and letters of recommendation and tolerated, with some annoyance, delays and cancellation of flights.

Access to national archives and libraries was frustrating. When libraries claimed there were no documents, I insisted on checking personally and usually succeeded in finding some material. In Warsaw I checked several Polish documents. When I came across Mazzei's name I asked for an interpreter and discovered that these pages were instructions for Mazzei in Paris written by King Stanislaus. In Austria I had hoped to find correspondence between Mazzei and the Grandduke of Tuscany. There was none. Instead, I found correspondence between the Empress of Austria and Cardinal Marcantonio Barbarigo, founder of the Religious Teachers Filippini.

I cannot forget my trip to Vienna. I had arranged to meet a history professor in Vienna. The flight from Milan was cancelled and, because of the delay, I arrived late evening. The professor's apartment was located in a well-known sixteenth-century "palazzo." At that hour he no longer expected me and was disconcerted when I appeared at his door, completely exhausted. He did not know what to do with me, explaining that he lived alone and was sorry, but... To calm him, I interrupted, "Oh, Professor, don't worry, all I need is a bed!" His astonishment amazed me. Of course, I implied that I would go to a hotel, but the professor did not understand. Wringing his hands and totally frustrated, he asked me to sit down while he went to another room to telephone his neighbors.

Shortly after, he came back smiling and informed me that the Count and Countess Piatti, whose family had come from Italy centuries earlier, would be honored to have me as their guest. Not only was I received hospitably, but they arranged for dinner to be served. Later we chatted in the very room where Wolfgang Amadeus Mozart (1756-1791), at age five, gave a concert. The fireplace, the furniture, everything was the same as it had been in the seventeenth-century.

Countess Piatti showed me to my bedroom and explained that, as a child, Mozart had slept in that very bed.

The next morning, when I left the "palazzo," I was able to read the plaque at the main entrance commemorating Mozart's visit to the Piatti residence. The Countess accompanied me to the airport, giving orders to her chauffeur to tour the city and go through the park toward the airport while she acted as my guide.

In Grenoble I contacted Madame Fabre whose husband Jean Fabre had transcribed 280 letters written by King Stanislaus to Mazzei. The original correspondence was lost during World War II. Madame Fabre agreed to send me microfilm of the transcriptions. In Paris, after having been told there were no more documents, I located additional ones in the Ministry of Foreign Affairs.

In Lucca, Italy, I found ten documents. One day riding along the mountainside to the town of Fibbialla outside the walls of Lucca, not only did I see the very olive trees and vineyards that attracted Mazzei, but I also found among the records of the local Church a document which confirmed the fact that Antonio Giannini and others departed for America. The pieces all came together. Imagine my excitement as I read the words "in America, Settembre 1773." There was no doubt. These were the names of the farmers hired by Mazzei.

There were some sleepless nights on trains. When I arrived in Milan on May 18, 1979, I learned that TWA, my airline carrier, was on strike! In order to deliver a paper on Philip Mazzei at the Harvard University Conference on *The Presence of Italian Culture in the U.S.*, it was necessary to depart from the Rome airport.

At Harvard I was able to make a significant statement about an unidentified 7-page document published by Julian Boyd in *The Papers of Thomas Jefferson*. I announced that I had found this document-draft in Mazzei's own hand. In the 1776 document "Instructions of the Freeholders of Albemarle County to their delegates in Convention," Mazzei clearly stated his position. He was a historical figure in his own right.

My plans to continue research in Boston suddenly changed because I fell at Harvard. In fact I returned home with a swollen ankle that required a cast—an unexpected ending to an exciting trip abroad.

I hobnobbed with the famous, the near-famous, and the infamous as I traveled and lectured about Mazzei. I also accumulated many awards. I was included among the recipients of the 1978 Columbus Citizens Committee awardees during the Columbus Day celebrations in New York: Vic Damone, singer; Peter Sammartino, founder of Fairleigh Dickinson University; Lee Iacocca, industrialist; Peter Rodino, congressman; and Billy Martin, baseball player.

In one of my many scrapbooks there is an old photo with Billy Martin, kissing me on my forehead. He was attacked by other women in the area demanding to be kissed, too. His response: "I only kiss nuns." That photo appeared in a New York newspaper!

Although Jefferson and Mazzei remained an ocean apart geographically, the vicissitudes of war, political and personal crises, time itself, did not weaken their mutual regard nor put an end to their communion of interests and endeavors. What is most revealing is the fact that our eminent statesman and third president devoted so much time and effort to Mazzei, even during the most turbulent and trying periods of his own life. It honors Jefferson as a man of integrity and commitment; it honors Mazzei as one who must have merited such commitment.

Mazzei's interests and the range of his correspondence provide unusual insights into the tumultuous early years of the French Revolution. Mazzei was privy to many of the epochal events of those years. Hundreds of letters were exchanged between Mazzei and King Stanislaus of Poland, a man who, at that time, was himself creating a revolution with his famed Polish Constitution of May 3, 1791.

In 1792 Mazzei was in Warsaw as a confidant of King Stanislaus during the Polish struggle against a Russian invasion. He then returned to Tuscany to his new home in Pisa, and was married in 1796.

At the age of eighty, Mazzei began his memoirs—*My Life and Wanderings*—a rich source-book for the life and mores of the eighteenth century. He speaks of his many friends among whom were the first five presidents of the United States: George Washington, John Adams, Thomas Jefferson, James Madison, James Monroe.

Philip Mazzei was a modern man: ecology-minded, he advised Jefferson to enact laws to protect forests; agriculture-minded, he introduced southern European cultures; people-minded, he advocated education of slaves before their emancipation; feminist-minded, he opposed the idea of men as the stronger sex and held that women have rights, too; fiscally-aware, he wrote a pamphlet showing that he understood the dangers of monetary inflation. Mazzei was indeed a "Citizen of the World."

Because of my research on Philip Mazzei, in 1985, in the category of Individual Achievement, Freedoms Foundation at Valley Forge selected me for the George Washington Honor Medal for excellence, citing me for having "uncovered for all Americans a beautiful, exciting and important aspect of our great concept of freedom...one that otherwise would have gone untold or avoided." Princeton University Professor Robert R. Palmer described my research as "a permanent monument that will last centuries in our great libraries."

On July 4, 1996, an impressive ceremony was held in the renowned Villa Medici in Poggio a Caiano—the summer residence of Lorenzo il Magnifico—the town where Philip Mazzei was born. There, in the presence of dignitaries and friends, Mayor Piero Cambi conferred honorary citizenship on me for having promoted Italian culture and having Philip Mazzei re-evaluated during the 1976 bicentennial of the United States of America. An exhibit was held in Town Hall and a large catalog describing Mazzei's memorabilia and books was printed. The media marked the occasion with much fanfare and publicity.

Philip Mazzei supported the first attempt to compile and preserve the American State Papers. His signature on the document dated August 23, 1774, precedes Jefferson's. Little did he dream that one day I would publish his own papers, sponsored by the very Continental Congress project that began with his signature and continues today under the auspices of the National Historical Publications and Records Commission.

Mazzei writes about a world "tribunal" in his *Memorie*. He refers to conditions in Europe in 1789: "What I had more than anything else at heart, was preventing the scourge of war by instituting a tribunal made up of delegates from all civilized countries with powers to settle disputes and compel the parties involved to abide by its decision." Was his idea a forerunner of the United Nations? How noble were his ideals!

So many people, around the world, were thrilled by the discovery of an Italian figure of such historical momentum. In Italy a documentary was produced and an English version was circulated in the United States. At the Center for Mazzei Studies, meetings were held with bankers, attorneys and producers (Chris Mankewicz, Giacomo Pezzali, Vincent Labella) for a full-length film; several scripts such as, *Merchant of Fortune, Eagles of Monticello, World Citizen* were also reviewed, but plans did not materialize for lack of funds. However, inspired by my research on Philip Mazzei, Rose Basile Green, author and poet, honored me with a poem entitled, *World Mounted Marchione*:

> Sister Margherita Marchione strives
> For Teachers Filippini more to rise;
> Classrooms for Villa Walsh she now contrives
> "My future home" to be shared otherwise.
>
> Giuseppe Prezzolini stirred her brain
> Others at Fairleigh Dickinson to lead;
> Philip Mazzei research helped her explain
> The facts of history the world would read.
>
> Across Atlantic Sister's flag unfurled,
> Relating U.S.A. to Italy;
> Now, as a citizen of the whole world
> She is to all what current saints should be.

As once Columbus proved the world is round,
Marchione mounts as unity is bound.

Significantly, Mazzei both transmitted European ideas to the new Americans and in return carried American ideas across the Atlantic. A friend of the most renowned political figures of his time, he may be considered the first Italian immigrant to promote economic and political relations between the United States and Italy.

Philip Mazzei belongs in the company of the Founding Fathers of the United States of America. He also belongs to the group of Italian immigrants who, not being able to achieve the dream of liberty within their own country, sowed its seeds throughout the world, risking their fortune, even their lives, in order to live as free men.

I have been blessed by the kind words of friends and associates who spoke highly of me when interviewed by the media. In an interview for the *Sunday Star Ledger* (September 2, 1984), Professor Filomena Peloro, an FDU colleague, who participated in the Mazzei activities on campus, stated: "She is relentless in pursuit of her objectives. She also has the sort of warm personality that makes one feel she has been a friend for years, a very short time after a first meeting. This warm feeling carries over to her students, the university staff, and everyone with whom she comes in contact. Her inspiration and contributions in the fields of literature and history have made the world richer."

Professor Max Renzulli, an American historian at FDU, called the Mazzei books "definitive." My teacher at Columbia University, Professor Maristella Lorch, said: "She was a very lively and motivated young lady who wasn't afraid of anything. Her writings on Mazzei are very substantial and very well written with charm and elegance."

When interviewed by the *Daily Record* (October 11, 1987), Sister Filomena DiCarlo, secretary at the Mazzei Center, remarked: "Sister Margherita is a challenging person. She cares about her work for the Italian community and about spreading Italian culture. Her dedication and commitment to the Italian-American cultural scene have been exemplary. Students, colleagues, and friends have recognized her unusual talents and accomplishments. She has an indomitable spirit of independence, dedication, and tenacity that posterity will not fail to acknowledge."

Although I have been much honored as an international scholar, it pleases me to know that I made an important contribution to the American Bicentennial Celebration.

Chapter Nine: Awards

"Hundreds of young students learned from her
not only the beauty of Italian literature,
but the way to understand it."
(Prezzolini, April 11, 1971)

My esteem for Giuseppe Prezzolini makes me especially cherish this quotation from a letter he wrote to Lucille De George, founder of the Amita award. My Columbia University mentor was congratulating her for having selected me for its Education award—given annually to American Women of Achievement who inspired the youth of our Country. (The letter was included in the 1971 souvenir booklet).

"Sister Margherita is a worthy example of Italian blood, of Christian idealism, of American education.... She is an extraordinary teacher, a great organizer, a faithful friend. Filled with the spirit of sacrifice she has been the animator of students at all levels of education with whom she came into contact. We who have seen her develop and grow, applaud the Amita Society that has the merit of placing her among the best descendants of the Italian people who have enriched America" (Lugano, Switzerland, April 11, 1971).

Other local, national, and international awards bring back happy memories. One was the September 15, 1984 National Italian American Foundation award dinner in the Washington-Hilton. Present on the dais were President Ronald Reagan and the other presidential candidates—George Bush, Walter Mondale and Geraldine Ferrara. This was the first time both Republicans and Democrats attended such an occasion before an election.

Awardees are chosen for outstanding career achievements in selected fields of human endeavor—science, art, literature, music, industry, and education. For example, I was honored for achievements in the field of literature. Others recognized on that occasion were:

actor Daniel J. Travanti, composer Gian Carlo Menotti, scientist Robert Gallo and businessman Arthur J. Decio.

I addressed the three thousand guests and accepted the award in the name of all Italian-American women. The media quoted me: " 'I'd like to remind you that the last woman to receive this award was *Sophia Loren!*' When the applause ceased, Sister Margherita added: 'And I'm happy to follow in her footsteps.' "

The beautifully-designed award was created by Tiffany & Company. Executed in the elegance of pure spatial form and simplicity, it suggests a balanced union of reason and emotion. Deeply etched with Leonardo da Vinci's best known design, "Proportions of the Human Figure," the three surfaces of the clear crystal pyramid express a synthesized statement of the universality, beauty and strength of the human experience.

The National Italian American Foundation is a non-partisan, non-profit organization and the major advocate in Washington, DC, for Italian-Americans, the nation's fifth largest ethnic group. It serves as an American presence on a broad scope for Italian-American interests, providing educational and cultural grants, serving a liaison role for organizations, conducting conferences on topics of importance, and working with the media to provide a realistic portrayal of Italian Americans.

Among those working to improve the image of Italian Americans was Peter Sammartino, vice president of the Northeastern Region of the NIAF. In his book, *Of Colleges and Kings* (Cornwall Books, 1985), he states: "No other ethnic group has had as wide an influence on the birth and early development of the United States as the Italians.... When we consider the sum total of early explorations, the force of ideas, the basis for law, the influence on art, architecture, and music, the sheer cumulative weight indicates that our country would not have been what it is today without the contributions of Italians.... This has been a forgotten page of history." Indeed, Sammartino's efforts to disseminate Italian culture should not be forgotten.

Over this half century, I have amassed a wealth of honors. Among others are the Columbia University Garibaldi Scholar award

(1957), Fulbright Scholar (1964), UNICO National Rizzuto award (1977), Star of Solidarity of the Republic of Italy (1977). Freedoms Foundation—George Washington Honor Medal (1985). I received the National Italian American Bar Association "Inspirational" award, the Columbus Day Woman of the year award (1987), and the "Toscani nel Mondo" award in 1990.

My association with Ramapo College of New Jersey began when Attorney Robert Corman, our Jewish neighbor and member of its Board of Trustees, called one day to inquire whether we provided baby-sitters. He was in desperate need for that very evening. When I explained that we did not have that kind of service, he was disappointed. I told him not to worry for God would provide a baby sitter. Then I began making telephone calls.

Determined to assist our Jewish neighbors, I contacted Ceil Gallis in Nutley, NJ, and asked her to help Robert and his wife Laura that evening. She came to their aid. This was the beginning of a long friendship. Not only did she take care of Juliane who was only three months old, but also Daniel, their second child, when he was born. Months later the Cormans learned that Ceil was my sister.

This was more than thirteen years ago. Recently both Ceil and I attended the Shabbat Service at Temple B'nai Or when Juliane was called to the Torah as a Bat Mitzvah. She was remarkable as, at age thirteen, she publicly proclaimed her Jewish ancestry in Hebrew and affirmed her appreciation of her rich spiritual heritage and its values and ideals. It was a most inspiring ceremony.

In 1990, I received the honorary Doctor of Humane Letters degree from Ramapo College. In my commencement address, I referred to one of Dante's famous characters of the *Divine Comedy*, Ulysses—a hero who challenges the unknown and goes down to death in his insatiable quest for knowledge. Dante has him speak:

> Consider your origin:
> You were not formed to live like brutes,
> But to follow virtue and knowledge.

I reminded the graduates that just as Dante regarded great mental powers as a precious trust, so too should they be aware of the extraordinary power of their intellect and of the importance of their achievements. Thomas Carlyle said: "What we have done is the only mirror by which we can see what we are." Plato wrote: "The life that is unexamined is not worth living."

I also told them that this commencement ceremony called for the examination of their aspirations and future mission: "As we approach the Third Millennium, everyone is touched by a feeling of expectancy; time seems to pass ever more quickly, things seem to change more rapidly.

"Pope John Paul II, in his *Encyclical on Social Concern*, reminds us that we should be aware of 'the urgent need to change the spiritual attitudes which define each individual's relationship with self, with neighbor, and with nature itself.'

"We are informed of the indiscriminate application of advances in science and technology. We hear of the depletion of the ozone layer, unrestricted deforestation, industrial waste that defiles the atmosphere and the environment. But do we really understand and value the sacredness and oneness of the world? What is our position on the need for ecological harmony, diversity, interdependence?...Every day well lived makes every yesterday a dream of happiness and every tomorrow a vision of hope. Respect and honor this day as you continue to weave the tapestry of your life...."

In recognition of my contribution to the Italian-American community, I was given the "Arts award" by the New Jersey Christopher Columbus Quincentennial Observance Commission (October 17, 1992). Awards were also given to: Michael Bongiovanni (Science); Arthur Imperatore (Business); The Antonio and Francesca Marchetta Family of New Brunswick ("La Famiglia"); Joe Piscopo (Entertainment); Honorable Peter Rodino, Jr. (Government).

In expressing my gratitude for the lovely crystal reproduction of Columbus' three small ships, the *Santa Maria*, the *Pinta* and the *Niña*, I addressed members of the family of my birth, my religious family, and my world family: "We are all in this world to serve one another, and to do it with love. For all God's gifts, visible to us in the marvels of creation and in one another, join me in thanking God for His many blessings and loving care, as we ask him to bless the leaders of all nations and the Church, to bless our families and friends."

In tribute to my leadership in the State, I also received many Resolutions from both the New Jersey Senate and the New Jersey General Assembly, and many times I have been included in *The Congressional Record* and recognized as a scholar, educator, and author. I was the recipient of a *Michael* from the New Jersey Literary Hall of Fame (1993), joining among others, poet Belva Plain, writer Mary Higgins Clark, and Pulitzer Prize winner, Carl Sagan.

I received the "Philip Mazzei-Thomas Jefferson International award" in Florence, Italy. In 1996, both Poggio-a-Caiano (Philip Mazzei's birthplace near Florence) and Pontecagnano (my parents' birthplace, Province of Salerno) honored me with citizenship. Among several books, I am included in *Past and Promise, Lives of New Jersey Women* (1992) and *Poverty, Chastity, and Change: Lives of Contemporary American Nuns* (1996).

On September 13, 1997, the Religious Teachers Filippini also honored me with the Humanitarian award. I received a papal blessing personally signed by Pope John Paul II. Besides family and friends, many ecclesiastical and civic personalities were among the 800 guests at the Parsippany Hilton. One of the congratulatory pages in the souvenir journal listed my family: three sisters, Jean, Marie and Ceil; twenty-one nieces and nephews; forty great nieces and nephews; twenty-two great-great nieces and nephews!

Entertainment for the evening was provided by Jerome Hines with several young opera singers and comedian Joe Piscopo who was master of ceremony. In a surprise act, to the tune of "The Macarena," Joe Piscopo gave his own interpretation to my life:

Let me tell you something, please listen up, Mister;
I want to tell you about a 'Super-Nun Sister'—
If we didn't see her everyday, we would surely miss her...
'SISTER MARGHERITA'

"AIYY!"

She's a genius and a scholar and there's no one like her, 'Nope!'
She works with parents, priests and nuns giving everybody 'hope'
Has friends the world over, including our Beloved Pope...
'SISTER MARGHERITA'
"AIYY!"

(At this point, Joe Piscopo called several young nuns on stage to dance the Macarena as he continued singing. This "brought the house down.")

You can call her, ask a favor and will get not one complaint
She even teaches me Italian but 'Perfetto' I sure ain't
And Our Lord only knows she has the patience of a Saint...
'SISTER MARGHERITA'
"AIYY!"

So that's the story of Sister Margherita Marchione
Once you get to know her, you will never feel alone
Saint Lucy Filippini is forever heart and home...
'SISTER MARGHERITA'
"AIYY!"

The guests joined Piscopo with the refrain and everyone was pleasantly entertained by the Sister Margherita "Macarena."

The celebration was memorialized by a long article in the *Congressional Record*. Among the many awards received that evening were: The Distinguished Service Award from the Ambassador of Italy to the United States, a Proclamation from the Governor of New Jersey, and Resolutions from both the New Jersey Senate and the New Jersey General Assembly. The occasion also marked the launching of a campaign for funds toward a new Home-Health Care Facility for Retired Sisters.

After the closing remarks, I surprised everyone by presenting a $25,000 royalty check to Sister Frances Lauretti for the new Retirement Facility. Accepting the check in the name of the Religious Teachers Filippini, Sister Frances responded: "Didn't I tell you that Sister Margherita always has the last word?"

On March 15, 1998, at Alvernia College in Reading, PA, I received *La Festa della Donna Award*, a celebration of Italian-American Women and their dedication in preserving the values of the Italian culture in America. The College of Education and Human Services Alumni Council presented me with the Seton Hall University Humanitarian award (October 10, 1999). I also received the *Woman of the Year Award* from many organizations, and countless citations from governors, senators, congressmen, assemblymen, freeholders and other important civic and religious leaders.

Throughout the years, I was privileged to meet with several Italian presidents. I convinced President Francesco Cossiga, when as Prime Minister he was in Washington, DC, to issue the 1980 Filippo Mazzei Italian stamp. Despite many difficulties, he succeeded.

I once shocked a cab driver by asking him to take me to the Quirinale for an appointment with the President of Italy. He did not believe me and said: "Questo lo devo vedere!" ("This I have to see!") The guards received me graciously and assured him he could leave. The cab driver was speechless.

I recall with pleasure other visits to the Quirinale in Rome. In January 1982, I accompanied Giuseppe Prezzolini when he traveled from Switzerland to Rome to meet President Sandro Pertini for the "Penna d'Oro Award" ceremony. The Italian Government arranged the details of our flight to Rome and our stay at the Hassler Hotel. I scheduled Prezzolini's appointments and accompanied him everywhere. At a dinner with many dignitaries, I was the only woman present and I sat between him and Giovanni Spadolini, Prime Minister of Italy who hosted the dinner.

In 1996, I sent the manuscript of my book on the Holocaust to President Oscar Luigi Scalfaro who commented: "Your work…is a testimony to the charity offered by the Church and Pope Pius XII, who demonstrated his love for justice and peace by a life of prayer, heroic sacrifice, and generosity. May it be a source of meditation for those who insist on misrepresenting the truth." Months later, when I met with him in the Quirinale, President Scalfaro renewed his approval of my work and, ending our conversation, said: "And now, before you leave, let's stand and together pray the *Ave Maria*."

There were deeply spiritual moments during pilgrimages to Italy (Rome, Florence, Venice). Once, because of the cancellation of our return flight, our trip was blessed with two extra "expense-free days" in a luxurious hotel on Lago Maggiore and with vouchers for the entire group of students and teachers for a return trip, compliments of TWA.

Never will I forget the precious private audiences in the Vatican, or the joy-filled moments accompanied by groups of students, in Saint Peter's Basilica or in Castelgandolfo when we shouted, "Viva il Papa, Viva il Papa!"

Chapter Ten: Audiences with Popes

"Love one another, my dear children!
Seek rather what unites,
Not what may separate you
From one another."
(Pope John XXIII's *Last Testament*)

"Have you seen the Holy Father?" Invariably, this was the question Giuseppe Prezzolini asked me whenever I met him in Italy or in Switzerland between the years 1957-1982. This was one reason why I had an audience with the Pope whenever I was abroad.

I also had closer connections. In the 1950s, Pope Pius XII's niece, Elena Pacelli Rossignani had ear surgery in the United States. Mother Ninetta invited her to be our guest at Villa Walsh, in Morristown, NJ., after the operation. I was her companion, and one summer we spent about ten days with my family in Fleetwood, NY. When she returned to Rome, she sent my parents a hand-painted autographed scroll with the Pope's blessing and his white "zucchetto" for their golden jubilee. Our friendship continued throughout the years. (Even today my trips to Rome include a visit to the nursing home where Elena now resides.)

During my first trip to Italy (May 1957), as a Columbia University Garibaldi Scholar, I visited Elena Rossignani Pacelli and her mother Elisabetta, Pope Pius XII's sister. They arranged an audience for me. Accompanied by Elena, I had the opportunity to meet the Pope in the Basilica of Saint Peter.

We sat in front of Giovanni Lorenzo Bernini's impressive bronze baldachin beneath the dome. With a small group of people, at the end of the audience, we were permitted to approach His Holiness. I held his hand, kissing his ring as Elena introduced me and reminded him about her visit to the United States several years earlier.

Pius XII's piercing eyes penetrated my soul and I still see him—a tall, dignified, and ascetic figure with a brilliant glance, a loving smile, and animated gestures. He had a magnetic personality full of intelligence and nobility of spirit. He asked about my research on Rebora, the poet who had joined the Rosmini Fathers after his conversion in 1929. I asked the Pope to bless my work. The memory of this precious meeting remains with me. I also possess a photograph with the Holy Father and Elena that was taken during the papal audience.

When I think of Pius XII, I feel inspired. He had a warm, gracious personality. Recognizing the habit of the Religious Teachers Filippini, he chatted genially with us for several minutes. All the accounts I had heard about Eugenio Pacelli's great learning, his personal holiness, his deep piety were reinforced by this personal meeting. Everything anyone ever said about him, all the numerous Roman stories that circulated about him, all the news reports and biographical acounts seemed to agree on one thing—he was an extraordinarily sincere, dedicated and holy man.

I have examined his life in the light of the documents which some historians still ignore. How can I not dedicate myself to Pope Pius XII with the same fervor that impelled me to write about Clemente Rebora, Giovanni Boine, Philip Mazzei, Giuseppe Prezzolini, and other historical figures?

Few people are acquainted with Pius XII's encyclicals and accomplishments. He was a great diplomat and statesman whose life will always be part of world history. His true portrait, personal and political, has been distorted. Yet, twelve volumes of documents—over five thousand—are available.

When Angelo Roncalli was elected Pope (1958), I was ecstatic. While researching the circumstances of Clemente Rebora's conversion to Catholicism, I learned that Pope John XXIII (then Apostolic Visitator in Bulgaria) was instrumental in helping the poet take this step when they first met in Milan. He sent Rebora to His Eminence Cardinal Aldefonso Schuster who, after he was baptized, administered the Sacrament of Confirmation upon him in the Cathedral of Milan in May 1930.

No doubt Pope John XXIII was pleased when he received a special copy of my book, *L'imagine tesa* (The Life and Works of Clemente Rebora), published by Edizioni di Storia e Letteratura in 1960. In it, I speak about his association with Rebora.

Critics hailed it as "a work of perfect spiritual honesty, of notable accuracy and keenness; it is a dedicated, critical and biographical reconstruction of one of the most unforgettable figures of our tormented older generation" (Lavinia Mazzucchetti, *Il Ponte*, 1961). Giannino Zanelli in *Il Resto del Carlino* wrote: "a very rare life, perhaps unique in the world, which deserved such a singular document. It is almost a revelation, thanks to the one who wrote it and to the way it is written."

A ceremony in Sacred Heart Cathedral, Newark, NJ, on June 13, 1962, followed by a dinner in their honor, marked the occasion of my parents' sixtieth wedding anniversary. Pope John XXIII granted my request for his special blessing. *The Bergen Record* photographed the presentation of the autographed papal blessing as my parents kissed Archbishop Thomas A. Boland's ring. The photo and an article appeared in the newspaper the following day.

When my book on Clemente Rebora was reprinted in 1974, Pope Paul VI personally asked the Vatican newspaper, *L'Osservatore Romano*, to review it. He also suggested that they request another copy from the publisher because he preferred to keep the copy he received in his private library. In a letter dated September 17, 1974, His Holiness thanked Prezzolini for my bilingual anthology, *Twentieth Century Italian Poetry* (Fairleigh Dickinson University Press, 1974), in which I translated some of Rebora's poems.

Charles Angoff, an influential presence in American literary circles, had this to say in the Foreword: "The poems in the present anthology also carry insights into the all-enveloping mystery, and they posit guides for us to find greater joy and comfort in God's universe. Saint Francis knew this, and Dante knew this. But so do so many of the modern Italian poets who have graced the land of Italy and of the whole world with their writings. There isn't a single feeble poem in the entire volume. They all glow with, to quote Sister Margherita's excellent phrase, *metaphysical* lyricism."

The anthology seeks to convey an image of the role of religion in the broad panorama of contemporary poetry. In inspiration and content, these poems may be classified as *religious* or, at least, *spiritual*. The translations attempt to give an accurate, line-by-line rendering of the original text. The section "Notes on the Poets" provides biographical data on those represented. Of the ninety poems, twenty-two— some in their respective authors' handwriting—appear for the first time. Interspersed are many original sketches by Sister Filomena Puglisi, suggesting the mood of a poem; several of the poems have illustrative holographs.

In 1966, I was privileged to have a private audience with Pope Paul VI. I experienced feelings of trepidation and awe mingled with a sense of belonging to him and to the Church. The Pope is usually briefed about the person who approaches him. As I knelt before him in Castelgandolfo, I kissed his hand and asked him to bless my family, friends, students and, in particular, the Filippini Sisters. His Holiness graciously extended his blessing to all I mentioned and, in a very paternal way, urged me to continue my apostolate. His words were words of wisdom and understanding and I experienced a moment of ecstasy as I looked into his piercing eyes and held his hand.

The conversation was in Italian. While chatting, I told Paul VI that Prezzolini had commissioned me to give his regards. He interrupted me, questioning, "Giuseppe Prezzolini?" The Pope was shocked to hear his name. He couldn't understand how I knew this professor who professed no religion. I explained that Prezzolini had been my mentor at Columbia University and I had just visited him in Vietri sul Mare. I did not tell the Holy Father that I had heard about their recent forty-five minute conversation. After referring to the greetings from our mutual friend, Prezzolini, His Holiness told me to pray for his conversion and to teach him how to pray.

Holding his hand and looking at him, without blinking an eye, I blurted out: "Your Holiness, if you did not succeed, how do you expect me to?" The Monsignori near him were horrified. But Paul VI simply laughed and said: "Yes, Prezzolini is a good man and a dear friend. We must continue our prayers for him." Pope Paul VI's evident amusement reassured me that my question had not been misunderstood. In a photograph in my possession, one can see his smiling face. With paternal solicitude Paul VI gave me rosary beads and blessed me. This was the first time I was alone with a Pope. I wonder if Pope Paul VI remembered laughing heartily when he spoke to me in 1966!

Pope John Paul I, a well-known scholar, was interested in Italian literature and had written several books. I did not have the opportunity to meet him, but no doubt he was well acquainted with my work on Clemente Rebora. He died shortly after his election to the papacy.

With the publication of each book that I thought would interest Pope John Paul II, I arranged to meet him, either at a private audience, or with groups of students and teachers at a general audience. After attending Mass in the Pope's private chapel, I presented Volume II of Rebora's *Correspondence* (Edizioni di Storia e Letteratura, Rome, 1982).

Rebora's letters have value, not only for their autobiographical and spiritual elements, but also for the originality of their language and style—seldom relaxed, at times restless and tormented, and not infrequently almost poetic, as he outlines his innermost thoughts, his stirring emotions, his struggle for recognition as a writer. These letters are annotated. They reveal the details of his life as a teacher, lecturer, and writer, as well as information about his friends, his interest in Tagore, his conversion to the Catholic faith.

Pope John Paul II had already received my book on the Holocaust, *Yours Is a Precious Witness: Memoirs of Jews and Catholics in Wartime Italy* (Paulist Press, 1997). Before the official book-signing ceremony, I also decided to present the Italian edition entitled *Pio XII e gli Ebrei* (Editoriale Pantheon, Rome, 1999) to him. I arranged for the publisher to bring me a copy of this book to be presented to His Holiness during the March 10, 1999 audience. The appointment with the publisher was for eight a.m. I waited almost two hours. Finally, only ten minutes before the Holy Father arrived, did I have the book in my hands. I immediately autographed it. But there was no way I could wrap it decently. So I had to approach the Holy Father with the unwrapped book. I apologized, explaining that I had just received it. I had no control of the situation.

The Holy Father understood my embarassment and tried to console me by holding my hand, patting me on my cheek, touching my shoulder, examining the book. He then handed it to the archbishop near him and continued the conversation. Apparently he was pleased to have the book. The papal photographers remarkably recorded the entire audience. I have about one dozen extraordinary photographs depicting every move and expression.

The next day (March 11, 1999), I had an appointment at eleven a.m. in the Palazzo Quirinale with the President of Italy, Oscar Luigi Scalfaro. Arrangements had been made by the Minister of the Diplomatic Corps, Franco Mistretta. The purpose of the visit was to present my book on Pius XII. But, again, I had no book. Nor did the publisher have one. He telephoned to say there was no way he could provide a copy because he could not get to his office. All roads leading to the Vatican were blocked. Traffic near the Vatican was stalled because the President of Iran was on his way for an audience with the Holy Father. I grabbed the photos from the previous day, took a cab, and arrived on time. Minister Mistretta was waiting to accompany me to President Scalfaro.

I greeted him and immediately apologized, saying: "Your Excellency, I do not have a copy of my book, but here are pictures of it." I then showed him the photos with the book and the Holy Father looking at it. It was a real comedy, as I described the situation! We finally were serious and the President explained that he knew Pius XII, and was impressed with his sanctity, his extraordinary intelligence, and great sensibility during the Holocaust. The President felt, however, that his statue in Saint Peter's Basilica, sculpted by Giacomo Manzù, was too austere.

"Historians," said President Scalfaro, "have not treated the Pontiff justly." Referring to the English version of my book, *Yours is a Precious Witness* he added: "Your work is a testimony of the charity offered by the Church and Pius XII. May it be a source of meditation for those who insist on misrepresenting the truth." I assured him he would soon have the Italian version.

Many wonderful comments by Jews and Catholics alike greeted the book. Dorothy Teko, of the *New World Press* wrote: "Your perspective on a delicate subject is both refreshing and edifying, and such memoirs are certain to do much good."

Tom Depoto of the Newark *Star Ledger*: "The author has set out to balance the record in a manner that is effective. She shows that the Catholic Church was not a passive body while atrocities were being committed.... Any discussion of the Church's role, and the role of ordinary citizens, too, must include this work."

Lee Wixman of the Palm Beach *Jewish Times*: "This book rights the old wrong that people thought for years—that the Pope did nothing."

Michael Bobrow, a New York free-lance writer: "As a Jew who served as a newspaper correspondent overseas, I know how highly Pope Pius XII is regarded by the Orthodox Jews of Israel. His Holiness knew that making noisy bombastic speeches in downtown Rome was not the effective way to save Jewish lives."

In the *St. Louis Post Dispatch*, Rabbi Robert Jacobs, Executive Vice President, St. Louis Rabbinical Association: "Memoir after memoir attest to the saving role of the Italian Catholic Church. The accumulating impact is profound. The Pope's own words to Cardinal Paolo Dezza in 1943 are significant: 'They lament that the Pope does not speak [against the Nazi atrocities]. But the Pope cannot speak. If he were to speak, things would be worse.'"

Cardinal John O'Connor, Archbishop of New York: "The author does indeed offer a 'precious witness' to a story of Gospel love. She has carefully combined solid historical research with fascinating anecdotal material to shed light on the generous and often sacrificial response of the Church to the horrendous plight of the Jews in Italy during the Holocaust."

Robert A, Graham, S.J., former editor of *America* and one of the four editors of the twelve volumes of Vatican documents: "This new book is fantastic and hits the bull's eye! Why did we have to wait fifty years?"

In an effort to restore historic truth to the role of Pius XII and the Catholic Church during the Holocaust, I appealed to every bishop, archbishop and cardinal in the United States, informing them of my book. When it was published, I asked Bishop Frank Rodimer for a letter to every bishop to accompany a complimentary copy of my book. They graciously acknowledged receiving their copies.

Archbishop Theodore McCarrick wrote (July 1, 1998): "I am so proud of what you have accomplished and I am inspired by your own formidable courage and perseverance in defending the name of this good Pope, Pius XII. ... I did bring up the question of our support of him at the bishops' meeting in Pittsburgh last week. I also spoke to His Eminence Cardinal Keeler about it too. ...We must keep working on this and we must make the history to be a true reflection of the reality of the times."

Copies of the book in Italian, *Pio XII e gli Ebrei*, were finally made available on March 12, 1999, when the official presentation took place in the Vatican Radio Sala Marconi on the occasion of the sixtieth anniversary of the Incoronation of Pius XII. Speakers were: Cardinal Edward Idris Cassidy, Senator Giulio Andreotti, and Father Peter Gumpel, S.J. The exceptionally interested audience, comprising the media, scholars, clergy, and friends, filled the room with the crowd extending into the hallway where an exhibit on Pius XII had been arranged.

A few months later I returned to Rome and again I was privileged to attend the Eucharistic Liturgy in the Pope's private chapel. Immediately after, he listened to me as I spoke about my research on Pius XII. I gave him the manuscript of my new book, *Pio XII: Architetto di pace,* scheduled to be printed in December. However, when I arrived in Italy for a lecture tour on this topic, the publisher informed me that it would not be ready for several months.

Again, sadly, I had to apologize: "I'm sorry, Your Holiness," I murmured. "I was scheduled to bring you my book, but it's not ready, so I brought you the jacket." Recognizing my disappointment, the

Pope examined it carefully, blessing me and my work in defense of Pius XII.

This was the third time in one year that I had an audience with Pope John Paul II. How privileged I was to be near him! In addition, as I mentioned, his photographers recorded every detail of my dilemma during these visits. I have many treasured photographs.

Cardinal Cassidy wrote the Preface for three of my books on Pius XII. He considers my research for the millennium book, *Pope Pius XII: Architect for Peace*, "...a valuable contribution to the study of Pope Pius XII and his times. The author has shown here how distorted and untrue are the allegations that Pope Pius XII could have done more to avert the consequences of the Nazi design..."

This book describes Pius XII's passionate work for peace, his concern for prisoners of war and the support provided to them by the Vatican, and his particular care for Jews during World War II. Yet, Pope Pius XII continues to be the target of attacks by the media. It is enormously difficult to correct deep-rooted prejudices, ingrained misrepresentations and constantly repeated partial truths. But that is precisely what we must try to do—not so much for the dead victims—but for the sake of future generations.

The great strides made in Jewish-Christian relations—spiritually, politically, morally, and intellectually—should not be jeopardized by those who are unwilling to learn the truth and are covertly attacking traditional Christian morality. Indeed, such individuals are not only seriously unjust, but also anti-Jewish because Christian morality is Jewish morality.

Sir Martin Gilbert, an outstanding Jewish historian, paints a deeply personal and cultural portrait of the Holocaust in *Never Again: The History of the Holocaust* (Universe Publishers, 2000). Gilbert's new book demolishes John Cornwell's book, *Hitler's Pope: The Secret History of Pius XII*, that charges the Catholic Church with having led to the Holocaust. In an interview, Gilbert noted that Christians were among the first victims of the Nazis and that the Churches took a very powerful stand. ... On the question of Pope Pius XII's alleged silence, he added, "So the test for Pacelli was when the

Gestapo came to Rome in 1943 to round up Jews. And the Catholic Church, on his direct authority, immediately dispersed as many Jews as they could." Gilbert thanks the Vatican for what was done to save Jewish lives.

In an earlier book, *The Holocaust: A History of the Jews of Europe during the Second World War* (New York: Holt, Rinehart and Winston, 1985), Sir Martin Gilbert stated: "In addition to the six-million Jewish men, women and children who were murdered, at least an equal number of non-Jews were also killed, not in the heat of battle, not by military siege, aerial bombardment or the harsh conditions of war, but by deliberate planned murder."

Anne O'Hare McCormick, in her *New York Times* weekly column "Abroad" (August 21, 1944), credited Pope Pius XII with having saved Rome: "The Vatican was a refuge for thousands of fugitives from the Nazi-Fascist reign of terror. Jews received first priority—but all the hunted found sanctuary in the Vatican and its hundreds of convents and monasteries in the Rome region. What the Pope did was to create an attitude in favor of the persecuted and hunted that the city was quick to adopt, so that hiding someone 'on the run' became the thing to do. This secret sharing of danger cleared away Fascism more effectively than an official purge. The Vatican is still sheltering refugees. Almost 100,000 homeless persons from the war zone and devastated areas are fed there every day."

After the war, numerous tributes and public gratitude were given to the Pope, the Church and the clergy for saving the Jews throughout Europe. The World Jewish Congress presented a large monetary gift to the Vatican "in recognition of the work of the Holy See in rescuing Jews from Fascist and Nazi persecution." (*New York Times*, October 11, 1945)

Chapter Eleven: Defending Pius XII

"I have fought the good fight,
I have finished the race,
I have kept the faith."
(St. Paul to Timothy 4:7)

Pope John Paul II's message for the Millennium is clear: "Let us build a new future in which there will be no more anti-Jewish feeling among Christians or anti-Christian feeling among Jews... Only a world at peace, with justice for all, can avoid repeating the mistakes and terrible crimes of the past" (March 25, 2000).

Via the educational route, problems of world starvation, racial bitterness, and world peace can be approached. It is the educator's privilege to help students develop and pursue an ideal, a vision, an impossible dream—for what students love, believe in, and desire will determine their future. Interested in the life and activities of my students, I challenge them to fulfill their mission in life.

As my teaching career began, America was playing a leading role in world affairs. This was a momentous period in history—a period that led to dictatorships, World War II, and the Holocaust in Europe. I was ignorant of these horrors and, like so many Americans, was indifferent to the pain and suffering of so many people. Fifty years later, interviewing several of our Sisters (Religious Teachers Filippini) in Rome, I learned how they risked their lives to save 114 Jewish men, women and children. I began to understand the terrible sufferings during the Holocaust and the role of Pope Pius XII in saving Jews and other refugees.

In October 1994, I was at a meeting in Rome, when the Jewish congregation presented a document to the Religious Teachers Filippini, "recalling those who risked their lives to save Jews from Nazi-Fascist atrocities." Rabbi Elio Toaff stated: "We do not want to forget the good that was done by many Italian citizens who saw the persecuted Jews not as people to abandon. They saw them as their brothers."

At that time I learned that Sy Rotter, an American Jew, was producing a film on the Jews in Italy during the Holocaust, entitled *A Debt To Honor*. I was intrigued and began researching about him and searching for his whereabouts. A graduate of Berkeley and Cornell University, he was chairman of Documentaries International Film & Video Foundation in Washington, DC. I tried to contact him in Washington, but it was not an easy task.

"Yes," I was told, "he is scheduled to be in Rome to film the fifth in his video documentary series." I requested that he telephone me upon his arrival. But no call came. Instead I heard from the Sisters of Sion that he had already gone to northern Italy. Determined to contact him, I telephoned his hotel every day. My messages were unanswered.

Then, one Saturday evening Sy telephoned. He made it clear that he could not see me for lack of time. "Furthermore," he added, "I just completed six hours of filming. The documentary on the Jews in Italy during the German occupation will be only thirty minutes."

"But Sy," I interjected, "you must see me!" I was almost in tears. Sy politely questioned, "Why must I see you?" "Because I'm a nun," I blurted out. "Oh," he said, I know many nuns…" Impulsively, I interrupted: "But we are different." There was silence. "What I mean is… our legacy and mission dates back to the seventeenth century and we are interested in all areas of education and social work. Futhermore, I have documentation to show that our Sisters rescued many Jews."

After listening to me, Sy very gently said, "I'm sorry. There can be no more filming. I leave for Israel early Monday morning." Pausing for a moment, he then continued, "but…I'll see you tomorrow at 4 p.m." I was satisfied and arranged to meet him in our convent on Via Botteghe Oscure near the Vatican, where sixty Jews had been hidden and where some of the Sisters who rescued them still resided.

I was aware that Sy did not know the area. So, upon my arrival the next day, I went to the third floor terrace, and watched the passers-by. Soon I noticed a tall, stately gentleman searching for numbers along the busy street. I waited until he was near Piazza Santa Lucia Filippini, and then leaned over the balcony shouting: "Sy, here I am!" Startled, he looked up and pointed in my direction, "Sister Margherita?" "Yes," I yelled, "I'll be right down."

I quickly covered three flights of steps and, by the time Sy crossed the piazza, I was at the door. He was surprised when I greeted him with a kiss on both cheeks—Italian style. That kiss broke the ice and we began a tour of the areas in the convent where the sixty Jews had been housed and cared for by the Sisters.

Contrary to his intentions, before Sy Rotter left for Israel, he arranged for a TV crew from RAI to film several Sisters. When I returned the next morning to serve as interpreter, little did I realize that much of that interview would be used in the documentary *A Debt To Honor*.

When interviewed, Sister Maria Pucci, an eyewitness in the convent on Via Caboto, not far from the Jewish ghetto of Portico d'Ottavia, said: "We were young, frightened. We knew that if caught harboring Jews we would be shot by the Nazis or Fascists. Yet, when twenty-five Jewish men, women, and children arrived, we opened our doors. They lived in our auditorium which we closed to the public. There they were barricaded with supplies and merchandise from their stores. They also occupied two well-fortified rooms in the area of the kindergarten. What a scene that first day—they were desperate! We gave them what they needed, especially blankets to keep warm. Children were crying, hugging their mothers. Everyone was frightened. During air raids we all fled to the shelters. We prayed with the Jews. Our prayers were mixed with tears."

When asked why the Sisters protected Jews, she answered: "Why? But these were our neighbors. We respected and loved them. We responded to the Pope's plea to open our doors!"

Sister Lelia Orlandi vividly recalled the bitter night during one of those terrible November storms. Clara Coen-Capon and her husband Luciano, with their one-year-old infant, knocked on the convent door in Cave, near Rome. Fully aware of the risk that, by protecting them, the Sisters would also be shot by the Nazis or the Fascists, Sister Lucia welcomed them. When she was 100 years old, she told this story on national Italian TV.

Many Jews were hidden in our convent located on Via Botteghe Oscure. Donated to the Religious Teachers Filippini by Pope Gregory XVI in 1836, this is an imposing structure, known as the Ginnasi Palace because one of its entrances is located on Via Arco dei Ginnasi. At the end of the war Jewish women presented, in gratitude, a five-foot statue of the Madonna that today still stands in the very wing where Jews lived for more than a year.

The building has a very large courtyard and various wings with classrooms for Kindergarten to Normal School. When the war began, many young boarders were sent home. An entire wing—dormitories, dining room, laundry, bathrooms—housed the Jewish people who were saved from the concentration camps. All this is seen in the documentary which chronicles ordinary people whose extraordinary acts of courage saved eighty-five percent of Italy's Jewish population from the horrors of the Holocaust.

When Sy Rotter completed the documentary narrated by Alan Alda, he suggested that I have the premiere showing of *A Debt To Honor* in Morristown, NJ. Therefore, on May 23, 1995, during the fiftieth Anniversary of the Holocaust, I arranged a symposium—*Holocaust "Rescuers in Italy" Day*—held in Mother Ninetta Hall auditorium at Villa Walsh.

Publicity and invitations were sent to various organizations sponsoring the event: The National Endowment for the Humanities, The National Italian American Foundation, Order Sons of Italy in America, Temple B'nai Or, The Anti-Defamation League, The Italian Embassy, The United Jewish Federation of Metrowest, and Unico National.

The Villa Walsh Academy Ensemble provided musical selections in both English and Hebrew. Sy Rotter gave the opening remarks, followed by greetings from Christine Todd Whitman, Governor of New Jersey, and a Proclamation by Murray Laulicht, representing the NJ Commission on Holocaust Education.

Immediately after the film, a panel discussion took place with Sy Rotter as Moderator. Panelists were: Shirley Horner, Columnist, *New York Times*; Robert A. Scott, President, Ramapo College of NJ; Rita Mannella, Deputy Consul, Italian Consulate General of NY; Maria Lombardo, Director, NEH Project: Holocaust in Southern Europe; and Sister Margherita Marchione, Professor, Fairleigh Dickinson University.

Rabbi Donald Rossoff's Sisterhood of B'nai Or in Morristown, NJ, hosted the reception after each program. Guests were able to view the Holocaust Exhibit of books and photographs in the lobby. Both afternoon and evening sessions of the symposium were filled to capacity (800 seats) with standing room only.

The record of the Religious Teachers Filippini shows that, in the midst of hatred and destruction during the war, their charity had no bounds. Also in consonance with the Pope's wishes, the Filippini Sisters in the United States not only visited the Italian prisoners of war and internees sequestered here, but they began shipping large weighted wooden cases containing medicine and clothing to the Vatican to help care for the needy.

This charity continued through 1966 when, as a Fulbright student, I crossed the Atlantic on the *Michelangelo*. My research trips to Italy were always by plane, but this time I had a special mission. I accompanied twenty cases of clothing and medicine addressed to His Holiness, Pope Paul VI.

To my amazement, although my ticket was Tourist Class, as I boarded the ship, I was told my room would be in Cabin Class and that I would have courtesy of the ship at all times. I was given a private tour of the *Michelangelo*, from the Captain's deck to the baggage rooms. My schedule was a busy one as I accepted invitations to dine at the Captain's table and to be of assistance to others. I even gave someone English lessons! There were many interesting people: a student from FDU, an author of updated Italian textbooks, several university professors, newspaper reporters and others with whom I chatted, dined, and exchanged ideas. I was labeled the ship's mascot.

Throughout the trip to Naples the Atlantic Ocean was like a lake and, I must add, the return trip in September was the same. However, our arrival in Naples was delayed by a few hours because of an SOS from a tanker which had exploded. This caused some excitement. We rushed to its assistance and did not leave the scene until help came from Gibraltar. I will never forget the efficiency of the crew and the spirit of charity and love for humanity manifested on this occasion. The entire trip was delightful.

It was a thrilling experience. Professor Prezzolini and his wife, who were living in Vietri sul mare (Salerno), greeted me at the pier in Naples and helped me expedite the delivery of twenty huge cases of clothing and medicines for the Pope's poor.

Obviously Pius XII's charity is well-known to the generation who lived through World War II; many were the beneficiaries of his endeavors to help the poor in Italy. However, some of the victims may have too deeply buried their memories or too easily forgotten the past. This should not happen. It is imperative that today's youth learn the true facts.

While it is difficult for succeeding generations to judge the past without having suffered the horrors of war, they must re-examine history and discover the way to arrive at historical truth. They must understand the action undertaken by the Church to put an end to the evils committed during the Holocaust.

It is time to restore truth to the role of Pope Pius XII during World War II and the Holocaust, to recall the saving of hundreds of thousands of Jewish lives, and to address also the unjust attacks both upon his proved, unequalled, and historic efforts in this regard and upon his virtuous character. It is ironic, and should be a source of serious concern that, since the issuance of the Vatican document on the Shoah, these attacks have grown in frequency and vituperation. They have appeared in such major publications as *The New York Times* and *Atlantic Monthly*, and have also been expressed by spokesmen from major organizations.

This matter has taken on a particular urgency, however, with the recent publication of *Hitler's Pope: The Secret History of Pius XII*

(Viking, New York, 1999) by John Cornwell, a scandalous book that not only distorts the truth about the extraordinary efforts of Pius XII and the Church to save the Jews during World War II, but actually also depicts this saintly Pope—whose cause for beatification is underway—as a collaborator of the Nazis. Cornwell's book has received approving reviews in *Time* magazine, *The New York Times*, the *Washington Post*, and other leading American publications. This is unlike the reception given to the book in Europe, where perhaps people have a firmer historical sense about the period. There is a need to set the record straight about the facts in the United States, where this apparent lack of historical knowledge leaves people susceptible to deliberate and careless "revisionist history," warping their views of Pope Pius XII and the Catholic Church.

The British journalist John Cornwell contends that Pope Pius XII helped start World War I, World War II, betrayed German Catholics, and assisted the Holocaust. He deals in rumors, half-truths and misrepresentations. Twice in one month I had the frightening experience of confronting Mr. Cornwell. I agreed to debate him because I felt I had to stand up for the truth as I know it.

Although I am keenly aware that there were many scholars and trained historians who could have dealt with Cornwell's demonizing of Pius XII, and I would have been only too happy to have them debate in my place, the TV and radio talk show hosts often turned to me. Could it be that the good Catholic scholars were unwilling to face the criticism and scorn that a defense of the Church today invites? Probably the media wanted someone as different from Cornwell as they could find—an old-fashioned Nun.

All I knew was that someone had to speak out. And if that someone had to be me, it had to be. I was seventeen when Eugenio Pacelli became Pope (March 2, 1939)—the "Pope of Peace," as newspapers everywhere described him. Like most Catholics of my generation I revered the new Pope and prayed that he would be able to prevent the dictators of Germany, Russia and Italy from plunging the world in a bloodbath of war. Unlike most Catholics I was a young nun whose order had a special connection with the papacy from 1707 when the then Pope Clement XI called our Sisters to open schools in Rome. Pius XII was often in my prayers.

Thus, when the great onslaught against Pius XII took over the media a few years ago, I was compelled to investigate more deeply and to publish what I discovered. In my writings I try to remind readers of the single, undeniable truth that defined Pope Pius XII's life: he was Christ-like. He was a man who devoted himself totally to finding peace, completely dedicated to healing and helping all the victims of war. His critics may ignore his total dedication to peace and loving charity, but they cannot change the facts of his life. It was a life of total dedication and giving.

Even John Cornwell acknowledges the saintly life of Pius XII. In his book, that author gives the reason for writing about the Pope: "Convinced, as I had always been, of Pius XII's innocence, I decided to write a new defense of his reputation for a younger generation. I believed that Pacelli's evident holiness was proof of his good faith."

However, it is difficult to respect the credibility of an author who claims to recognize the Pope's "good faith," when he places the provocative photograph on the jacket of the book depicting part of an ordinary ceremonial accorded Pacelli, years before Hitler came to power. It conveys the deceitful impression that Pius XII was pro-Nazi.

When the extermination of Jews began, the Dutch bishops issued a statement that precipitated a Nazi acceleration of roundup of Jews. On p. 287 Cornwell contests the statement that there were 40,000 Jews deported from Holland, calling this figure exaggerated. Not true. Deportation was not limited to Jews of Holland, but included "the Lowlands." The reference to the roundup that took place throughout the entire region includes priests and religious. Newspapers spoke of "deportation of 40,000 Jews of the Lowlands."

My first exchange with the British historical revisionist began when Wally Kennedy, producer of TV Channel WPVI (ABC *Sunday Live*) in Philadelphia, called me and asked if I would be on their October 3, 1999 program. I agreed to a telephone interview. I knew full well I would not have the "media presence" to expose Cornwell's errors. In no way could I respond properly to the insidious attacks in a

20-minute segment. In addition, as I soon learned, Cornwell would play the lead role, with all the time he wanted to speak; my part would consist of mainly shouted interjections. According to a later note from the producer, my contribution "provided the balance we wanted."

Present for the interview with Cornwell, who was in the New York studio, were Carol Saline, who described herself as a practicing Jew and journalist; Christine O'Donnell, who informed us she was a Catholic turned Protestant and has now returned to Catholicism; and Frank Desimone, a serious Catholic who admitted he had detailed knowledge of Pius XII. These panelists had definite and passionate viewpoints concerning Pope Pius XII.

At one point when Cornwell accused Pius XII of not protesting, I broke in and shouted: "There were 60 written protests against racial and religious persecutions sent to the Nazis on behalf of the Jews. Pius XII's Radio wartime speeches, and messages in the Vatican newspaper, provoked the Nazis to call him *a mouthpiece of the Jewish war criminals*." My comment was ignored as though the fact that the Pope repeatedly protested had no connection with the charge that the Pope was "silent."

Wally Kennedy addressed me, "Why didn't the Pope speak out against the Nazis?" "Because he was concerned," I answered, "that a public condemnation would mean the loss of more lives. Because he had agreed with the World Jewish Congress, the World Council of Churches, and the International Red Cross that they should avoid provocation that would undoubtedly have had serious consequences."

When Kennedy asked Mr. Cornwell if Pacelli ever met with Hitler, he said they never met but there had been negotiations for years before the signing of the Reich Concordat. He also insinuated that Pius XII was responsible for the demise of the Catholic Center Party.

When I finally had the opportunity, I responded: "Contrary to your allegations, Mr. Cornwell, Pius XII was always an opponent of anti-Semitism and did everything in his power to preserve Germany's Catholic Center Party. The Vatican agreed to the Concordat with Germany only after Hitler's reign of terror forced the Catholic Party to dissolve itself."

In his book, Cornwell brands this saintly Pope with the very serious charge of being an anti-Semite based upon a description of the 1919 terrorists' uprising in Munich. This typewritten report was prepared by a Monsignor who had investigated the incident. It was sent to the Vatican under Pacelli's signature.

The report describes the conduct of a Communist leader and his mistress—both atheist Jews from Russia who were terrorists—to whom the papal representatives were obliged to pay homage. In this six-page letter there is nothing against the Jewish people.

Yet, Cornwell states: "This association of Jewishness with Bolshevism confirms that Pacelli, from his early 40s, nourished a suspicion of and contempt for the Jews for political reasons." How can a description of terrorists be reasonably defined as anti-Semitic? Furthermore, this is not a newly-discovered document. Cornwell is unaware that it was published in 1992.

Later in the interview, Wally Kennedy asked Cornwell: "At what point do you think the Pope should have stepped up to a microphone and said, Nazism is mortally sinful and to be a subscriber of the theories of Hitler is to be anti-Catholic? Do you believe beyond a shadow of a doubt that Pius XII knew not only that there were gassings going on, but about the magnitude of the numbers of Jews put to death daily?"

Cornwell answered: "There is evidence from July 1942. Pius XII could have spoken out in his 1942 Christmas message. He could have addressed the consciences of millions of Germans. When Pius XII did speak, it was a denial of what was going on; he reduced the millions to hundreds of thousands. He never mentioned the word Jews; never mentioned the word Nazis. ... He lulled the consciences of millions of people, millions of Germans."

I was indignant. At this point I interrrupted Mr. Cornwell when he falsely claimed that *only* in the 1942 Christmas message Pius XII referred to the extermination of Jews. "This is not so. The Pope spoke out long before!" I tried, unsuccessfully, to say that Pius XII repeatedly addressed the consciences of not only Germans but of the

Marie and Frank Lotito's wedding reception.

Crescenzo and Felicia Marchione on their Golden Jubilee with family.

(Above) Sister Margherita, Giuseppe Prezzolini and Jakie, Vietri sul Mare, Italy.
(Below) Prezzolini at age 100, in Lugano, Switzerland
    Columbia University Graduation Day, May 18, 1960.

(Above) Sister Margherita with Peter and Sally Sammartino.
(Below) Sister Margherita, Sally Sammartino, Olga DeVita, Filomena Peloro,
in Washington, DC, for the Philip Mazzei Stamp.

(Above) Amita Award Ceremony: Sister Margherita with Lucille DeGeorge
        and Mrs. Henry Cabot Lodge, Jr..
(Below) Marie, Jean, Ceil with nieces Fran, Alexis, Joan, Kristen, and
        Marlene.

(Above) Joe Piscopo and Sister Margherita on the occasion of the Gala in her honor, September 13, 1997.
(Below) Members of the Marchione Family.

(Above) Pope Pius XII.
(Below) Mother Ninetta Jonata with Elena Rossignani Pacelli, Pope Pius XII's
    niece, at Villa Walsh, Morristown, NJ.

(Above) Sister Margherita with Pope Paul VI, July 27, 1966.
(Below) Sister Margherita with Pope John Paul II, December 8, 1999.

entire world over and over. There was no way the Pope could have had more specific information before his Christmas message of 1942.

The truth of the matter is that the British Foreign Office possessed information on the Warsaw ghetto by December 3, 1942. But Churchill wanted more evidence. On December 17, the Allies from London, Washington and Moscow finally issued their joint Declaration on the German persecution of the Jews.

The Holy See could not verify Allied reports on the number of Jews being exterminated. Owen Chadwick, in *Britain and the Vatican during the Second World War* (Cambridge University Press, 1986), explains that the Pope was very careful to guard against exaggeration: "Like the minds of most of western Europe, the mind of the Pope was not bad enough to believe the truth. Like the high officials of the British Foreign Office he thought that the Poles and the Jews exaggerated for the sake of helping the war effort."

The day after the Pope's election (March 3, 1939), the Berlin *Morgenpost* stated: "The election of Cardinal Pacelli is not accepted with favor in Germany because he was always opposed to Nazism." On October 28, 1939, the front page caption of *The New York Times* was in very large print: "Pope Condemns Dictators, Treaty Violators, Racism; Urges Restoring of Poland." Again on March 14, 1940, the caption read: "Pope is Emphatic About Just Peace; Jews' Rights Defended." In an editorial published in 1941, *The New York Times* considered the voice of Pius XII "a lonely voice in the silence and darkness enveloping Europe this Christmas and praised the Pope for having "put himself squarely against Hitlerism."

Pius XII's encyclical *Summi Pontificatus* (October 20, 1939) condemned racism and totalitarianism: "...The blood of countless human beings, even noncombatants, raises a piteous dirge over a nation such as Our dear Poland, which, for its fidelity to the Church, for its services in the defense of Christian civilization, written in indelible characters in the annals of history, has a right to the generous and brotherly sympathy of the whole world, while it awaits, relying on the powerful intercession of Mary, Help of Christians, the hour of a resurrection in harmony with the principles of justice and true peace."

Scores of protests, personally signed, were sent to the German Foreign Minister and to the German Ambassador. These are published texts: one so damning that it was included in the official documents used against the Germans on trial at Nuremberg. Among those on trial was Herr von Ribbentrop, Hitler's Foreign Minister. He was asked if they had received protests from the Vatican. He replied: "We had a whole desk full of them."

The Pope's frequent Vatican Radio messages were in many languages. On February 19, 1943, speaking in French, he invoked "the curse of God" on whomever abuses the liberty of men. Broadcasting in German in April 1943, he protested a long list of horrors, including "an unprecedented enslavement of human freedom, the deportation of thousands for forced labor, and the killing of innocent and guilty alike."

In his June 2, 1943, allocution to the Cardinals (published that same day in *L'Osservatore Romano*), Pius XII clearly referred to the Jews: "Do not be astonished.... There are those who, because of their nationality or their descent, are pursued by mounting misfortune and increasing suffering and extermination." The Germans and Italians were so astonished that they suppressed this section from all their reports of what the Pope had said. But the Vatican wireless broadcasted it to Germany. I had the *Times* text before me and shouted: "The paper described his confrontational meeting with the German Foreign Minister." I quoted: "It was learned today ... that the Pontiff, in burning words about religious persecution, also came to the defense of the Jews."

It took great persistence to continue reading in *The New York Times* its Christmas 1941 editorial praising Pius XII for having "put himself squarely against Hitlerism." Other headlines were (August 6, 1942): "Pope Is Said to Plead for Jews Listed for Removal from France"; (August 27, 1942): "Vichy Seizes Jews; Pope Pius Ignored. These arrests are continuing, despite appeals to Marshal Henri Philippe Pétain by leading Catholic clergymen, with the support of the pope." Pius XII publicly defended the Jews whenever the bishops informed him about Nazi atrocities.

I also added that the Vatican Radio (October 15, 1940) explicitly condemned "the immoral principles of Nazism," and the *Osservatore Romano* condemned "the wickedness of Hitler" citing Hitler by name (March 30, 1941). The London *Times* (October 1, 1942) praised Pius XII: "There is no room for doubt. He condemns the worship of force ... and the persecution of the Jewish race."

Later *The Tablet* of London reported that Nazi leader Goebbels issued pamphlets in many languages which condemned Pius XII as a "pro-Jewish Pope" (October 24, 1942). There were many references to the "fundamental rights of Jews" (December 3 and 5, 1943). While Germany occupied Rome and martial law prevailed, *The New York Times* (December 4, 1943) stated: "Vatican denounces decision to intern and strip all Jews in Italy."

To round off the very chaotic interview, Kennedy, in the usual American media fashion called for a poll among the five people present. He asked for responses to the question: "Should Pope Pius XII be canonized?" The Catholic criminal attorney and I immediately said "Yes." The Jewish reporter and John Cornwell reported strong "No's." The Catholic founder of an activist organization, SALT, preferred to make reference to the Bible which speaks in favor of Jews. Her counterpart did not agree and there ensued a loud debate between the two women participants. I could not believe what happened!

The program was suddenly over. I felt almost as though I had not said anything. All the facts and figures and accounts of the millions Pius XII had helped were still in my mind, unspoken. I thought of Michael Bobrow, an American Jewish journalist, whose cousin was saved by nuns in a convent in Belgium. He wrote to me recently: "The canonization of Pope Pius XII would be an act of supreme justice, charity, and truth..."

And I remembered the words of Carlo Sestieri, a Jewish survivor of the Holocaust in Rome: "Only the Jews who were persecuted understand why the Holy Father could not publicly denounce the Nazi-Fascist government. Without doubt, it helped avoid worse disasters."

Sestieri had been hidden in the Vatican; his wife in a nearby convent. Both were saved.

Providentially, three days later I was given a second chance to answer Cornwell's libelous opinions. On a thirty-minute Radio interview from Ann Arbor, MI, with Al Kresta of WWCM, Cornwell and I again faced off. I listened to the author's remarks and then I began by telling Mr. Cornwell that his book unjustly defames the memory of Pope Pius XII who was a humble, holy, selfless humanitarian. He was not the ambitious or power-hungry leader described in the Cornwell book.

I accused Mr. Cornwell of misinterpretations, false statements, omissions, and inaccuracies. I was given the opportunity to cite specific errors. I pointed out, for example, that in dealing with the March 24, 1944 Rome massacre, he accuses Pius XII of having had prior knowledge of plans for this massacre. I reminded him that he knew this was an old lie which had long ago been disproved, and that he not only repeated the falsehood but compounded it with new falsehoods. His book states that Pius XII's sister and nephew sued perpetrators of this lie in a Roman court.

It was not the pope's sister and nephew who brought this protest to court, it was his niece! It was Elena Rossignani Pacelli, my friend, who, in 1957, had arranged for me to meet Pope Pius XII! She brought suit for defamation against film producer Carlo Ponti, author Robert Katz and director George Cosmatos. After the trial and appeals, the producer, author, and director were found guilty of calumny against Pope Pius XII on February 7, 1981.

When I accused Cornwell of totally twisting the Roman court's decision in this famous case, he heatedly insisted that he had not falsely reported the verdict. I quoted from *Hitler's Pope*, p. 380: "The Pacellis lost, but appealed, and the case was eventually judged inconclusive." Even then he would not admit that the Pacellis had won, that the court had ruled in their favor and found Pope Pius XII had been falsely accused. He would admit nothing. He was silent.

I cannot adequately describe my feelings of repugnance as I listened to Cornwell repeat over and over his misrepresentations and inaccuracies. There are many examples that could be cited.

On pages 274-276 of his book, Cornwell portrays Cardinal Henri de Lubac—the great French Catholic anti-Nazi theologian—as being progressive and totally opposed to Pius XII. The truth of the matter is that Cardinal de Lubac was a great admirer of Pius XII and wrote a book of wartime memoirs, *Christian Resistance to Anti-Semitism: Memories from 1940-1944* (Ignatius Press, San Francisco, 1990) in which he discusses Pius XII's influence on Catholic rescuers of Jews. Nowhere does Cornwell mention this book!

On page 262, Cornwell quotes Cardinal Tisserant out-ot-context to suggest that the Cardinal denounced Pius XII in a private letter to Cardinal Suhard (*Le Monde,* March 26, 1964). In "Interview," *Informations Catholiques Internationales* (April 15, 1964), as well as in other Catholic papers, Cardinal Tisserant clearly stated that he was not criticizing Pius XII whom he admired, but criticizing members of the Curia for not carrying out the Pope's policies.

Concerning Pius XII, Cardinal Tisserant said: "The Pope's attitude was beyond discussion. My remarks did not involve his person, but certain members of the Curia. ... If the consequences of a protest were to fall on himself alone, Pius XII would not have been in the slightest way concerned. Everyone knows that he was ready to go to a concentration camp. But he weighed before all else the mortal risks to which the victims of Nazism could be exposed in the case of a protest... ."

Cornwell's allegations were made in a calm, superior manner. But at one point in the TV interview my indignation upset him. I strongly exposed his injustices to Pius XII. He admitted that he was upset. He spoke of his position being misunderstood, of more explanation being necessary, of a disturbing "anger" in "the Sister's response." His sense of irritation with me was ever more evident in the radio interview where I had more time to speak. I was able to express my outrage at this sensationalized and propagandistic and inaccurate book, thanks to

Al Kresta of WWCM. The script is available on the internet (www. catholicfamilyradio.com).

Critics should consider the wisdom of Pius XII's words and actions. Jewish physicist Albert Einstein wrote: "Being a lover of freedom, when the Nazi revolution came in Germany, I looked to the universities to defend it, knowing that they had always boasted of their devotion to the cause of truth; but, no, the universities immediately were silenced. Then I looked to the great editors of the newspapers, whose flaming editorials in days gone by had proclaimed their love of freedom; but they, like the universities, were silenced in a few short weeks....

"Only the Church," Einstein concluded, "stood squarely across the path of Hitler's campaign for suppressing the truth. I never had any special interest in the Church before, but now I feel a great affection and admiration because the Church alone has had the courage and persistence to stand for intellectual truth and moral freedom. I am forced thus to confess that what I once despised, I now praise unreservedly." (*Time* magazine, December 23, 1940).

Unlike Cornwell, Jewish historian Pinchas Lapide, a practicing Jew, strongly defended Pope Pius XII: "If fairness and historical justice are keystones of Jewish morality, then keeping silent in view of slanderous attacks on a benefactor is an injustice. ... Far more than two million Jews did indeed survive, thanks to the help of the Church, bishops, priests, laymen. ... The Talmud teaches us 'whoever saves a life receives as much credit as if he had saved an entire world.' If this is true—and it is just as true as the most typical of all Jewish principles: that of the holiness of human life—then a Jew must also defend loudly a great saver of Jewish life." (*Die Welt*, July 16, 1964).

Cornwell's real objective is to destroy the papacy and the church as we know it. He writes in *Vanity Fair*, p. 192: "A future titanic struggle between the progressives and the traditionalists is in prospect, with the potential for a cataclysmic schism, especially in North America." By denigrating Pius XII, depicted as authoritarian, traditional and Roman, by painting John Paul II with the same brush,

Cornwell is contributing to the goal of many confused Catholics—changing the Church into a social institution.

Hitler's Pope, by John Cornwell, depicts this saintly Pope as a collaborator of the Nazis. Instead of objectivity, Cornwell favors sensationalism. He ignores what does not fit into the image he wants to convey and omits the factual record of Jewish-Vatican relations that earned the gratitude of Jewish leaders throughout the world.

My books on this topic are in English and in Italian: *Yours Is a Precious Witness: Memoirs of Jews and Catholics in Wartime Italy* (Paulist Press, 1997) and *Pio XII e gli Ebrei*, (Editoriale Pantheon, 1999). These were followed by *Pius XII: Architect for Peace* (Paulist Press, 2000) and *Pio XII: Architetto di Pace* (Editoriale Pantheon, 2000).

I try to confront the insidious attacks against the Papacy and the entire Roman Catholic Church, offering an abundance of incontestable evidence to obliterate the myths and lies. Included in *Pius XII: Architect for Peace* are an annotated bibliography and a response to the September 1998 statement by the International Jewish Committee on Interreligious Consultations criticizing the 1998 Vatican document on the Holocaust entitled *We Remember: A Reflection on the Shoah*.

Robert A. Graham, S.J., one of the editors of the *Actes et documents du Saint Siège relatifs à la Second Guerre Mondiale* (Acts and Documents of the Holy See Relative to the Second World War), stated: "A study of the Vatican documents is the only way to understand the truth and to do justice to those who stretched a helping hand to the Jews in those tragic days."

There are more than five thousand documents, published between 1965 to 1982, in this French edition of the twelve volumes. I included a selection from Volumes 1, 5, 6, 7, 8, 9, 10 in the Appendix of *Pius XII: Architect for Peace*. A summary of the documents from Volumes 1 and 10 follows:

Volume 1 (*Le Saint Siège et la guerre en Europe [The Holy See and the War in Europe, March 1939-August 1940]* 1970, 558pp.)

Rome, May 6, 1939:
Britain's first response to Pius XII's peace conference proposal.
Washington, May 15, 1939:
Pope informs President Roosevelt of the steps taken toward peace talks.
Rome, July 11, 1939:
Apostolic Delegate to Sumner Welles with regard to the international situation.
Vatican, August 16, 1939:
Alleged Press information, sent by Great Britain's Minister.
Rome, August 26, 1939:
Great Britain's Lord Halifax's thanks Pope for the message of peace.
Rome, August 26, 1939:
From London, proposal suggested: Make Danzig and Corridor a free city.
Washington, February 14, 1940:
Roosevelt thanks the Pope for receiving Myron Taylor, as intermediary to work toward peace and harmony among peoples.

Volume 10 (*Le Saint Siège et les victimes de la guerre [The Holy See and Victims of the War, January 1944-July 1945]* 1980, 684pp.)
New York, February 18, 1944
Acknowledgment to the Pope on behalf of the persecuted Jews in Europe.
Vatican, April 1, 1944
Request for intervention on behalf of Hungarian Jews.
Washington, June 13, 1944
Solidarity of North American Bishops with Bishops of France to protect art.
Vatican, June 24, 1944
The "War Refugee Board" reports massacre of Jews in Hungary.
London, July 3, 1944
Request for intervention on behalf of Hungarian Jews.
New York, July 21, 1944
Acknowledgment of Pope's efforts on behalf of Italian Jews
London, July 21, 1944
Holy See's intervention in Hungary; final appeal to Horthy is requested.
Vatican, August 7, 1944
Intervention on behalf of civilian internees in Egypt.
Rome, August 12, 1944
Under-Secretary to the Minister of War's suggestions for an audience.
Istanbul, August 18, 1944
Information on the charitable work of the Delegation on behalf of Jews.

Vatican, September 15, 1944
Request for information on prisoners of war and internees.
Vatican, October 4, 1944
The Pope supports North American Agency for help given to the Italians.
London, October 14, 1944
Request for intervention on behalf of Hungarian Jews.
Vatican, October 18, 1944
Intervention for foreign Jews in Slovakia
Rome, November 15, 1944
The Holy See's efforts on behalf of the Jews
Vatican, November 17, 1944
Request on behalf of Italian prisoners interned by the Allies in Italy.
Vatican, December 14, 1944
The Holy See's efforts on behalf of Slovak Jews.
Rome, February 1, 1945
Request for Pope's intervention on behalf of Jews.
Vatican, March 2, 1945
Return of Italian civilians from Albania.
Vatican, March 3, 1945
The Holy See's attitude regarding the post-war situation.
Washington, March 9, 1945
Report on the conditions of Poland occupied by the Russians.
Vatican, April 16, 1945
Assistance offered to the Pope by American Catholics for his charitable works.
Vatican, April 19, 1945
Request on behalf of the Italian internees in Germany.
Vatican, April 23, 1945
The Pope acknowledges offering from the Diocese of Boston for war victims.
Vatican, May 3, 1945
Acknowledgment of the Pope for assistance by the Catholics of the United States.

Pope Pius XII continually condemned Nazi policies during World War II, speaking amply and effectively. He sent over sixty official Vatican protests. The Nazis understood his diplomatic language, and so did the whole world. *The New York Times* headlines were: *Pope Pius XII Denounces Atrocities in Poland, Vatican Reveals Terrors in Poland.* The article stated: "Jews and Poles are being herded into separate ghettos, hermetically sealed and pitifully inadequate for the economic subsistence of the millions destined to live there" (January

23, 1940). In its editorial the *Times* refers to *The Vatican's Indictment* against the Nazis—*Vatican Amplifies Atrocity Reports, Weight of Papacy Put Behind Exposure of Nazi Excesses in Poland:* "Now the Vatican has spoken, with authority that cannot be questioned, and has confirmed the worst intimations of terror which have come out of the Polish darkness" (January 24, 1940). Countless other similar headlines appeared before the 1942 Christmas message!

On March 1, 2000 the Israeli government finally released the Adolf Eichmann *Diary*, describing the extermination of Jews by the Nazi regime and the actions taken by Pope Pius XII when Jews in Rome were deported on October 16, 1943. Eichmann clearly states that the Vatican "vigorously protested the arrest of Jews, requesting the interruption of such action; to the contrary, the Pope would denounce it publicly."

No one can deny that, during the period of the Holocaust, Pius XII performed acts to stop the evils of Nazism. Israel was obliged to make the *Diary* known when historian David Irving brought a libel suit in London against the American professor Deborah Lipstadt for calling him "a dangerous spokesman for Holocaust denial."

To prove that the Holocaust existed, the Israelis—relying on Eichmann's credibility—released a *Diary* they had in their possession for the past 40 years.

Why did the Israeli government wait so long! Gideon Hausner, the prosecutor in the Adolf Eichmann trial, cautioned that publication of the memoirs could compete with the verdict. That is why Prime Minister Ben-Gurion ordered the manuscript locked away for 15 years. Only last year was it decided to make the memoirs public immediately, and a copy of the manuscript has been sent to London, after a request by defense lawyers. The book will serve as evidence of the Nazi genocide. A photocopy and typed versions of the text in the original German were made available at the Israel State Archives in Jerusalem. Thus the humanitarian work of the Vatican was made known in the very words of a Nazi leader condemned at the Nuremberg Trials. These memoirs reveal the truth.

Holocaust scholar Jenö Levai, invited as an expert at the Eichmann trial in Jerusalem, insisted that bishops of the Catholic Church "intervened again and again on the instructions of the Pope. ... the one person who did more than anyone else to halt the dreadful crime and alleviate its consequences, is today made the scapegoat for the failures of others" (*Hungarian Jewry and the Papacy: Pius XII Was Not Silent,* Sands and Company, London, 1968).

The Holocaust took place during a complex and dark period of human history. One must not fail to remember that Rome was occupied by the Germans. The Church was the only institution that had the courage to denounce the Nazi action. Eichmann's words confirm the thesis of those historians who have collected documents on the action undertaken by the Vatican to defend Jews.

Several years ago, I interviewed Princess Enza Pignatelli Aragona who personally informed Pope Pius XII about the October 16, 1943 Nazi raid in the Jewish ghetto. The story is told in my books *Yours Is a Precious Witness: Memoirs of Jews and Catholics in Wartime Italy* (Paulist Press, Mahwah, NJ, 1997), and *Pio XII e gli Ebrei,* (Editoriale Pantheon, Rome, 1999). Having no transportation, the Princess telephoned and awakened her friend Gustave Wollenweber, who was an aide in the German Embassy and asked him to bring his car and drive her to the Vatican at once. Ironically, a German diplomat of an anti-Semite government was accompanying an Italian princess to the Vatican to protest the arrest of Jews!

Some critics do not want to accept the truth and make allegations stating that the Vatican is withholding evidence regarding its participation in World War II. These writers continue to state that Pope Pius XII was "silent" about the Nazi atrocities and deny that he did everything in his power to alleviate the sufferings of the Jews during the Holocaust.

It is time to dissect the "big lie" that the media continues to spread about Pope Pius XII's "silence." It is time to accept the actual role of Pope Pius XII during World War II and the Holocaust in saving the lives of hundreds of thousands of Jews, and to counter the unjust attacks upon his proved, unequalled, and historic efforts in this regard.

Further corroboration of Pope Pius XII's efforts are found in Eichmann's *Diary*, in a chapter regarding Italy, where he explains that on October 6, 1943, Ambassador Moelhausen sent a telegraphic message to Foreign Minister Ribbentrop in which he said that General Kappler, SS commander in Rome, had received a special order from Berlin: he had to arrest 8,000 Jews who were living in Rome, to deport them to northern Italy, where they would be exterminated.

General Stahel, commander of the German forces in Rome, explained to Ambassador Moelhausen that, from his point of view, it would be better to use the Jews for fortification works. On October 9, however, Ribbentrop answered that the 8,000 Jews of Rome had to be deported to the Mathausen concentration camp. Adolf Eichmann emphasized this fact when he gave evidence under oath in the military prison of Gaeta on June 27, 1961, stating that this was the first time he heard the term *Final Solution*: "At that time, my office received the copy of a letter, that I immediately gave to my direct superiors, sent by the Catholic Church in Rome, in the person of Bishop Hudal, to the commander of the German forces in Rome, General Stahel."

Eichmann wrote in his diary: "The Church was vigorously protesting the arrest of Jews of Italian citizenship, requesting that such actions be interrupted immediately throughout Rome and its surroundings. To the contrary, the Pope would denounce it publicly. The Curia was especially angry because these incidents were taking place practically under Vatican windows. But, precisely at that time, without paying any attention to the Church's position, the Italian fascist government passed a law ordering the deportation of all Italian Jews to concentration camps."

A good number of them hid in convents or were helped by men and women of the Church. According to the Nazi leader: "The objections given and the excessive delay in the steps necessary to complete the implementation of the operation, resulted in a great part of Italian Jews being able to hide and escape capture."

Adolf Eichmann organized the deportation of millions of Jews to death camps during World War II. After Israeli agents seized him in Argentina and brought him to trial in Jerusalem, he wrote his memoirs in an Israeli jail. In the summer of 1961, over a period of four months he laboriously penned his autobiography which he apparently intended to publish as a book entitled *The False Gods*. Totaling 1,100 pages the book includes drafts, diagrams and footnotes, recounts at length Eichmann's defense in his trial: that he was no more than a cog in the Nazi machine, that he was not anti-Semitic but misguidedly drawn to the nationalist ethos of Nazism. He also portrays himself as an official with limited authority who was simply following orders. In one diagram of his *Diary* Eichmann places himself at the bottom of the Nazi hierarchy.

Experts who witnessed that era, agree that, if Pius XII had engaged in more confrontation with the Nazi leaders, more lives would have been lost. Robert Kempner, the American deputy chief of the Nuremberg war crimes tribunal stated: "All the arguments and writings eventually used by the Catholic Church only provoked suicide; the execution of Jews was followed by that of Catholic priests."

At the Nuremberg trials, Ernst von Weizsäker, Germany's Chief Secretary of Foreign Affairs until 1943, and then ambassador to the Holy See, testified: "It was well-known everybody knew it—that the Jewish question was a sore point as far as Hitler was concerned. To speak of interventions and requests submitted from abroad, requests for moderation of the course taken, the results of these, almost in all cases, caused the measures to be made more aggravated, and more serious even, in effect."

Albrecht von Kessel, aide to Ernst von Weizsäker in the Roman embassy, also testified: "I am convinced, therefore, that His Holiness the Pope did, day and night, think of a manner in which he could help the unfortunate Jews in Rome. If he did not lodge a protest, then it was not done because he thought, justifiably, that if he protested, Hitler would go crazy, and that would not help the Jews at all, that would give one the justified fear that they would be killed even more quickly. Apart from that, the SS would probably have been instructed to penetrate into the Vatican and lay hands on the Pope."

Pius XII was not a "silent" Pope. The wisdom of his words and actions is supported by the evidence. Obviously Adolf Eichmann's testimony, during the Nuremberg Trials and in his *Diary,* should be examined by the experts. He had already been condemned and had no apparent motive to fabricate when writing his memoirs.

Yet, despite all the documentation, some critics do not want to accept the truth and continue to reiterate the contention of several contemporary Jewish leaders that the Vatican is withholding evidence about its participation in World War II.

In St. Louis, Missouri (January 27, 1999), Pope John Paul II stated: "If you want Peace, work for Justice. If you want Justice, defend Life. If you want Life, embrace the Truth—the Truth revealed by God."

As I tour the country, my topic—*The Truth about Pius XII and the Holocaust*—is an important contemporary issue affecting the Magisterium of the Catholic Church. At the Franciscan University of Steubenville, during a two-day national conference of The Society of Catholic Social Scientists, I reiterated that one of the purposes of that particular group of Catholic scholars is "to defend the Church and comment in the media." Since it is the duty of every Catholic to defend the Church, I challenged them to join me.

However, I concluded: "I pray you will be more successful than I have been. You may have read the March 18, 1998 *New York Times* editorial statement: 'A full exploration of Pope Pius XII's conduct is needed. He did *not* encourage Catholics to defy Nazi orders.' And, three days later, Peter Steinfels wrote; 'The Vatican Document skirts the issue of the Pope's *silence*!' "

The allegations that followed on April 26, 1998, in *The New York Times* magazine article, "John Paul II's Jewish Dilemma," maligned the character of both Pius XII and John Paul II, offended Catholics, and denigrated the Catholic Faith. In fact, I had the honor of being singled out in a flippant manner. I was described as "a faithful remnant." Why? Because I had written many "pro-Pius letters to the editor"—none of which were ever published!

Was I insulted? No, indeed. I was honored to be mentioned, because, at times, remnants are useful! Besides, I've had other titles. I was called The Independent Nun, The Literary Nun, The Flying Nun,

The Whirlwind Nun, The Feisty Nun… but **none** pleases me more than the latest title—The Defender of Pius XII.

It is imperative that Catholics and Jews respond to the allegations, implications, and indictments regarding Pope Pius XII. Is there no way to stop the calumnies about the silence of Pius XII and the unfounded charges that Christianity led directly to the Nazi death camps? How can Catholics ignore the truth, and not fight back? How could Pius XII thwart a world power with military domination over a continent from murdering the civilians it defined as its enemies? In no way could Pius XII have taken a public stand against the Nazis without endangering the lives of other human beings. The thousands of Jews hidden in convents and monasteries would have been sent to concentration camps along with those who were trying to save them.

Rabbi Marc Saperstein wrote in *The Washington Post*, April 1, 1998: "The fundamental responsibility for the Holocaust lies with the Nazi perpetrators. Not with Pope Pius XII. Not with the Church. Not with the teachings of the Christian faith."

Archbishop Eugenio Pacelli, who for many years represented the Vatican in Germany, helped prepare a powerful Vatican statement condemning anti-Semitism. It was issued March 25, 1928, long before any major voice in Europe condemned the Nazis: "Moved by Christian charity, the Holy See is obligated to protect the Jewish people against unjust vexations. It particularly condemns unreservedly hatred against the people once chosen by God; the hatred that commonly goes by the name of anti-Semitism."

As Nuncio in Germany, Cardinal Pacelli applied this teaching and spoke out repeatedly against Nazism. In 1933, when he was Vatican Secretary of State, he negotiated a concordat with the Germans to protect the rights of Catholics. In 1935, he spoke before hundreds of thousands in France, and *The New York Times* reported (April 29): "Nazis warned at Lourdes." Cardinal Pacelli, who had visited the United States in 1936, appealed to our government to throw open its doors to Jewish refugees. His request was unsuccessful.

Cardinal Pacelli was elected Pope on March 2, 1939. He immediately exhorted his representatives to oppose the racial laws and to intervene on behalf of persecuted Jews. The Nazi press accused him of being anti-German, and the International Communist newspaper called him a "relentless opponent of Hitler!"

On August 24, 1939, while the Nazi and Communist governments were signing the Non-Aggression Pact—which included Poland's partition between Germany and the Soviet Union—Pius XII sent a radio-message from Castelgandolfo calling Hitler to negotiation and peace. His statement was clear: "Nothing is lost with peace; everything can be lost with war." The Pope's efforts to stop Hitler's army went unheeded. Meanwhile, the Nazis invaded Poland, September 1, 1939.

But even before the war, as Secretary of State, the "Voice" of Cardinal Pacelli had been raised. In 1937, he helped draft the encyclical *Mit Brennender Sorge* (With Burning Anxiety), a strong condemnation of Nazi ideology. In response to the Nazi invasion, Pius XII issued (October 20, 1939) his first encyclical—*Summi Pontificatus* (On the unity of Human Society)—condemning racism and totalitarianism.

Pius XII spoke of the thousands of families enduring death and desolation, lamentation and misery. The encyclical clearly condemned Fascist laws and the rights assumed by the State: "Safety does not come to peoples from external means, from the sword, which can impose conditions of peace but does not create peace. ... The new order of the world must rest on the unshakeable foundation, on the solid rock of natural law and of Divine Revelation."

John Cornwell speaks favorably about Pope John XXIII, and neglects to mention that he, too, was a great admirer of Pius XII and collaborated with him during the war to save the Jews. (Pope John XXIII was beatified by John Paul II on September 3, 2000.)

In his book Cornwell says that the 1942 Christmas message was the first time Pope Pius XII spoke out. The truth of the matter is that the Pope did speak out against the National Socialist regime and his words have been reported in newspapers throughout the world. There are literally hundreds of documents: Inaugural encyclical, October 1939; Christmas messages, 1941, 1942; Papal discourse, June 2, 1943; Discourse to abolish suffering without distinction of nationality or race, June 2, 1944; and countless other important statements against the Nazis.

In his 1940 Easter homily, Pius XII spoke about the bombardment of defenseless citizens, infirm and aged people and innocent children. On May 11th he condemned the invasions of Belgium, Holland, and Luxemburg, and referred to a world poisoned by lies and disloyalty and wounded by excesses of violence.

The record shows that Pius XII, a spiritual leader who condemned Nazi "idolatry of race and blood," wrote and spoke a great deal during World War II. His writings and speeches were recorded on the Vatican Radio and/or were printed in the *Osservatore Romano*. The record amply supports the conclusion that his was a strategic approach to protect Jews and other refugees from retaliatory Nazi terrorism.

As a result of my research, I have been able to publish articles defending Pius XII, not only in newspapers, but also in magazines, e.g., *Ambassador, Catalyst, Catholic Heritage, Crisis, Culture Wars, Homiletic & Pastoral Review, Inside the Vatican, La Follia, Share, Sisters Today, Social Justice Review, The Catholic Answer, The Priest, and others.*

A story entitled "Holy See is Eager to Rescue Hebrews" (*The Catholic Review*, November 5, 1943), tells of the arrest of Roman Jews, the concern of the Vatican, and the Pope's offer of gold to ransom Jewish hostages. The same issue contains a reprint of an appeal for prayers on behalf of the Pope, made by Rabbi Lazaron of the Baltimore Hebrew Congregation. The Rabbi speaks of Pius XII as a prisoner in the Vatican, declaring: "The Pope has condemned anti-Semitism and all its works. Bishops of the Church have appeared in the streets of Antwerp, Brussels, The Hague and Paris, with the Star of David on their arms. Humble priests...have joined with Protestant ministers in protecting Jews...at the risk of their own lives."

Pius XII was not going to inflate his reputation for prophetic denunciation at the expense of others. Dismissal of the papal language as "evasive" is a denial of the evidence in the context of the diplomatic language the Holy See habitually uses. The nuncios who worked on behalf of Jews were in a good position to know and be influenced by the Pope's attitudes. They did not feel hampered either by a supposed sympathy to Nazi Germany or by an unsympathetic attitude to helping the Jewish victims of Nazism.

Addressing the Curia in June 1943, Pope Pius XII stated that his every word needed to be weighed carefully "in the very interest of those who suffer so as not to make their position even more difficult and more intolerable than previously, even though inadvertently and unwillingly."

Archbishop Amleto Giovanni Cicognani, Apostolic Delegate of the Holy See to the United States, encouraged the Catholic Bishops to make a strong appeal with regard to the Jewish plight. It was issued on November 14, 1942: "Since the murderous assault on Poland, utterly devoid of every semblance of humanity, there has been a premeditated and systematic extermination of the people of the nation. The same satanic technique is being applied to many other peoples. We feel a deep sense of revulsion against the cruel indignities heaped upon the Jews in conquered countries and upon defensless peoples not of our faith. We join with our brother bishops in subjugated France: 'Deeply moved by the mass arrests and maltreatment of Jews we cannot stifle the cry of our conscience. In the name of humanity and Christian principles our voice is raised in favor of imprescriptible rights of human nature.' We raise our voice in protest against despotic tyrants who have lost all sense of humanity by condemning thousands of innocent persons to death in subjugated countries as acts of reprisal, by placing other thousands of innocent victims in concentration camps, and by permitting unnumbered persons to die of starvation."

Excerpts from letters I received some fifty years later register the concern of present members of the hierarchy in the United States.

The Archbishop of Denver, Charles J. Chaput, O.F.M. Cap. (May 4, 1998): "I know your name from the good work you have done in explaining and defending the actions of Pius XII during the Second World War. I am also familiar with the article to which you refer, and found its tone tragic, strange and troubling all at the same time. I do not know a great deal about the issues in question, but I certainly share your fatigue at the barrage of criticism the memory of Pius XII seems to endure so undeservedly."

The Bishop of Austin, John McCarthy (May 7, 1998): "My heartfelt thanks for your kind letter in which you once again come forth heroically to defend the good name of Pope Pius XII. I have read your book and am very grateful for your important work in this area. I admire you for trying so generously to right a tragic wrong ....May God continue to bless your work."

The Bishop of Trenton, John M. Smith (May 11, 1998): "Thank you for your informative letter of April 29. Your work to undo the anti-Catholic revisionist history is a great example of scholarship in defense of the truth. Your recent book, *Yours Is a Precious Witness: Memoirs of Jews and Catholics in Wartime Italy,* has made an important contribution to the presentation of the truth concerning the role of Pope Pius XII in protecting Italian Jews and defying the forces of Fascism."

The Bishop of Peoria, John J. Myers (May 12, 1998): "I certainly agree with your concern about the gross distortion and untruths which are being put forward by superficial people pertaining to the role of Pope Pius XII and the attitude of the Church towards the Jewish people during World War II. I encourage you to quietly keep promoting the factual information which you have available. In the long run, we must trust the Holy Spirit will lead people to the truth which will set them free."

The Bishop of Brooklyn, Thomas V. Daily (May 13, 1998): "Thank you for your letter of April 26, 1998, and your sterling defense of Pope Pius XII. Recently, I was reading one of your fine articles that defended him even in more detail than you expressed in your letter to me. To say the least, it was certainly reassuring, and because it was the truth, most consoling.... Surely Pope Pius XII, who during his life here on earth, lived the Gospel message of Jesus Christ as found in the sixth and seventh chapters of Saint Matthew's Gospel, is at peace and please God, is praying for those writers, government officials, politicians, etc., who have not treated him nor his memory with fairness."

The Bishop of Lincoln, Fabian W. Bruskewitz (September 17, 1998): "I completely agree with your view of the PBS production of 'Reflections on Vatican II.' Allow me to tell you of my deep appreciation and admiration of your excellent work in trying to stem the defamatory articles and avalanche of untruth which is attempting to smear the memory of Pope Pius XII. May God reward you for your labors, and protect you from the dangers that come to those who must heroically stand for historical and theological truth."

The Archbishop of New York, John Cardinal O'Connor, (March 2, 1999): "Thanks for all that you do to bring about a more complete and honest portrait of Pope Pius XII and the Catholic Church during those difficult and tragic years. Your work is a great service to the universal Church." On May 5, 1999, I sent the late Cardinal O'Connor my reaction to Father Andrew Greeley's op-ed piece that had appeared in *The New York Times,* and requested that my response be placed in the archdiocesan newspaper, *Catholic New York.* He sent my correspondence to the editor. In his own hand (May 11, 1999), the Cardinal replied to me, "You're terrific! I'm glad you're on our Holy Father's side. You'd make a formidable opponent!"

The Archbishop of Philadelphia, Anthony Cardinal Bevilacqua, (December 6, 1999): "Your efforts to promote a true understanding of the efforts of Pope Pius XII to help the Jewish community during World War II and his responsibility to protect the Church against the onslaughts of Nazism are greatly appreciated. While any efforts to promote the truth are often met with opposition initially, I am confident that your efforts will bear fruit."

Dr. Joseph Lichten, a Polish Jew who served with the Polish Government in exile during World War II and a former director of the Intercultural Affairs Department of the Anti-Defamation League of B'nai B'rith, suffered personal tragedy from the Nazis. It is paradoxical that he has provided one of the best personal defenses of Pope Pius XII. Dr. Lichten wrote thirty-five pages of documentation in support of his belief that Pius XII did "everything humanly possible to save lives and alleviate suffering among the Jews," and that "the evidence moves against the hypothesis that a formal condemnation from Pius would have curtailed the mass murder of Jews."

During the war, *The New York Times* (October 15, 1944) noted the gratitude of Jews who universally praised Pope Pius XII for his humanitarian efforts. According to eyewitness Herbert L. Matthews: "No Pope could have done more along the simple lines of charity and helpfulness than Pius XII. ... The pope's role has remained what it always has been and what he chose that it should be—that of peacemaker and conciliator."

Shortly after Pius XII's death, an article in *The Jewish Newsletter* (New York, (October 20, 1958) expressed the uniqueness of his extraordinary contribution: "It is to the credit of Pope Pius XII that ... instead of preaching Christianity, as the Christian Churches had done for centuries, he and the churches practiced its principles and set an example by their acts and lives, as did the Founder of Christianity."

The only link the prisoners of war had to a voice of friendship was that of Pius XII through the Vatican Information Bureau. Their hope for the future was based on the interest expressed by the Pope, as he inspired and comforted them with the visits of his representatives.

In the Vatican, Pius XII maintained throughout the war not only a diplomatic network, but he also increased the number of Papal Guards from three hundred men in September 1943 to four thousand within nine months in order to save the lives of these Jews and others hunted by the Nazis.

Members of the Papal Guards protected the Vatican walls and the extraterritorial buildings, but the main reason for the increased number was to assist in hiding the identity of targeted victims, regardless of race or religion. The hunted were given Vatican identification and lived in the Vatican itself or in one of its extraterritorial buildings. When services were no longer needed at the end of the war, the Pope kept these endangered persons in the Papal Guards. Their work was to distribute food and clothing to the needy in Rome and its suburbs.

Pius XII was personally interested in the life of each individual brought to his attention. Young and old appealed to him for help in locating missing relatives. In order to correspond with the families of the prisoners, the Holy Father established the Vatican Information Bureau. Requests for information came from every country in the world. All received his attention. This was the only archive in the world completely dedicated to transmitting news to the families of prisoners of war.

I am convinced that Pius XII was a wise and saintly man. I truly believe that Pius XII did everything he could have done to foster peace and help all victims of war and oppression. There is great need to demolish the false interpretations of the so-called "silence" of Pope Pius XII that have circulated for half a century. Some critics "know not what they do."

Everyone understood Pius XII's reference to Jews. His thoughts were expressed clearly and emphatically. His style was that of a diplomat who deliberated over every word he uttered. He used trenchant terms to protest the atrocities: "the wrath of God," "acts which cry to God for vengeance," "woe to those who...oppress and torture the unarmed and the innocent." He expressed his concern for: "all victims of this war," "those expelled from their native land," "those who are suffering on account of nationality or race," "those threatened with extermination."

The Vatican was the one major refuge for thousands of persecuted people, and its Information Bureau was the sole means of communication available to prisoners of war and their families. In my book, *Pope Pius XII: Architect for Peace* (Paulist Press, Mahwah, NJ, 2000), I have tried to make clear the role of the Church in this period, to defend Pius XII's actions, and to make the truth known.

To set the record straight, the Catholic League for Religious and Civil Rights recently sponsored a full-page ad in *The New York Times* entitled "Was the Church Silent During the Holocaust?"

The ad provides the answer to that question by quoting from the 1941 *New York Times* Christmas editorial: "The voice of Pius XII is a lonely voice in the darkness enveloping Europe..." Editorial comments in *The New York Times* prove conclusively that Pius XII was not silent during the Holocaust as his current accusers shrilly maintain.

Vatican documents reveal that the Jewish community received tremendous help from Pius XII. He used his own personal funds to ransom Jews from the Nazis; his nuncios in Croatia, Romania and Hungary intervened—at their own peril—to stop deportation; he was in constant communication with German generals who sought to overthrow the Hitlerian regime. The Pope was playing a dangerous game and he knew it! The Pope's "silence" was a carefully crafted strategy to protect Jews and Catholics alike. Nazi reprisals continued.

The New York Times stated (August 13, 1943): "The arrests are linked with strong anti-Nazi and anti-war movements in the preponderantly Roman Catholic section of Germany, in which Catholic students as well as priests are said to be active." When the Catholic bishops sent a pastoral letter on February 21, 1943, that was read from all Catholic pulpits in the Netherlands, the newspaper quoted a portion of that letter (March 14, 1943): "In all the injustices that are now being committed, our sympathy goes out particularly to the youths who are being violently taken away from their parental homes. It goes out to the Catholic believers of Jewish origin and to those persecuted for their belief in religious freedom. ... The church does not wish to take sides in the conflict between States and people attempting to solve immense problems of national collaboration, but only as long as they respect divine law. With the mandate of Christ as guardian of Christian principles, it must not fail to proclaim inviolate the word of God, which is to obey Him rather than man."

The National Socialist Mayor of Rotterdam's response to the pastoral letter was also quoted in that same issue of the *New York Times*: "When the terrorism of the church widens its scope and calls for sabotage, as it did in these letters, the time has come for the party to react in an appropriate manner." Consequently, Jewish converts to Catholicism, including Saint Edith Stein, were rounded up and sent to the concentration camps; Jewish converts to Protestantism were left unharmed.

When Corinne C. Boggs was appointed U. S. ambassador to the Vatican, I was invited to a reception at her home in Rome. After she read *Yours Is a Precious Witness: Memoirs of Jews and Catholics in*

Wartime Italy, "Lindy" Boggs wrote (July 21, 1998): "I am truly inspired by your writings on Pope Pius XII. Your clear approach will serve as a great education tool for future historians, bring truth to the forefront and pay tribute to a great Pontiff who did all he could for humanity."

Among numerous letters of appreciation, the following reflects the sentiments of many readers: "Your letters—full of facts and devotion to the Church and one of her outstanding Shepherds—are a shining exception to what one reads in the media. To me, Pius XII is a Saint. I suppose we shouldn't be surprised when someone, as transparently saintly as Pius XII was, gets slandered by an ignorant and crass world. … Apparently things haven't changed much in 2000 years. And you are like one of those courageous women who stood by the cross when the others had fled. God bless you, and please keep up the very good work you are doing. With great admiration, Carroll McQuire (January 23, 1999)."

Chapter Twelve: Other Activities

**"...for she teaches temperance
and prudence, justice and courage"**
(Book of Wisdom, 8:7)

What prepared me for a career that included public speaking? I do not know how this developed. I only know that I did not take courses, or have private instruction and coaching. I simply accepted invitations whenever I was invited to speak. The first time was Mother's Day in 1950, when I delivered a Communion Breakfast talk for the Children of Mary in Torrington, CT. Since then, nationally and internationally, I have spoken countless times.

The topics I spoke on were as diverse as the groups I addressed: "The Blessed Virgin Mary" for many parish groups and societies; "Vocation Promotion to Religious Life" at gatherings for young ladies; literary, historical, or just general topics for numerous groups: National Italian American Foundation, Rotary, Kiwanis, Sons of Italy, Unico National, Israel America Foundation, and other national, civic or religious organizations throughout the United States and Europe. I also participated in programs on university campuses and at conferences and panels on Italian Literature.

Of course there were Bicentennial talks on Philip Mazzei and the American Revolution and, recently, lectures, TV, and radio interviews on the topic of *The Holocaust and Pope Pius XII*. It is impossible to recall the times I have spoken on radio and TV. Among these innumerable occasions, the more recent are: *Catholic Answers Live* which airs from California connecting with over fifty radio stations; *Religion on the Line* with Father Paul Keenan of the New York Archdiocese; *American Forum* on Family Radio hosted by former Ambassador to the Vatican, Ray Flynn; WWCM, *Al Kresta in the Morning* from Ann Arbor, MI; and other stations, locally and nationally (WXXI, ABC-TV, NBC, CBS, PBS, EWTN...).

I shall never forget what happened several years ago when Raymond Arroyo and the EWTN crew from Alabama came to Villa Walsh to interview me. I had also been asked to arrange interviews for several Polish survivors of the Holocaust. In fact, I am reminded about the EWTN visit every time I look around the Mazzei Center. To prepare for the taping, I organized my office so that the room would be cleared of all piles of papers. I stored them in large boxes and removed them from view.

As luck would have it, the EWTN-TV equipment could not fit in the Mazzei Center, so the crew scouted around for a new location. They settled for the beautifully-decorated concert hall of the nineteenth century Southern colonial mansion on top of the hill. Two segments for the EWTN program *The World Over* were accomplished and the crew was satisfied. Every day, however, as I work in the Mazzei Center, I see those boxes of papers that still need to be sorted out!

Months later I was invited to Alabama where segments were prepared on the Holocaust for the EWTN Johnette Benkovic two-part, two-hour program, *The Abundant Life* (November 9 and 16, 1999). Participants in this panel were: Bill Doino, a free lance historian and colleague of Robert Graham, S.J.; Liz Altham, contributing editor to *The Latin Mass* and *Sursum Corda* magazines; Jeffrey Rubin editor, *The American Life League* and *The Conservative Book Club*.

More recently Raymond Arroyo's special two-hour live program, *Pope Pius XII: The War Record*, was a great success and aired many times. I joined panelists Dr. Ronald Rychlak, professor of History at the University of Mississippi and Rabbi Marc Saperstein, professor of Jewish history and director of the program in Judaic Studies at George Washington University.

One of the panelists was from Rome, Father Peter Gumpel— relator for the cause of Pope Pius XII at the Vatican's Congregation for the Causes of the Saints. He is convinced that Pius XII was an extraordinary man who faced terrible situations with courage and great wisdom, and who was in his personal life an exemplary and great priest, bishop, cardinal and pope. Regarding the reason for the lengthy investigation, Father Gumpel explained that not only did Pius XII lead the Church as Pope for twenty years, but he had been Nuncio and Secretary of State for more than two decades previous.

It is unjust that false statements are being circulated by the media with regard to the cause for beatification of Pope Pius XII. Indeed some articles reduce the beatification of Pius XII to a political struggle and repeat the charges that he did not speak out to condemn the Nazis for their persecution of the Jews. This is not true.

On March 31, 2000, following the Israeli Papal visit, I was asked to appear on NBC's Channel 4 special forum *Journey to the Holy Land*. The focus of the discussion was on Pope John Paul II's visit to the Holy Land. Also appearing on the program were Father James Loughran, Director of the Ecumenical Commission of the Archdiocese of New York, Imam Izak El Pasha of the Malcom Shabazz Mosque, Rabbi David Woznica, Director of the Bronfman Center, of the 92nd Street Y, and Reverend Eileen Lindner, Associate General Secretary of the National Council of Churches. Other members of the panel were Abe Foxman of the Anti-Defamation League and Dr. Hani Awadallah of the Arab-American Association. Hosts were Chuck Scarborough, Lynda Baquero, Gabe Pressman and Ralph Penza.

During this hour-long town meeting held at the Y's Kaufman Concert Hall, located at 92nd Street and Lexington Avenue, I tried to set the record straight. I was able to defend Pope Pius XII and stress the Vatican documents, including the important papal decree on anti-Semitism issued on March 25, 1928, long before World War II.

Pope John Paul II's visit was a historic turning point that will promote better relations and understanding in the Jewish world. He fulfilled his spiritual pilgrimage to link the Old and New Testaments. In fact, the Israeli press became enthusiastic when the Pope visited the Memorial to the Holocaust in Yad Vashem. People learned about Christianity which in schools had been misinterpreted or eliminated. Now it is necessary to review the comments on Christianity in history books. The Pope asked that the spiritual message of the Bible be rediscovered and that the promises of Abraham and their fulfillment in Jesus Christ be acknowledged. Christians must be a bridge to reconciliation and recognize the great dignity of Jews and Muslims.

Pope John Paul II's interreligious services included Muslims, Palestinians, Israeli. He repeated that we are all sons and daughters of the same God. He spoke about brotherhood, love and peace among all groups in the Holy Land. Religion should never be used to justify violence. His message to the youth of today was "Be not afraid, have courage in faith, and preach the Ten Commandments and the Eight Beatitudes." He wanted all Catholics to re-kindle their faith in the Eucharist.

The pilgrim Pope was leading his people to conversion and repentance with the hope of preserving the Christian heritage and presence in the Holy Land. He spoke about love of God that translates into love of neighbor and is manifested by our actions. His message transcends all political aims. At Yad Vashem he prayed for unity, understanding, forgiveness. He invited all men and women to follow his example. He insisted that anti-Semitism is not condoned by the Catholic Church. The Pope's last visit in Jerusalem was to the "Wailing Wall," the western wall built by Herod to enclose the Temple's courtyard. It is a sacred place for Jews where they pray and weep in memory of the ancient splendor of Jerusalem and the Temple, once the center of all Jewish life, definitively destroyed in 70 A.D. by the Romans. They place small votive messages in the crevices of the slabs of stone.

Pope John Paul II's petition for forgiveness was the prayer he read in Rome on March 12, 2000—a commitment to genuine fraternity with the people of the Covenant. It was a very emotional moment: the Pontiff walked up to the Wall alone, prayed there for a few moments, and placed a piece of paper with his signature in one of the crevices. He then placed his right hand on the Wall, before blessing himself.

The Pope's final words were: "Only a world at peace, with justice for all, can avoid repeating the mistakes and terrible crimes of the past. Let us build a new future in which there will be no more anti-Jewish feeling among Christians or anti-Christian feeling among Jews." In his official response, Prime Minister Barak praised John Paul II, saying, "You have done more than anyone else to bring about the historic change in the attitude of the Church toward the Jewish people, and to dress the gaping wounds that festered over many bitter centuries."

Among this Pope's previous actions were: in 1979, a visit to the Auschwitz concentration camp near Krakow, in Poland; in 1990, he endorsed the Prague settlement that declared anti-Semitism a sin against God and humanity and one for which Christians should repent; in 1993, he announced full diplomatic relations with Israel. These actions and the heartfelt words at Yad Vashem have conforted many Jews. Although critics remain, there have been some wonderful expressions of gratitude.

Headlines (March 26, 2000) in Rome's Sunday edition of the newspaper *Avvenire* were: "Today I, an Elder Brother, Feel Like Wojtyla's Son. Over the Last Weeks, I Wished I Were a Christian."

Paolo Alazraki stated: "I am a Jew, but over the last weeks, I wish I had been a Christian. To have such a religious father, so majestic in his simplicity, so powerful in his humility, so wise in his strength to combat and overcome, with the gentleness and enormous force of faith, the resistances that he met within his 'circle' to the petition to 'forgive us,' first made to himself, then to his faithful, and finally to the entire world, and to his sublime words of strength and charity spoken in Palestine."

Alazraki emphasized that all this happened in Israel, land of Canaan, land of the Patriarchs and also land "of our deepest self, in the ancient roads of the salt and silk caravans, the birthplace of extraordinary civilizations. Those who forgive are not weak; those who ask forgiveness are strong. My Rabbis and a great part of Israeli Judaism have acted wrongly in not understanding, not interpreting, not rejoicing over this immense gesture of reconciliation which opens new, extraordinary possibilities in favor of mutual respect among peoples and, therefore, a better life for them and among themselves, and also greater economic development because it will allow, especially in the Middle East, but not only there, the freeing of those creative, mercantile and intellectual forces that for dozens of centuries have characterized the mind of Jews and Arabs."

All of the foregoing has "positive influences also for Europe," according to the Jewish writer. "This young, shaky but serene old man, who is conscious of the importance of his actions and the steps he is taking, reflected in his face, has sublimated, gone beyond, made the suspicious, uncomfortable postures of the Rabbis and Muftis, probably pressured by political authorities, look almost ridiculous. What did they want with the condemnation of Pius XII, the humiliation of their 'younger brothers'?"

The writer congratulates the Jewish people and Prime Minister Barak, "an angel of peace with a good face who has given the Holy Sepulcher as a 'present' to the Vatican." Behind this news, were five years of struggles and mutual recriminations over the administration of the Holy Places. "Praised be the Lord, whoever he is and wherever he is. Praised be this Pope," the writer states, overwhelmed with gratitude to the Holy Father, and not knowing how to thank him.

"Perhaps, giving him, but only for this Jubilee year, something of my religious being, which is what matters most to me in the world. This year, with my Jewish friends, I myself will try to meet Christians again, as they did during the first three centuries of this era, when they prayed together in the same synagogues and only after Constantine's reign, sadly, went on different roads.

"Dear Wojtyla, this is my gift for a year. And the promise to become a promoter of a huge forest of new trees, right there, on the border (which I hope will soon disappear forever) between Gaza and Israel, in your name, with our names, but also our hearts, engraved. What you have done for all is immense. Like faith, like love. Extraordinary things that are often lost, re-found, and lost again."

The writer ends his article: "This is my present for the Jubilee. I have no debts and no credits. Therefore, I can celebrate it worthily, in my deepest interior and with all Jews and Christians who have understood your gesture. So be it! So be it!"

As I remark on the distinguished individuals I have met recently, I realize how many names I have not mentioned of friends who were part of my life and the many activities that were an intimate part of my career over the past fifty years. Whenever, for example, Dr. Peter Sammartino required someone to fill a slot in one of the organizations he founded or merely sponsored, I was recruited.

The American Institute of Italian Studies, incorporated by the Board of Regents for and on behalf of the State of New York Education Department, was originally organized by Judge Edward D. Re, of Saint John's University. When he left for duties in Washington as chairman of the United States Customs Court, Peter Sammartino was made chairman of the board and I became president. Both the board of trustees and the board of advisors consisted of administrators, professors, businessmen, and writers—Ambassador John Volpe, Fairleigh S. Dickinson, Jr., Dr. Anne Paolucci, Archbishop Lydio Tomasi, Dr. Rose Basile Green, Joseph Muscarelle, Sr., Professor Filomena Peloro and others. Meetings were held at the Columbus Club in New York City for many years. Later the AIIS office was moved to the Philip Mazzei Center in Morristown, NJ.

Objectives of the AIIS included the fostering of an understanding of the Italian contribution to world literature; the development and dissemination of cultural information and materials concerning Italians and Italy for use in schools and organizations at all levels; and the publication of books on how Italy has contributed to the founding and contemporary history of the United States.

To understand the history of Walsh College one must go back to 1928, when the Religious Teachers Filippini founded a Normal School in Trenton, for the training of young women interested in becoming Sisters. It was relocated two years later when the Motherhouse was moved to Morristown, NJ. In 1948 the name was changed to Villa Walsh Junior College and subsequently shortened, in 1957, to Villa Walsh College. It was authorized in 1960 to award the Associate in Arts Degree.

But there was a decline in the number of women becoming members in the 1960s. When a change in administration of this non-profit, two-year institution of higher education took place (1966), I became president. I consulted Dr. Peter Sammartino, Chancellor of Fairleigh Dickinson University. He realized that it could no longer continue with its limited enrollment, and suggested that lay members be added to the Board of Trustees to try to save the college. It was renamed Walsh College in 1970.

Walsh College would now offer a non-sectarian program leading to the Associate in Arts Degree for young women who wished to begin their education in a junior college and transfer to a senior college for the Bachelor's Degree.

Carl Sandburg wrote: "One thing I know deep out of my time, youth when lighted and alive and given a sporting chance is strong for struggle and not afraid of any toils or punishments or dangers or deaths."

The Public Relations office began its recruitment for young women to benefit from the kind of education that would provide academic, cultural, spiritual and social experiences. Applicants with wholesome character traits, high motivation, a willingness to serve, and the quality of the student's previous performance were considered. They would join other young women interested in becoming Religious Teachers Filippini.

Moved by the idealism of young people, applicants found in Walsh College a program of service that included not only the theory of good works, but also the practice of good works among the less fortunate in nearby communities. Its doors were opened in September 1970 for women of all denominations. Twenty-five applicants were accepted.

Under Dr. Peter Sammartino's direction, the curriculum was revised to meet contemporary needs. The basic idea was to provide maximum flexibility in the curriculum for a program that would combine meaningful knowledge, with relevant experience, with dynamic citizenship, in order to attain a maturing personality.

Each student was obliged to take a six-credit course called *Persistent Problems of Living.* This was a seminar to be designed jointly each year by instructors and students. It was concerned with ecology and the responses of our economic system to the problems generated in such areas as: environmental pollution; population trends; food, nutrition and hunger. Included in the seminar were: the causes of poverty, urban housing and standards of living, crime control, the effect of esthetic standards on environment, the rationale for taxes. The role of the citizen in the community and the pursuit of the ideals of peace were also paramount throughout the discussions.

The curriculum also included independent reading programs styled on the British tutorial system; outside community service work in hospitals, child care, geriatric centers, and ghetto areas; a course in Western Civilization with emphasis on events that had a profound influence on the present day.

Students at Walsh College would study Pius XII's directives for modern woman. His call was for Catholic women to enter public life: "She must compete with man for the good of civic life" (October 21, 1945). Addressing the Federation of Italian Women, Pius XII stated: "There is no field of human activity that must remain closed to women (October 14, 1956). No Pope had spoken in this manner. His official pronouncements on the subject of womanhood are unprecedented.

Students at Walsh College were enthusiastic and the results were excellent. Financial support from the laity was available. Many friends offered their assistance. Licia Albanese, the renowned Italian opera star, gave a solo performance in Ninetta Hall auditorium and earned approximately $20,000. People like Mrs. Grace Dickinson became sponsors and donated generously toward our Endowment Fund. Among the board members were: Archbishop Thomas A. Boland, Dr. Peter Sammartino, Mrs. Alice Dreyfuss, Chairman of the Board of United Advertising Corporation, Mrs. Thelma Dear, Jr., and Mr. Arthur J. McGinnis, President of Simmons-Boardman Publishing Corporation. Everyone was stunned when the administration of the Religious Teachers Filippini voted to close Walsh College. I was heartbroken! Neither the lay members of the board of trustees nor I had been consulted about the decision to close the college.

After only one semester, how could the evaluation of a selected group of administrators be valid? I definitely did not agree. Walsh College had succeeded financially and educationally, yet the board of trustees had not been involved in the decision to close its doors. However, I reluctantly informed the board of trustees in writing

(March 10, 1971) and received their unanimous support and approval of my actions. Although the college had not been given a fair chance for survival, the board instructed me, representing them as president, not only to transfer its Endowment Fund to an irrevocable Trust for Educational Purposes, but also to cancel the College Work-Study Grant and other funds awarded by the United States Office of Education. I then immediately and successfully arranged for the transfer of students to other colleges.

Although saddened by the closing of Walsh College, I learned some valuable lessons. Misfortunes and mistakes help us grow and become better people. Change can benefit us. God can derive good from unexpected changes that occur in our lives. We must also learn to accept failures realistically as a part of life and philosophically make the best of them. No experience in life is ever wasted or bad if we learn from it and succeed in making the world a better place.

I also had beautiful memories of this innovative and educationally-sound experiment! The catalog alone represented years of experience donated by Sally Sammartino who had been director of admissions for Fairleigh Dickinson University for over a quarter of a century! Although disheartened, I continued teaching at Fairleigh Dickinson University and, with Sally and Peter Sammartino's encouragement, resumed research projects and other educational activities. They warmly supported all my future projects, including the Summer Institutes in Italy under the auspices of Fairleigh Dickinson University. Students received six undergraduate credits. They were held in different Italian cities: Rome, Salerno, Tivoli. During the six-weeks course in language and culture, we visited the main cities of Italy on weekends.

Unfortunately, we lived in a "pensione" on Via Lombardia in Rome. These accommodations did not guarantee water at all times. Classes were held in a building conveniently located near the well-known Hotel Excelsior. When the lack of water at the "pensione" posed a problem, students and faculty would saunter into the lobby in small groups and nonchalantly head for the bathroom where water was always available.

The Salerno area "pensione" had small balconies which the students enjoyed. However, one heavily-built student accidentally broke the lounging chair when he sat on it. Although I knew it could be easily repaired, before our departure I asked the proprietor what he thought I should pay. He answered, "Well, I'll have to replace that chair with a new one!" "Fine," I said, "what is the price?" When he mentioned an exorbitant amount, I responded, "Oh, in that case, the chair is mine. I'm sure it can be repaired." This took the proprietor by surprise. Obviously, he expected to have the chair as a bonus. Instead, I gave it to a young Italian boy who said he would make good use of it. The last FDU summer group was located in Tivoli near the famous Roman ruins and Villa D'Este, with its beautiful fountains and gardens.

Students came from different parts of the United States and returned home with friendships and knowledge that come not from books but from interacting with people abroad. They not only studied and were challenged to speak the language, but they visited museums and monuments in Rome, Naples, Florence, Siena, Lucca, Venice. Among other dignitaries, they were privileged to see the Pope and, while touring the American Embassy (former palace of Italy's Queen Margherita), they were greeted by American ambassadors to Italy John Volpe, Richard Gardner, or Maxwell Rabb.

These FDU Institutes were followed by the establishment of Corfinio College-on-Wheels. (See Chapter Eight.) An anthropological approach was used in this innovative program—a program structured to take students to nearby towns and cities where they would learn, through observations and interviews, about the lives of other people, their aspirations and their problems. Materials for use in the culture and language courses were developed to provide insights into the nature of Italian life styles and gain new perspectives in the context of the social services and international trade and business. Language proficiency was of primary importance.

One summer while walking in Rome to make arrangements for the students' arrival, I fell on the sidewalk. With my leg in a cast, I met the group at the Leonardo da Vinci Airport in Rome and greeted them while sitting in a wheelchair. The following weeks we toured Italy as usual, with the added attraction that I was often in the arms of strong, young men who transported me up and down stairs, in and out of classrooms, to and from the "Pulmino" (Corfinio Scuolabus), until the cast was removed in Florence in Santa Maria Novella Hospital where Philip Mazzei himself—the subject of so many of my endeavors—was a resident surgery student in 1747!

Carmen Prezioso, chairman of the Language Department of Princeton High School, is worthy of his family name, "precious." An instructor from the first to the last session of Corfinio College, he was friend and guide to all the students. Each summer he helped develop Corfinio College into a unique, unforgettable program. Nothing was too difficult for him to accomplish with his friend Edward Golda of Union College, Grace Gaetani of FDU, and several other instructors who accompanied the group. Students and staff appreciated their guidance, culture, and dedication.

As director of activities, Carmen Prezioso's responsibility was to interact with students after classes were dismissed each day, and to encourage them to mingle with the local residents. Occasionally there were a few problems. One student was smitten by the baker's son who offered her a ring which she wore with pride. Carmen thought that the young girl needed a little fatherly advice. During a very hot day in June, while walking in the Corfinio piazza where the bakery was located, he invited her into the bakery and said: "My dear, if you were to marry this person, this is where you would be spending most of your time, making bread, cooking and taking care of children. Is this what you want?"

Wherever she went this young lady seemed to attract young men. They followed her on bikes, motorcycles, cars. Carmen told me about the problem. I gently admonished her and said: "My dear, you seem to attract too many admirers. I'm afraid for your safety. Since you have a grandmother in Italy, I called her and suggested that you visit her. Your grandmother is delighted to have you continue your study of Italian with her." Perhaps tired of so much attention, the young girl consented and the problem disappeared.

We offered the students many experiences. While in Naples we visited "La Certosa di San Martino"—a museum that had a world-famous collection of many historic and artistic life-size nativity scenes. When we arrived, however, there was a large sign at the gate: Chiusura Estiva! (Closed for the summer!). I desperately tried to attract attention, but there was no one in sight. Disappointed, I roamed from door to door, trying to get help. When I noticed a large church bell in the courtyard, I decided to ring it. Suddenly, a worker appeared, informing me that no visitors were permitted because of repairs. I then asked to speak to the person in charge of the museum. A few minutes later a kind-looking gentle monk appeared. I explained that these students had traveled many miles to see the museum and could not return next year, so would he please make an exception. Not only did he grant permission, but he personally gave us a guided tour.

We started the second year of Corfinio College with a bang! Italy was recovering from the 1984 earthquake. We saw evidence of it as we traveled by bus from Fiumicino Airport to Popoli, our new residence. Families whose homes were destroyed were temporarily occupying the upper third of the hotel. We were very tired the first night so we retired early. About 10:30 p.m., there was a strange sound and many students found themselves in the middle of the room as the beds shifted. So did I. We were indeed experiencing an earthquake. The tenants on the third floor were screaming. When I realized I was not dreaming, I rushed to the students in my robe and told them to proceed to the lobby. The proprietors, accustomed to these tremors, explained that there was nothing to fear and, shortly after, advised us to go to bed.

Our first or last stop was always in Rome where we were right at home, living in the "pensione" staffed by the Religious Teachers Filippini. We were within walking distance of the Vatican and always arrived early for the Papal Audience. When the gates were opened by the Swiss Guards, the entire group of students and faculty would run to the auditorium. I usually had a special place and the privilege of speaking to the Holy Father as I presented one of my books with a small monetary offering from the group. Often some students had the opportunity to kiss the Pope's ring and talk with him while the photographers took pictures. That very afternoon the photographs would be delivered to the "pensione" and the students were then able to order copies. What excitement and joy these Corfinio College students experienced when they examined the photographs showing some of them actually touching the Pope!

There were other occasions that neither I nor the students will ever forget. Once, en route to the airport in Milan, we traveled from Venice by train. We were located in the last trains because seats could not be reserved elsewhere. As usual before our departure, students had additional packages and gifts with them. The thought of losing students or luggage haunted me. My instructions were for them to remain on the platform upon arrival in Milan, until I could hire a porter. But none were available. As my frustration grew, I desperately realized I had to find a solution to arrive on time for our plane. So I literally ran toward the train station, hailed a porter driving a rickshaw-type, powered vehicle with about eight wagons attached for luggage. He had a kind face and was sympathetic when I told him we were Americans in need of help.

Pleading for assistance, I explained my predicament about getting the entire group and their luggage to the airport. I hopped on, not realizing that the seat accommodated only one human being, and found myself half seated on the man's lap. I could not jump off without breaking some bones because the vehicle had started to move toward the students at the very end of the platform. It was a sight to behold, as I hung on for dear life to the driver who had not even noticed my embarrassment. As we approached, the students began cheering, laughing, and screaming to their heart's content, sorry that their cameras were packed in their suitcases. We all followed the vehicle to the bus. I compensated the driver generously and was at peace only when the group of about thirty students and teachers finally boarded the airplane for New York!

I also recall in this regard Geoff Hannauer, a high school graduate, who had no intention of going to college. Owing to his experience in Italy, he eventually went to Oberlin College and then pursued a major in Italian at Middlebury College. The following letter to me is revealing: "Images of last summer in Italy have kept me warm during the often bitter cold months in northern Ohio. Thought of the Tuscan countryside in full bloom or a sun-drenched Saint Peter's Square distract me from my studies almost daily, and I can only hope that my memories will stay as vivid for years to come. ...

"The program left me with a passion for Italy, its culture and of course its language that I know will stay with me forever. I felt warmly welcomed to what was for me in an unknown country and I relished every day, every new city and town, every plate of pasta and drop of Chianti. Perhaps I've never said that as often as I should have, for which I'm sorry. I know now that had I gone to Italy on my own as I had originally planned, my experiences would never have been so rich nor my desire to return and continue my studies so strong.

"Many Corfinio College alumni share these feelings. While some students were successful with books and quizzes, others were successful on the streets in everyday life, learning Italian culture first hand and, after only a few weeks, had acquired the ability to truly take a bite out of Italian life in action. Watching David and Tony, in broken but effective Italian, haggle with a "fruttivendolo" for a pair of bananas, was for me a sign of success. Or seeing Richard tell a particularly rude waiter that he understood and didn't appreciate that nasty remark about Americans... and get an apology, indicated success.

"The program is unique in its richness and left deep impressions on everyone involved. I assure you, no one came home unchanged. It is my humble opinion that the program was overall, greatly successful. May you open the eyes of college students to the beauties and wonders of Italian culture and history for many generations."

Indeed, the FDU Summer Institutes developed into a special program incorporated as Corfinio College, that became a non-profit, non-sectarian co-educational program in Association with Edison College of NJ, offering seven undergraduate credits which were banked in Thomas Edison College in Trenton and transferrable to any other college in the United States. Eligible applicants included seniors in high school, college students, as well as older persons interested in exploring the Italian language and culture. In addition to daily language study, Corfinio College shifted locations to five different regions in a six-week period, thereby offering students/teachers wider living knowledge of Italy, its customs, its art, and its people.

The 1988 session included twenty-five students from eight states and nine different universities. It began as usual in Corfinio (the center of national unity in 90 B.C., when the inhabitants rebelled against Rome and formed a separate state called Italica). In this town, students examined the hidden treasures from its prehistoric origins up through the era of the glorious Roman Republic. It was in Corfinio that the term "Italia" was first used. A large bronze plaque found on the ruins of the main road as one enters Corfinio narrates its history.

Aside from visiting the usual sites in the Abruzzo Region—Corfinio, Sulmona, l'Aquila, Scanno, Popoli—there were special trips to Pescara and Capestrano where students visited the "Scriptorium," a library stacked with miniature scriptures, examples of the first publications of the Gutenberg press, papal bulls and epistles from the fourteenth century.

Sessions in Florence were conducted in conjunction with Campus in Tuscany, a service organization directed by Sergio Pezzati and sponsored by the "Associazione Filippo Mazzei." A former professor of Berkeley University delivered a conference on the Renaissance and students reviewed a film, "The Florentine Experience." Another interesting class was a cooking lesson given at an excellent restaurant in the hills of Fiesole. The chef and his wife prepared a menu with the help of the students. While in Tuscany, two trips—to Lucca and Siena—were added to the program. Students were received at the Mayor's office and then invited to a reception. A tour included a tunnel through which Dante once walked and a visit to the top of a tower where vegetation and a large tree thrived. In Florence they visited the Uffizi Gallery, the Accademia delle Belle Arti, the Medici Palaces, the Duomo, Santa Croce, etc.

In Prato, the president of the Bank, Dr. Silvano Bambagioni, invited the students to visit the museum and personally gave a tour of the thirteenth-century Cathedral of Prato. One summer, during our annual visit to Poggio a Caiano, Philip Mazzei's birthplace, there was a theatrical performance at the Villa Medici. For this production of Thomas Mann's "Fiorenza," the actors were Arnold Foa as Lorenzo il Magnifico and Virginio Gazzola as Savonarola. This live performance was being filmed for Italian Television.

In Poggio a Caiano there was also a private tour of the palace, dinner, and a preview of the Philip Mazzei documentary (which has been shown in the United States), followed by a discussion with its producer, Massimo Becattini. I might add that from the beginning of the project, efforts to produce a film had not been lacking. In fact there were several attempts made by the Philip Mazzei Foundation, but none of them succeeded in obtaining sufficient funding. However, the project had considerable loss of funds because of several seemingly well-meaning directors whose interest, however, was undoubtedly personal gain.

En route to Venice students always stopped in Padova to visit the Saint Anthony Basilica; and, not far from there, to view the Giotto paintings in the famous Scrovigni Chapel. In Venice there was participation in the fantastic Feast of the Redeemer, with fireworks illuminating the Grand Canal on the Piazza San Marco during a sleepless night. From Rome, students traveled for a weekend in Naples and, later in small groups, visited Capri, Pompei, and the Vesuvius.

Perhaps the January 1989 news release in *Il Popolo Italiano* best describes how students felt about Italy. "Corfinio College Alumni gathered together in the Morristown administrative office to celebrate its sixth anniversary and reminisced in a typical Italian fashion: they ate, talked, laughed, and saw slide pictures of the wonders they had mutually experienced, especially in the cities of Rome, Florence, and Venice.

"Who can ever forget the welcome each class enjoyed from young Italians with names like Giovanni and Massimo and Antonio? And how about the hotel in Popoli with 'exquisite' local fare in a home-like setting, complete with babies and toddlers? Students remembered the Fourth of July festas with Achille and his old (now new) restaurant. Some still recalled the *al fresco* dinners prepared annually by the townspeople of Poggio-a-Caiano, the birthplace of Philip Mazzei, when an escort of police cars and the mayor in full regalia greeted them.

"Perhaps their strongest memories were the private interviews with Ambassador Maxwell Rabb in the American Embassy in Rome and with Pope John Paul II in Saint Peter's Square where they had special seats, photographs, and even the opportunity to chat with him. These students became American ambassadors and citizens of a larger world—a world where art and beauty and friendly communication became more than mere words. They admit it was difficult to return to the United States the same person. Indeed, many times it was just difficult to return.

"Corfinio College has left its imprint on each one fortunate enough to have participated in its unique program. To continue this rich tradition and give to others what they have been granted—an opportunity to experience the Italian culture in an intimate way and change the way they look at the world—Corfinio College Alumni Association has formed various committees...."

Another student, Margareta von Grote, wrote an article for a Florida newspaper: "No day goes by that I do not reminisce about the wonderful trip to Italy, which was filled with memories I shall treasure forever! ...The course for me, as well as for the other participants, deepened my intense love for Italy, its language and its people. The Pope actually talked with us and held our hands! Being in the Eternal City was truly a marvelous experience. Imagine, too, walking among the ruins of the Forum, traveling back into history down the Via Appia Antica, descending into the labyrinth of the Catacombs, and being able to attend *Lucia di Lammermoor* by Gaetano Donizetti (1797-1848) under the clear, starlit sky of Rome at the Baths of Caracalla. It is impossible to describe in detail all the wonderful places we were able to visit..." Unfortunately, the Corfinio College project, too, came to an end.

But there was always some new project to initiate. Frank Visceglia, benefactor of the Religious Teachers Filippini, donated funds for a group of Sisters to visit Italy. Thus began a ten-year project. This was to be a cultural and educational experience. Sister Frances Lauretti, Provincial Superior, decided that there would be a lottery and the Sisters who won would have expenses paid while others could also join by providing their own funds. I was asked to be the official guide in Italy. Each summer for approximately two-weeks, I directed a pilgrimage that included not only religious, but also lay people interested in joining the group.

Every year the pilgrimage began in Rome with an unforgettable papal audience, continued in Florence, and ended in Venice, with optional side trips. One of the highlights of each pilgrimage was a visit to honor our founders, Saint Lucy Filippini in Montefiascone and Cardinal Marcantonio Barbarigo in Venice.

In Tarquinia we visited the house where Saint Lucy was born in 1672, and the surrounding towns of Montefiascone, Viterbo, Grotte di Castro, and others where she walked the streets or rode a donkey to visit the schools she established for young ladies. Everywhere she would also gather the women and accompany them to church for meditation and prayer services.

In Montefiascone we attended the Eucharistic Liturgy at St. Lucy's crypt in the Basilica of Santa Margherita and the pastor gave us a tour of the priceless treasures and frescos. As guests of the Sisters, we visited the beautiful chapel where her death took place (March 25, 1732—the year George Washington was born). The chapel had been her bedroom and we were able to see her relics, prayer books, letters, etc., as well as those of Cardinal Barbarigo.

Saint Lucy would walk miles to visit the shrine of *Nostra Signora della Quercia* (Our Lady of the Oak Tree) and we always joined her in spirit on our pilgrimage. The ceiling of this church is beautifullly decorated with gold that was brought back by Christopher Columbus on one of his voyages to America. At the side of the sanctuary is a painting of Saint Lucy and other saints praying to Our Lady. The pastor explained: "The people of the town considered the Virgin their special protector and placed her picture in an oak tree. On two occasions the neighboring townspeople stole the painting and carrried it off to their towns. Both times the picture miraculously returned."

The people then built a church around the oak tree enclosed as part of the altar. The picture and the oak can be seen through a glass frame above the tabernacle. We were privileged to climb the steps and actually touch the relics. There, too, are remains of bombs that fell on Viterbo during World War II. Miraculously, no one was killed. Even hundreds of young men who served in the Italian army returned home safely, thanks to Our Lady of the Oak Tree.

In Venice we followed the footsteps of Cardinal Marcantonio Barbarigo. We visited the "palazzo"—now divided into apartments—where he was born and where the Barbarigo family lived for centuries. One must cross the bridge called "Ponte Barbarigo" that leads to the house. A large plaque gives its history.

Marcantonio was baptized in the Church of the Anzolo Raphael (Archangel Raphael), where we found the record of his baptism. A special side chapel with the original marble baptismal font was beautifully decorated. The Church has many treasured paintings by the Venetian masters. The pastor offered the Eucharistic Liturgy on the same altar no doubt used by Marcantonio who prayed the Holy Office with the priests of the parish, whenever he returned to Venice. Later the sacristan gave us a tour of the archives. He showed us the ancient missals with miniature paintings and unlocked closets containing ancient vestments, a chalice from the fifteenth-century and a crucifix from the thirteenth-century—precious items that Cardinal Barbarigo may have used.

These travels and experiences enriched the lives of many participants. Several students kept a diary! Sister Margaret Geraghty's account, which was mailed to the United States each day, kept the Sisters in Morristown, NJ, informed about what happened during the pilgrimage! An excerpt follows (July 8, 1992): "We arrived in Florence at about 9 a.m. after a pleasant ride north on the Autostrada. The weather was pleasant; the scenery, beautiful. We checked in at the pensione of the Sisters of the Assumption, conveniently located in the center of Florence. We have large comfortable rooms and bath. The food is good.

"Our first visit was to the Baptistry and the Duomo which are the great architectural marvels of Florence. As we returned for dinner, we went to the Church of the Annunciation, which is adorned with gold in quantity that boggles the mind; and the variety of the designs and the scenes depicted are difficult to grasp.

"After dinner everyone tried to solve the maze of the narrow, twisting and curving streets. For all their sophisticated modern conveniences, these cities are basically medieval; there is no way to alter the rock foundations and the structures carved out of them. Close your eyes to the cars and the clothing of the people and you are in the very Florence of Dante and his contemporaries. Through the ages the people have kept the flora—trees, bushes, flowers, in abundance. And, of course, that keeps the birds. All day long they fly and sing. So, in a bustling city you have a sense of the countryside. Yet, everything they use, especially electricity, is adapted to enrich and beautify their lives. Italy knows the balance of ecology and stays nature-friendly in the midst of technological progress."

Filippini pilgrimages in Italy winded down toward the end of the Second Millennium. So many expressions of gratitude came from the traveling group. Sister Santa Priolo was inspired to write a touching poem, *Symphonic Giftedness*:

Every note leaps in pure delight
Projecting pure serenity,
Radiating divine light.

   Receptive to eternal contemplation
   Mysteries unfold in simple cadenzas,
   As mysterious fugues cascade down...

Musical reverberations linger on
In rhythmic circles like sparkling stars
And thundering cloud bursts.

Contrary motion progressing toward perfection
Rejoicing in blissful contemplation,
Bringing infinite gratitude to the Master Musician.

Chapter Thirteen: Epilogue

> **"Would that I were in every corner of the earth**
> **to cry out everywhere and plead with all peoples**
> **of every sex, age, and condition: 'Love God, Love God'!"**
> *(St. Lucy Filippini)*

Historically, religious communities have been strengthened by overcoming social discrimination and other difficulties as they settled in the New World. They have helped in welcoming waves of European immigrants, encouraging their rich heritage, strengthening their courage and determination to act in a Christian manner collectively and individually. Indeed, women religious continue to pass on special traditions to others in the secular world at a time when technology overwhelms so many aspects of life. Their loving and faithful service should inspire others to join them in the fields of education, health care, social work and prayer ministry. I believe I was called to follow in the footsteps of Saint Lucy Filippini. Through self-discipline, contemplation, simplicity of life, dedication to others and daily prayer, I believe that I have achieved spiritual maturity

I committed myself to the service of the Church. While promoting the interests of the Church and the Italian-American community, I have listened to my heart, followed my dreams, overcome obstacles. And, as I serve humanity, I pray that I shall continue to give glory to God. Currently, my mission—the defense of Pope Pius XII—is a challenge that I embrace wholeheartedly.

"Sister Margherita does not fit the secular stereotype of the traditional nun," wrote Kenneth Baker, S.J., in *Homiletic & Pastoral Review* (April 2000). He added: "In her article, *The Nun Versus the Spin Master,* Sister Margherita Marchione points out the lies and errors about Pope Pius XII in John Cornwell's recent book entitled, *Hitler's Pope: The Secret History of Pius XII.*"

My life has been closely intertwined with so many people who have supported me. I am deeply indebted to my family, religious community and friends the world over. While the world prides itself by shocking the public with outrageous and suggestive displays in movies, videos, and magazines, the black habit I wear proclaims Christian morality and love of God and neighbor.

David and Alice Jurist are among my cherished friends. Several years ago, when I completed my research on Pope Pius XII, I consulted David, the president of Tanagraphics, Inc. As I handed him my manuscript, I explained that I was looking for a publisher. He took the copy and, in a few days, returned with bound copies for distribution to potential publishers. Soon after, Paulist Press sent me a contract. I am proud of David Jurist's "Foreword" in *Yours Is a Precious Witness: Memoirs of Jews and Catholics in Wartime Italy.* It appeared also in the Italian translation, *Pio XII e gli ebrei.* The following year I showed him *Pius XII: Architect for Peace.* No explanation was needed. Paulist Press accepted this manuscript, too.

For years David has been president of *The Tomorrows Children's Fund for Youngsters with Cancer.* Each year these children are guests at his home in Mendam, NJ., for a wonderful, unforgettable party. On May 16, 2000, I attended the dedication of a new building—The David Joseph Jurist Research Center for *Tomorrows Children.* Through his efforts, the Hackensack University Medical Center has been transformed into a leading national and international research authority. David Jurist will be remembered by me and many other people for his philantropy and love.

There are many other personal friends, whose love cannot be forgotten, like Shirley and Luke Lukawitz, who registered at Walsh College for evening classes in Italian in 1970. Not only have they continued their association with Villa Walsh, but recently they have become exceptional benefactors. Their generosity toward the Religious Teachers Filippini will be remembered *in perpetuum.*

Several years ago, Val Della Pello, a dear friend and benefactor, called me about his son who was to be married, but had not yet received the Sacrament of Confirmation. Because of his work, Vincent could not attend evening classes as requested by his pastor. This was a serious problem. Plans had been made for the wedding. His dad appealed to me. I contacted the pastor and arranged to assume responsibility for the young man's instruction.

Vincent came regularly early mornings, and was soon prepared to be confirmed, thanks to Sister Josephine Cucuzzella, who agreed to instruct him. He was very serious about becoming a good Catholic and studied diligently. I was honored when he asked me to be his sponsor. I walked with him to the altar at Assumption Church in Morristown. Bishop Rodimer was surprised to see me and looked at me perplexed, as if to say, "What in the world are you doing here?" I smiled and said, "Your Excellency, I'm Vincent's godmother!"

Among so many life-long friends I must mention Professor Filomena Peloro for whose constant support as a colleague, I will always be grateful. She has genuinely assisted me in my endeavors during the past fifty years. And it was she who introduced me to a new friend, Ralph M. Cestone, to whom I am deeply indebted for his generosity toward my defense of Pope Pius XII.

At Villa Walsh, among my administrative duties as treasurer, I cannot fail to mention the responsibility for the department of building maintenance. This was accomplished with the help of Sister Helen Sholander and her assistant, Sister Geraldine Frisk.

Sister Helen was an elementary school teacher for many years in New Jersey. After working as a missionary in Brazil and, subsequently, in Rome, Italy, at my request she returned to Villa Walsh as my assistant. While attending classes at the Morris County Vocational Technical School, she learned about landscaping, small engines, cars and boilers. When she received the Black Seal Fireman's License, local newspapers and NBC's Channel 4, celebrated the event, calling it "a mechanical miracle."

For years Sister Helen has taken care of the nitty-gritty associated with maintenance at Villa Walsh. Her task has been to supervise the personnel and keep the many vehicles, furnaces, and equipment in working condition. Her expertise is such that she can compete with any engineer. Only with Sister Helen's assistance has my task been possible.

Another person to whom I am indebted is Sister Filomena Di Carlo who has been my secretary from the early 1970s. She has participated faithfully and intelligently in my work and daily struggles at Villa Walsh. The services of these Sisters are priceless.

Among my fondest memories traveling in Europe was the day I joined Lady Irene and Lord Charles Forte for the family Christmas dinner in their lovely home at 86 Park Lane in London. It was wonderful to be their guest and experience the hospitality of a typical Italian family that had not abandoned its Italian roots. The meal was prepared by Lady Forte and everyone exchanged gifts. It brought back childhood memories of Christmas in Little Ferry.

I first met Lady and Lord Forte at a New York reception in their honor hosted by Peter and Sally Sammartino. Knighted by the Queen of England, Lord Forte was founder of the Trusthouse Forte Hotels, and President of the Italian Chamber of Commerce in the United Kingdom. He was also Consul General in London for the Republic of San Marino.

On another occasion the Forte family invited me and my dear friend, Sister Mary Paglia, to London. We were given the best suite in the Gouvernor Hotel, surrounded with such luxury that I questioned, "Is this area for all the people on the floor?" The answer was, "No, indeed, this is part of your suite." In fact, we were so embarrassed to accept all the courtesy extended to us, that we decided to use the coffeeshop instead of the dining room for our meals.

Insisting that his poem entitled, *The Spirit You Gave*, appear in the September 13, 1997 souvenir booklet honoring me, Sy Inwentarz, a former FDU student, expressed his sentiments:

> We came to you with little knowledge
> Of what the world could be,
> You embraced us with the joy of learning;
> A bouquet that set us free.
> Now these many years have passed,

The seed, the minds you cast.
When challenge stands before our eyes,
And we fail, but continue to try.
The towers we build and the progress we made,
Started with you and the spirit you gave.
On behalf of your students
For the contribution you made
To their joy of learning,
Thank you, Sister Margherita.

Yes, teaching was a rewarding experience in my life. I encouraged students to learn that in the eyes of God nothing else counts except honest effort and generous motives and that, with divine grace, success is within the grasp of everyone. Throughout my life's tasks, trials, joys or temptations, I have always enjoyed the thrill of happiness, free from all conditioning by others. I have truly welcomed into my life everyone indiscriminately and, irrespective of what people think, I have been capable of enjoying the company of man or woman, young or old, high or low, rich or poor, learned or illiterate, virtuous or sinful.

I firmly believe that love of God translates into love of neighbor and is manifested by our actions. The hope of society lies with those who do not rest while there is good to be done or suffering to be relieved. The Church is the champion of the sanctity of the home, where one finds the great bond uniting heaven and earth —the precious and priceless gift of faith.

My prayer is that God grant all—Jews, Protestants, Muslims, Catholics—the grace to respond to His call to be our best selves for the sake of the generation growing up and their children and their children's children.

Only where Christian families are established will there be a mother-country that generates noble men and holy women. I am grateful to God for having had a sound Catholic philosophy of life. I pay tribute to my parents whose steadfast faith, dauntless courage, and selfless dedication empowered me as a child. Nothing has ever weakened my faith, nothing has ever lessened my courage to be involved, nothing has ever dimmed my awareness of the need for wholesome family living.

My parents had faith in the true values that help Americans sustain the spiritual fabric of America—the America as it was, is, and, we hope and pray, will forever be. For faith and truth and wisdom are not features typical of any one age, nor do they belong exclusively to any one country or group of human beings. They are transtemporal, beyond time; they are at home wherever there is a human being who wishes to do good; they are lasting, changeless, universal. The *Book of Wisdom* (8:7) clearly reminds us of the virtues required of everyone: "...for she teaches temperance and prudence, justice and courage."

I take pride in my heritage. This makes me no less American. I have helped convey the highlights of Italian culture and improve the uninformed image of the Italian immigrants who, like my parents, possessed the will, the personality, the vision that helped make the United States an enviable country. These immigrants brought with them a spiritual element that we, their children and grandchildren, have imbibed. It is for us to accept the challenge, fulfill their dreams, respect their wisdom and protect our freedom.

Above all, my gratitude goes to our heavenly Father, whose light has illuminated and still illumines my life. Each day His light shines forth more radiantly than ever. Each day I bask in the beauty of Villa Walsh with the same enthusiasm I had on the day I arrived in 1935, in a setting made lovely by vast expanses of lawn, by rolling hills and wooded countryside, by many devotional shrines; a setting unbounded except for the sky that speaks of God's love.

Here I contemplate His love, immersed in mother nature on Tower Hill, bursting with the vitality of teenagers in the sportsfield, the crocus and daffodils and blossoms of hundreds of trees announcing the coming of new life, as well as the companionship of wonderful Sisters in Christ Jesus, our Lord and Master.

Here, too, I delight in the unforgettable sunrise and sunset, the bubbling and laughter of neighbors' children sliding down the snow-capped hills, the amazing deer and colorful birds chirping and singing, the Canadian geese and the wild turkey, the squirrels, chipmunks and cottontails competing with one another midst indescribable sights and sounds.

My memories of the twentieth-century are indeed wonderful. I was privileged to serve God for seventy years. I rejoice as He continues to show His mercy and goodness. My family, colleagues, and friends were always at my side with many acts of kindness, concern and love. Difficulties along the way were balanced by surprises as I received recognition and awards for my work. My life was a sheltered one, yet I had the exposure that enriched it, enabled me to become more compassionate, and allowed me to fulfill my dreams. God chose me to serve others as a teacher, an administrator, a writer.

For my daily prayer, I repeat the words of Mary, our heavenly Mother: *Magnificat anima mea!* My soul proclaims the greatness of the Lord! (Luke 1:46-55), as well as the *Shemà Israel's* call to response and commitment (Deuteronomy 6:4-7): "Hear, O Israel! The Lord is our God, the Lord alone! Therefore, you shall love the Lord, your God, with all your heart, and with all your soul, and with all your strength. Take to heart the words which I enjoin on you today... ."

May God increase in each of us the wisdom to promote dialogue and mutual respect as we seek the ideal of one world with *love* for one another, with *hope* in the integrity of future generations, and with *faith* in the Almighty Father of us all.

Books by Margherita Marchione

Clemente Rebora:

L'imagine tesa, Edizioni di Storia e Letteratura, Rome, 1960, 300pp.;
   reprinted and enlarged, 1974, 410pp.
Lettere, Vol. I, Edizioni di Storia e Letteratura, Rome, 1976, 680pp.;
   Vol. II, 1982, 450pp.
Clemente Rebora, Twayne's World Author Series, Twayne Publishers,
   1979, Boston, 183pp.

Correspondence of Giovanni Boine:

Carteggio Giovanni Boine-Giuseppe Prezzolini (1908-1915), Vol. I,
   Edizioni di Storia e Letteratura, 1971, Rome, 264pp.; reprinted, 1981.
Giovanni Boine-Emilio Cecchi (1911-1917), Vol. II, 1972, 233pp.;
   reprinted, 1982.
Giovanni Boine-Amici del "Rinnovamento" Tome 1 (1905-1910);
   Tome 2 (1911-1917), Vol. III, 1977, 1130pp.
Giovanni Boine-Amici de "La Voce" (1904-1917), Vol. IV, 1979, 690pp.

Philip Mazzei:

Philip Mazzei: Jefferson's "Zealous Whig," American Institute of Italian
   Studies, Morristown, NJ, 1975, 352pp.
Philip Mazzei: My Life and Wanderings, American Institute of Italian
   Studies, Morristown, NJ, 1980, 437pp.
*Philip Mazzei: The Comprehensive Microform Edition of His Papers, 1730-
   1816,* nine reels and clothound Guide and Index, Kraus International
   Publications, 1982, 172pp.

Philip Mazzei: Selected Writings and Correspondence, Cassa di Risparmi e
    Depositi, Prato, 1983, Vol. I - *Virginia's Agent during the American
    Revolution,* XLVIII, 585pp.; Vol. II - *Agent for the King of Poland
    during the French Revolution,* 802pp.; Vol. III - *World Citizen,* 623pp.
Filippo Mazzei: Scritti Scelti e Lettere, Volumes I, II, III (Italian
    Edition, same as above, 1984).
The Constitutional Society of 1784, Center for Mazzei Studies, Morristown,
    NJ, 1984, 49pp.
Istruzioni per essere liberi ed eguali, Cisalpino-Gogliardica, Milan,
    1984, 160pp.
Philip Mazzei: World Citizen (Jefferson's "Zealous Whig"), University
    Press of America, Lanham, MD, 1994, 158pp.
*The Adventurous Life of Philip Mazzei - La vita avventurosa di Filippo
    Mazzei* (bilingual), University Press of America, Lanham, MD, 1995,
    235pp.

Giuseppe Prezzolini:

Giuseppe Prezzolini: Un secolo di attività, Rusconi, Milan, 1982,
    160pp.
Carteggio Cesare Angelini-Giuseppe Prezzolini, Edizioni di Storia e
    Letteratura, Rome, 1982, 394pp.
Giuseppe Prezzolini: L'Ombra di Dio, Rusconi, Milan, 1984, 200pp.
Incontriamo Prezzolini, Editrice la Scuola, Brescia, 1985, 210pp.
Giuseppe Prezzolini: Lettere a Suor Margherita (1956-1982).
    Introduction by Margherita Marchione, edited by Claudio Quarantotto,
    Edizioni di Storia e Letteratura, Rome, 1991, XXXIV-378pp.
Carteggio Giovanni Abbo-Giuseppe Prezzolini, Edizioni di Storia e
    Letteratura, Rome, 2000, 233pp.

Biography:

From the Land of the Etruscans (St. Lucy Filippini), Edizioni di
    Storia e Letteratura, Rome, 1986, XIV-268pp.

Cardinal Mark Anthony Barbarigo, Religious Teachers Filippini,
Rome, 1992, 220pp.
Prophet and Witness of Charity (Tommaso Maria Fusco), edited by
Margherita Marchione. Paterson, NJ, 1993, 170pp.
Peter and Sally Sammartino (Biographical Notes), Cornwall Press,
Cranbury, NJ, 1994, 305pp.
The Fighting Nun: My Story, Tanagraphics, New York City, 2000, 207pp.

History:

A Pictorial History of St. Lucy Filippini Chapel, Edizioni del
Palazzo, Prato, 1992, 130pp.
Legacy and Mission: Religious Teachers Filippini, Villa Walsh,
Morristown, NJ, 1992, 50pp.
*Yours is a Precious Witness (Memoirs of Jews and Catholics in
Wartime Italy),* Paulist Press, Mahwah, NJ, 1996, 300pp.
Pio XII e gli ebrei, Editoriale Pantheon, Rome, 1999, 288pp.
Pope Pius XII: Architect for Peace, Paulist Press, Mahwah, NJ,
2000, 350pp.
Pio XII: Architetto di pace, Editoriale Pantheon, Rome, 2000, 413pp.

Poetry:

Twentieth Century Italian Poetry: A Bilingual Anthology, Fairleigh
Dickinson University, Rutherford, NJ 1974, 302pp.

Profiles:

Contemporary Profiles: NIAF Awardees, National Italian American
Foundation, Washington, DC, 1993, 265pp.
Americans of Italian Heritage, University Press of America,
Lanham, MD, 1995, 39 photographs, 246pp.

Photographs

The photographs appear in two groups, between pages 92 and 93, and pages 164 and 165.

1.

(Above) Early family photograph of grandparents, Luigi and Rosa Marchione, and my father, mother with baby Jean in her arms, sister Rose and uncle Pietro in center.
(Below) Crescenzo and Felicia Marchione holding Pope Pius XII's blessing on their golden jubilee of matrimony.

2.

(Above) Mamma with her brother Michael and sister Alfonsina.
(Below) Photos of Mamma and Papa.

3.

(Above) Papa interrupts work to play with Margherita, Ceil and Louis.
(Below) Margherita, dressed as an angel with wings, accompanied First Communicants to the altar of St. Margaret's Church in Little Ferry. Graduation Day: St. Mary's Elementary School, Hackensack, NJ.

4.

(Above) Sister Margherita was baptismal sponsor for George Gallis' children: Michael, Julie Ann and Alicia.
(Below) Papa with grandchildren: Louis, Jr. and Dolores Marchione (twins) and Joan Messner (center).

5.

(Above) Sister Margherita on her Investiture Day, June 12, 1938, with Mamma
　　　and Papa.
(Below) Sister Margherita on her Profession Day, August 31, 1941, with family
　　　and relatives.

6.

(Above) Profession Day, August 31, 1941, with family and relatives.
(Below) Sister Margherita with sisters Rose and Marie.

7

(Above) Ceil leaving the house in Little Ferry accompanied by Papa.
(Below) Bridal Party: Marie, Ceil, Nick, Louis.

8.

(Above) John Schettino, Palmina Pirro, Mrs. Gallis, Harry Gallis, Mamma and
　　　Papa.
(Below) George and Mildred Constantine, Harold and Jean Messner, Tom and
　　　Rose Pirro, Bob and Kay Messner.

9.

Marie and Frank Lotito's wedding reception.

10.

Crescenzo and Felicia Marchione on their Golden Jubilee with family.

11.

(Above) Sister Margherita, Giuseppe Prezzolini and Jakie, Vietri sul Mare, Italy.
(Below) Prezzolini at age 100, in Lugano, Switzerland.
    Columbia University Graduation Day, May 18, 1960.

12.

(Above) Sister Margherita with Peter and Sally Sammartino.
(Below) Sister Margherita, Sally Sammartino, Olga DeVita, Filomena Peloro, in
    Washington, DC, for the Philip Mazzei Stamp.

13.

(Above) Amita Award Ceremony: Sister Margherita with Lucille DeGeorge and
    Mrs. Henry Cabot Lodge, Jr..
(Below) Marie, Jean, Ceil with nieces Fran, Alexis, Joan, Kristen, and Marlene.

14.

(Above) Joe Piscopo and Sister Margherita on the occasion of the Gala in her
    honor, September 13, 1997.
 (Below) Members of the Marchione Family.

15.

(Above) Pope Pius XII.
(Below) Mother Ninetta Jonata with Elena Rossignani Pacelli, Pope Pius XII's
    niece, at Villa Walsh, Morristown, NJ.

16.

(Above) Sister Margherita with Pope Paul VI, July 27, 1966.
(Below) Sister Margherita with Pope John Paul II, December 8, 1999.

INDEX

The Top Ten People of 2002

There are many men and women of faith among us, many who are seeking to follow Christ by serving the poor, the Gospel, and peace. Here are 10 such people among a "cloud of witnesses."

Selecting 10 people out of many billions for recognition as "People of the Year" is evidently a partial and imperfect endeavor. There are so many people who have done so much during the year 2002 that choosing 10 from among them inevitably overlooks dozens, hundreds, thousands, even *millions* deserving of recognition, from children to old people, from mothers and fathers of families to vowed men and women religious, from doctors and nurses to poets and artists. Why then, do we even attempt this "foolish" task?

We do so because we think the wisdom outweighs the folly. And this is the wisdom: in a world where the most popular journals recognize "People of the Year" rock stars and fashion models, billionaire business tycoons and millionaire athletes, we think it is a special contribution we can make to the "culture of life" to choose 10 people who, in one way or another, are spending their lives on behalf of others: working with the poor, or for the poor; protecting the unborn, or praying for them; helping to build a more peaceful society in places where violent forces are threatening to bring chaos and war; helping to build the kingdom of God through their work and their prayer.

This year we chose 10 people, three women and seven men, three lay people and seven in religious life, from Italy, England, Russia, the United States, the Netherlands, Vietnam, and Poland. We propose these 10 people as models of the Christian culture Pope John Paul II sees as a sign of hope for our world.

— The Editor

[*Inside the Vatican* magazine, January 2002]

Sister Margherita Marchione

A leading scholar on the life of Pope Pius XII, this Italian-American nun has led the fight to defend Pius against charges that he did little on behalf of Jews during World War II.

Margherita Marchione, 81, a sister with the Religious Teachers Filippini, breaks every mold her heritage, calling, and age might suggest.

Her Italian parents, immigrants to America, were dismayed when their cherished youngest daughter at age 13 announced she was leaving home for the convent.

As a sister in a conservative order, she nevertheless attended the secular Columbia University in New York City, earning a Ph.D.

Now, at age 81, she travels the world, promoting causes that have earned her the name, "The Fighting Nun."

In a habit she's worn since 1938, only slightly modified, Sister Margherita balances her devotion to God and her passion for scholarship. As a dedicated member of her order, she still serves as the treasurer at the Villa Walsh motherhouse in Morristown, New Jersey, where we visited her. But she also is active in the secular world, serving on the New Jersey Historical Commission.

This tiny nun, a little more than five feet tall, has been described as charming, courageous, and compassionate. The woman we met deserves the epithet "feisty." Indeed, her latest "mission," as she describes it, tends to incite feistiness. She is a passionate champion of the canonization of Pope Pius XII.

But Pius, once internationally acclaimed as "saintly," is now widely vilified.

So, Sister Margherita has gone on the offensive. She has several titles in print on the subject of Pope Pius, including a biography, *Pope Pius XII: Architect for Peace.* Two books tackle head-on the history of the Holocaust in Italy and the Pope's role. *Consensus and Controversy: Defending Pope Pius XII,* and *Yours is a Precious Witness: Memoirs of Jews and Catholics in Wartime Italy* make a strong case for the active role the Vatican and Italians took to save many Jews. Her latest book is *Shepherd of Souls: A Pictorial Life of Pope Pius XII.*

Even in her autobiography, *The Fighting Nun: My Story,* she devotes more than two chapters to setting the record straight.

The British historian John Cornwell in his book, *Hitler's Pope: The Secret History of Pius XII,* claims the Pope's silence during the Holocaust condemned thousands of Jews to death by the Nazis. He further argues that Pius cut deals with Hitler in order to save German Catholics from persecution by the Nazis. Ultimately, Cornwell condemns Pope Pius as an anti-Semite who was a willing agent to Hitler's master plan.

"Absolutely untrue!" bellows the tiny nun. (She has argued with Cornwell on several occasions on radio and television.) Was Pope Pius silent? No, actually he spoke out officially on several occasions against Hitler and the actions of Nazi Germany. Moreover, those official statements had violent repercussions in Germany and Poland: in Dachau alone, 2,800 priests were imprisoned. More than half died there.

What Pope Pius determined was that the Church, and Rome, could do more good by acting quietly besides speaking officially against Hitler. To that end, convents, monasteries, even the Vatican itself, on the Pope's orders, were opened as havens for Jews. One amazing photograph in Sister Margherita's collection shows a dozen young Jewish mothers holding their infants in what is captioned "The Nursery." The tapestry visible in the background has the Pope's coat of arms: the Pope gave up his private quarters to house these women and their babies.

As a member of the Religious Teachers Filippini, Sister Margherita has access to the sisters of her order in Italy who participated in the sheltering of Jews. They share stories of setting up their cots throughout the convents, including the basements, so Jewish families could have the small bedrooms.

After the "Fighting Nun" takes apart her opponent's arguments, she asks the compelling question, "Why?"

"Controversy sells, and they are making money," Sister Margherita says of Cornwell and others.

But why are *Time* magazine, the *Washington Post* and most especially the *New York Times* so eager to promote and praise what has been proven to be inaccurate writing?

"By discrediting Pope Pius XII, the Church is discredited," Sister Margherita suggests. "He was widely admired and is now no longer widely known. If his voice of moral authority, thus the church's moral presence, can be taken out of the social ratio, the media's voice is empowered."

Fighting words from the Fighting Nun. She has a spirit and a voice that are hard to ignore.

[*Inside the Vatican* magazine, January 2003]